Praise for *Outside the Charmed Circle*:

"From diving into queerness, consent, and body awareness to demystifying sex magic and adjusting traditions, this book smoothly addresses many complicated issues that newcomers and experienced practitioners alike will appreciate and learn from."

—Laura Tempest Zakroff, author of *Weave the Liminal*

"*Outside the Charmed Circle* can guide you outwards and inwards to expand your experience of yourself and your understanding of others. The ideas, viewpoints, and practices are offered with a proper balance of challenge and reassurance that truly engage contemplation and action. This book is for anyone who dares to know themselves and to walk the ever-growing edges of awareness."

—Ivo Dominguez Jr., author of *Keys to Perception*

"*Outside the Charmed Circle* challenges us to examine and question our built-in assumptions about gender, sexuality, consent, and the power dynamics we unconsciously have about magic and the pagan community ... From step-by-step sex magic to the spiritual power of setting boundaries to the politics of consent with the gods themselves, this book has it all for those seeking to expand their horizons of gender and sex within magic."

—Tomás Prower, author of *Queer Magic*

"Misha Magdalene has written a user-friendly '101 and beyond' handbook for magical and social change. As a sexologist, it's now one of my top ten gender education books. As a polytheist pagan, one of my top five magical treatises. I won't leave home without it."

—Amy Marsh EdD, DHS, founder of the Glenhaven Center for Sex, Gender, and Culture

"The depth and heart that Misha Magdalene has put into this work is a triumph for this topic. This is a voice and perspective that's not only sorely needed, but proves once and for all that the circle is truly big enough for all of us."

—David Salisbury, author of *Witchcraft Activism*

OUTSIDE
THE
CHARMED
CIRCLE

About the Author

Misha Magdalene is a multidisciplinary, multi-classed, multi-geek, multi-queer witch with a slightly odd sense of humor who has practiced magic without a license (or a net) for more than thirty years. They're a queer, nonbinary initiate of the Anderson Feri tradition of witchcraft, theurgic sorcery, and curmudgeonliness. They're also an initiate of two lines of British Traditional Wicca, and have been known to dabble recklessly within the grimoire tradition. On a slightly more mundane level, they hold a bachelor's degree (magna cum laude) in Gender, Women, and Sexuality Studies from the University of Washington, which never fails to confuse people. They live on occupied Duwamish territory in the Pacific Northwest with their partner, their child, and a long-suffering bamboo plant named Smitty. They maintain an online presence at mishamagdalene.com and an ongoing blog, also titled *Outside the Charmed Circle*, at patheos.com/blogs/mishamagdalene.

Exploring Gender & Sexuality
in Magical Practice

OUTSIDE
THE
CHARMED
CIRCLE

MISHA MAGDALENE

LLEWELLYN PUBLICATIONS
Woodbury, Minnesota

FIRST EDITION
First Printing, 2020

Book design: Samantha Penn
Cover design: Shannon McKuhen

Llewellyn Publications is a registered trademark of Llewellyn Worldwide Ltd.

Library of Congress Cataloging-in-Publication Data
Names: Magdalene, Misha, author.
Title: Outside the charmed circle / Misha Magdalene.
Description: First edition. | Woodbury, Minnesota : Llewellyn Worldwide.
  Ltd, 2020. | Includes bibliographical references. | Summary: "Pagans,
  magical practitioners, focused on or concerned about LGBTQ+ issues,
  consent, and gender diversity within community"—provided by publisher.
Identifiers: LCCN 2019040307 (print) | LCCN 2019040308 (ebook) | ISBN
  9780738761329 (paperback) | ISBN 9780738761374 (ebook)
Subjects: LCSH: Magic. | Sex.
Classification: LCC BF1623.S4 M34 2020 (print) | LCC BF1623.S4 (ebook) |
  DDC 133.4/3—dc23
LC record available at https://lccn.loc.gov/2019040307
LC ebook record available at https://lccn.loc.gov/2019040308

Llewellyn Worldwide Ltd. does not participate in, endorse, or have any authority or responsibility concerning private business transactions between our authors and the public.

  All mail addressed to the author is forwarded but the publisher cannot, unless specifically instructed by the author, give out an address or phone number.

  Any internet references contained in this work are current at publication time, but the publisher cannot guarantee that a specific location will continue to be maintained. Please refer to the publisher's website for links to authors' websites and other sources.

Llewellyn Publications
A Division of Llewellyn Worldwide Ltd.
2143 Wooddale Drive
Woodbury, MN 55125-2989
www.llewellyn.com

Printed in the United States of America

Queer and trans folks, newbie Pagans, fledgling polytheists, baby witches, and neophyte magicians, I wrote this for you. Megan, I was able to write this because of you.

CONTENTS

ACKNOWLEDGMENTS

ALL FALSE MODESTY ASIDE, nothing of value I've ever accomplished has been a solitary effort, done in a vacuum. My best work has always been done in collaboration, and this book is no exception. The following company of good spirits were instrumental in the creation and completion of this text, and I'm endlessly grateful to every one of them.

First and last and always, my beloved life partner Megan Langley: my heart, my muse, my inspiration, my greatest supporter, my primary interlocutor, and the best alpha reader a writer could hope to find. You provided every kind of support a first-time author could hope for, and this book would literally not exist without you. Thank you for everything, dearest one.

Laura Tempest Zakroff, who kicked me under the bus once in Atlanta, and again in San Jose. #witchcraft, amirite?

Jason Mankey, my editor at Patheos Pagan, who took a chance on a totally unknown writer on the basis of a tipsy introduction, a recommendation, and a writing sample.

Tai Fenix Kulystin, who instigated the essay that mutated over time into this work, and who provided invaluable insight into the nature of Babalon.

Everyone at Llewellyn Worldwide, with special thanks to my editor Heather Greene, who managed to wrest the snark-hammer from my hands with grace and good humor.

Michelle Belanger, who graciously consented to write the foreword to this book.

Lon Sarver, who contributed pivotal thoughts on Dionysus and classical Greek culture, and Jay Logan, who graciously checked my work on Antinous.

The members of the Patheos Pagan Illuminati, whose spiritual and conspiratorial support was instrumental to the completion of this book.

Willow Moon, Chris Bartlett, Kyra Laughlin, and Kayla Rosen, my fabulous Bookfish: the team of beta readers who did the work of heroes in pointing out all the many places where my slip was showing.

Lauren Stein, James Larson, Haley Nichols, Makia Oaks, and all of the amazingly kind and tolerant staff of SoulFood CoffeeHouse in Redmond, WA, where a nontrivial amount of this book was written. Additional thanks to the Redmond location of the King County Library System, who put up with me using their Internet access and asking their staff all sorts of questions, ranging from the obvious to the perplexing.

Jean Marie Stine and Frankie Hill, who gave me invaluable guidance and timely advice on publishing and other matters germane to this text.

Rhea Shemayazi and Raven Bond, who inspired and encouraged me with their friendship, their writing, and the incandescent light of their love.

For those who find this sort of minutiae interesting, background listening for the writing of this book included Dirty Computer by Janelle Monáe, Thrice Woven by Wolves in the Throne Room, Dionysus by Dead Can Dance, Kilts and Corsets by Tuatha Dea, multiple albums by Rush and Queen, the first two seasons of Stranger Things, and lots of podcasts, including those listed in the appendix and several nerdy delights from the good folks over at LSG Media (www.libertystreetgeek.net). The author suggests pairing this book with a seasonally-appropriate beverage, good lighting, and a comfy chair.

This book is written in loving memory of Rheya Blackfire, Raven Bond, Niklas Gander, Ron Miller, and Valerie "Veedub" Walker.

CHARMED CIRCLE
FOREWORD

EVERY ONCE IN A WHILE, a book comes along that is so essential and insightful you actually resent it just a little for not having been there for you at an earlier point in your development. *Outside the Charmed Circle* is such a book—at least for me.

As I read to prepare my contribution, I found myself repeatedly stopping to copy down whole paragraphs because they resonated so deeply. It was actually pretty hard to get traction on the foreword, not because I wasn't into the material, but because the exact opposite was true: I wanted to share the book with my magickal students in House Kheperu. With my wife. With everyone who follows me on Twitter. I wanted to shout to the hills with a wild mix of frustration and elation, "SOMEONE GETS IT!!!"

Frustration, because where was this book when I was twenty and sitting in awkward silence during a Goddess meditation and all I could feel was how very Not A Woman I was?!? Elated because I live in this time where many of our communities are finally having these conversations about sex, identity, and gender; where, as an intersex person, I can have a wife and be legally married; where I can lead ritual at a public event as neither God nor Goddess but as a rightful representative of that which is betwixt and between— and I'm not the only one who's felt a little disenfranchised by the supposedly open-minded modern magickal community because accepting that role is a relatively recent thing.

Finally, readers. Finally.

Maybe that's a lot to unpack, and maybe you are from a more recent generation where it is only a matter of *politesse* to ask someone their preferred pronouns. But I came of age magickally in the late '80s and early '90s when "every woman is a witch" and all the covens I stumbled on spent at least one sabbat enjoining me to get in touch with my "female power"—except, as an intersex person, none of that felt like it applied. At all.

I was coming from Catholicism, which I'd left due in large part because they wouldn't let me be a priest. This was, of course, on the grounds that I wasn't male (I wasn't female, either, although I had no confirmation of this at the time. Intersex people were very rarely told of their condition and often deliberately misled about the real reasons behind everything from genital surgeries to infertility). Naïvely, I had expected a religion on the fringe like Wicca to be super open-minded about variations in identity and belief (also sexuality), and wow, did I have a comeuppance.

Every coven and circle that I found in the ten years I bothered searching were all aggressively gender-specific. Women were Priestesses. Men were Priests. The Great Rite was about the sexual union of the God and the Goddess. I could not, under any circumstance, perform the duties of the Priest. If I didn't want to draw down the Goddess, I was out of luck—and generally treated as if there was something wrong with me because I didn't really connect with the gendered facet of deity they felt appropriate to my assigned-at-birth sex.

Needless to say, I dumped Wicca just like I'd broken up with Catholicism. I never stopped practicing magick, however. That was such an integral part of my identity, I'd been doing it before I could fully explain what magick *was*—but I refused the label *witch*. Actively rebelled against it. The word had been indelibly painted in a color of gendered ink not suited to the likes of me.

To some extent, there's a happy ending to my early disenfranchisement with witchcraft. Unhappy with what I found, I wandered off and started my own thing, building from an archetype that was more suitably androgyne, way less focused on sex as a reproductive act, and inherently transgressive by its very nature: the vampire. If you recognize my name (and you're not really into ghost-hunting shows), chances are it's in connection with that community. And for the longest time, I was pretty sure only the vampire community really grokked how magick, sex, and neo-Paganism were about more than a gender binary. Over the past few decades, when I engaged with the Pagan or witchcraft communities at all, it was only on the fringe which, as a someone for whom liminality is writ not merely into their magick but into their very genetic structure, seemed entirely fitting.

I share this not to make this foreword all about me, but to give you context for why *Outside the Charmed Circle* is so electrifying on a profound and personal level. The book and all the concepts Misha Magdalene explains within it are a bridge. That bridge works to span the gap that has separated practitioners like myself (and pretty obviously the author themselves) from feeling both fully engaged with and fully accepted by the modern magickal subculture, particularly those aspects influenced by Wicca and witchcraft.

When I first heard the title, I assumed the "charmed circle" would turn out to be the very circle of witchcraft, a boundary set by the gender essentialists which those of us who are gender nonconforming are (and have been) obligated to navigate. Spoiler: that's not where the term comes from. To some extent, the "charmed circle" does apply to the modern magickal community, but it applies only insomuch as that community has existed in the past. Things are changing, and Misha Magdalene has some really fantastic ideas about how we all can facilitate those changes. A great deal of that work involves transforming ourselves—the best and most potent of all magicks (at least in my informed opinion).

Ostensibly, *Outside the Charmed Circle* is a treatise on queering sex magick, but to pigeon-hole it on the shelves as a sex magick book would be to overlook everything else it has packed between its pages. First and foremost, the work you hold in your hands is a Master Class on gender studies as they apply to the modern magickal movement. Misha Magdalene brings their considerable scholarship to bear on our entrenched assumptions about Gods and Goddesses, the Great Rite, and why, in a practice inherently liminal in nature, so many of us still labor under the binary distinctions dictated by our woefully intransigent mainstream Western culture.

But even that does not fully cover what you will find in this book. *Outside the Charmed Circle* is a know-thyself workbook, a much-needed discussion about consent, a frank and sometimes scathing assessment of the failings in our communities regarding the same, and an open dialogue with the reader that encourages questions, reflection, and honest wrestling with sometimes emotionally challenging material—and all of this presented with mindfulness, empathy, and gentle humor that I've come to think of as Misha's signature style.

This book has a lot to unpack, and I won't lie—it is not an easy book, either for brain or for heart. This book challenges you at every page: to ask yourself hard questions; to deconstruct your assumptions; to confront your ingrained biases; to love your body exactly how it is. The language at times is dense and Misha Magdalene makes no apologies for their scholarly background, tossing around terms like *hermeneutics* and *praxis* with the kind of blithe familiarity that only comes of being thoroughly steeped in academia. But don't let this intimidate you. Around the next corner will be a frank confessional of coming to magick through *Dungeons & Dragons*, some delicately worded distaste for Aleister Crowley, ruminations on the cultural meaning of the *Matrix,* and a peppering of *Babylon 5* references (which certainly won my heart).

Any good book is a conversation between author and reader, and Misha makes use of this in a conscious and active way. Throughout the text, there are key moments where the reader is encouraged to pause and digest. Helpful questions are offered to get you to engage with the material so you may better internalize complex concepts—particularly how they apply to you. If you are not a journaler by nature, for this book, you will want to be. As Misha states repeatedly throughout the book, their ideas and theories are not prescriptive, and only you will be able to make the final determination about how or if any of the material is something you can work into your personal practice. Your best guidebook will be the journal that grows out of your process, and with the carefully inclusive way the exercises have been written, even if you do not identify on the LGBTQIA+ spectrum, there are revelations in this book that can deepen your experience with your magick, with your practice, and with yourself.

At the beginning of this foreword, I bemoaned not having this book at an earlier point in my life, but the truth is, this book could only have come into existence in this moment, now: here in this time of cultural upheaval and (hopefully) cultural shift, where the "grab 'em by the pussy" mentality is openly challenged by initiatives like the #MeToo movement, where the gendered roles ingrained in our very language have come into question, where young people can choose a dress or a suit or none of the above and still have parents who love and accept them.

As a sometimes embittered Gen Xer, I can resent the fact that we didn't have books like *Outside the Charmed Circle* when I was coming of age, or I can rejoice that this book exists in this moment for those who need it now.

I choose joy.

Michelle Belanger
Walpurgisnacht, 2019

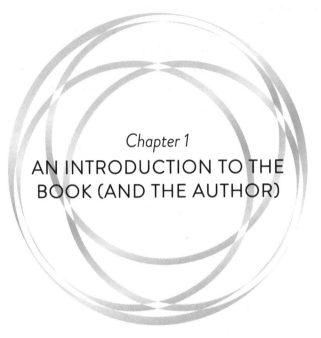

Chapter 1
AN INTRODUCTION TO THE BOOK (AND THE AUTHOR)

HELLO, BEAUTIFUL CREATURES.

At the beginning of a book like this, good manners suggest that I stake out the ground I intend to occupy early on. Not only does this give the reader a sense of where I'm coming from, but it also gives a sense of where I plan to go in the pages to follow. Start as you mean to go on, as the saying goes.

So, let's begin here: magic is queer. Whether you call it witchcraft, sorcery, or something else, all magic is innately, inherently queer, and the queerer it is, the more powerful it can be. Similarly, polytheism, Paganism, all forms of esoteric spirituality—all of them, queer.

Having read those words, dear reader, you're likely to be having feelings about some of them. How you're feeling depends on a lot of factors: who you are and what your background has been; how you define terms like *witchcraft*, *sorcery*, *magic*, or *queer*; and, perhaps most importantly, whether or not you identify with any of those terms. You may be amused, angry, curious, delighted, disgusted, or irritated. You may object to the connection between magic and queerness, or you may wonder what I mean by one or the other term.

Whatever your reaction, I want to ask you to pause a moment. Sit with that reaction, holding judgment in abeyance, and ask yourself what lies behind it. If you're responding positively, you may see yourself reflected in my statement, feeling the little surge of excitement that comes with validation. On the other hand, if your reaction is defensive, angry, or conflicted, you may suspect my motives. Perhaps you're worried that I'm smuggling aberrant sexuality or identity politics into magic, Neopaganism, or polytheism. You might be afraid that what I offer is a threat to your tradition and practice or even, perhaps, to your own identity.

In the words of an aphorism attributed to the mystic poet Victor Anderson, grandmaster of the Feri tradition of witchcraft: "Where there's fear, there's power." There's power in all words to shape both consciousness and reality, and the more potent the words, like *queer* and *magic*, the more they can scare us. For whatever it's worth this early in the game, I offer you my promise—my word, if you will—that I've chosen the words I use with the intent, not to provoke anger or fear, but to invite dialogue and contemplation.

Regardless of where or how you see yourself, dear reader, I cordially invite you to read on, and enter into a dialogue with these ideas and practices. I ask that you hear me out, learn what I mean when I say that magic is queer, and see where the patterns I draw and conclusions I offer might spark insights and new understandings for you. It's my hope that you'll find ideas to deepen your vision of both magic and spirituality, alongside techniques to incorporate into your own practice. It's possible that you'll find more of your own experiences of gender, sexuality, and magic reflected here than you expect, alongside the possibility of expanding the boundaries of your own perspectives. However, even if you come away from this book with nothing more than an understanding of how gender and sexuality inform others' magical practice, I'll consider the effort worthwhile. I hope you feel the same.

What This Book Is—and Isn't

Outside the Charmed Circle is an exploration of magic through the lenses of gender and sexuality. It's intended to give readers the tools to engage more fully with both their magical practice and their authentic gendered and sexual selves. In the pages to come, you'll find both discussions of theory and practical suggestions, along with personal anecdotes and examples drawn from across the spectrum of magical practice.

This book grew out of my own grappling with issues of gender, sexuality, and spirituality. It's informed by my own background of magical practice as a witch and sorcerer, as well as by the work of the multitude of magicians, sorcerers, witches, and writers on whose shoulders I'm standing. It's also been shaped by my work as a student and scholar in the fields of feminism and gender studies, most especially by my interactions with the work of theorists like Gayle Rubin, Audre Lorde, bell hooks, and Judith Butler. However, though I encourage you to check out all of those writers' works, it's not necessary to be familiar with any of them in order to read and work with this book.

Oh, did I mention that there's work in this book? Alongside the text in each chapter, you'll find practical work intended to deepen your experience and understanding of the concepts covered in that chapter. Some of them are intellectual exercises, some are meditative practices, and some are ritual magical workings. None of them are compulsory, and all of them are adaptable to your own style of practice.

So, that's what this book is. What it *isn't* is a comprehensive introductory text on magic. While I do offer suggestions and advice for folks who are new to magical and devotional practice, the focus of this book is on people who are looking to deepen and broaden their practice, and working to find or create their own spaces within their communities. This book is intended to be a supplement to the practice you already have, rather than a standalone system. (If you don't already have a magical practice of your own, I offer some ideas about developing one in chapter 9.) Similarly, this book isn't a guide to any particular tradition or style of magic. There are magical techniques in here, some of them quite powerful, but none are unique to any particular tradition. Rather, they're adaptations of techniques drawn from multiple streams of practice, created to fulfill our purposes here.

Another thing this book isn't and isn't meant to be, is a metric for validity. Even if I had a reliable metric for validity or legitimacy, I wouldn't presume to judge whose identities, experiences, traditions, or practices qualify. I have no interest in playing gatekeeper for either the queer community or the esoteric community. Where I provide definitions (as in chapter 2), they're intended to be descriptive, rather than prescriptive or proscriptive; they are points of entry for dialogue rather than any pretense of offering the final word on the subject.

How to Use This Book

As with most books, the material in each chapter builds on the ones before it. However, I've done my best to make these chapters stand on their own enough that you could conceivably skip over chapters that touch on issues you'd rather not grapple with right now. And make no mistake: some of the material in this book is potentially troubling, triggering, or dangerous. After all, we're talking about sexuality and gender, two topics fundamental to our very identities and selves, and about magic, the power of creation and transformation. If you're reading this book, I can only assume you're interested in all three of these forces and open to engaging with them in potentially transformative ways.

So how should you read it? Well, it's your book, and it's your experience. You're free to start at the beginning and plow straight through or spread it out over several days and bounce around the chapters in any order you like. You can do the practical work as you come to it in the text, or save the exercises until the end, or skip the explanations and *only* do the exercises ... though I don't really recommend that last one.

I recommend first glancing over the table of contents to get a sense of the general layout of the book, then coming back to read the rest of this introduction. Afterward, read chapter 2 and do the "Taking Measure of Your Self" exercise on page 57. Consider your responses to that exercise honestly and carefully. In what areas are you feeling confident? Where are you feeling challenged? What delights and comforts you, and what scares or discomforts you? If you're feeling pretty comfortable all around, go ahead and proceed forward through the book in an orderly fashion, or however you feel moved to read it. If you find, however, that some part of the exercise made you feel uncomfortable, sit with that feeling. Are you in a secure enough emotional place to explore this feeling, or would you be better served by not provoking it at this time? If you'd be better served by not provoking those feelings at this time, please feel free to give those exercises or chapters a pass for the time being. They'll still be here when you're ready to engage with them.

But what exactly is this book about? Who is it for? And just who do I think I am to be writing it?

What's in This Book?

My overarching thesis is that most modern forms of magical and devotional practice have valorized cisgender heterosexuality to the exclusion of all other expressions of gender and sexuality, and in doing so have cut themselves off from both the full spectrum of lived experience and a depth of magical practice. By accepting and embracing the broad range of gender and sexuality as lived realities, we can reclaim not only our lost power, but our own experiences of the numinous as well. Drawing on my own background as a queer magical practitioner and devotee, my intent is to provide both an intellectual framework and a set of practical tools that any reader—straight or queer, cis or trans, witch or magician or devotee —can use to develop and deepen their own practice. As for what that looks like … well, here's a sneak preview of what you can expect in the chapters ahead.

Words mean things, and the words we use to talk about our experiences shape how we understand those experiences. In chapter 2, I'll introduce the core concepts and terminology used in the rest of the book and engage with some of the preconceptions around gender, sexuality, and their relationships with spirituality. I'll outline and discuss some of the historical and contemporary myths that help us understand our experiences, encouraging us to embrace the ones which serve us and to dispense with those which don't. I'll also frame a contemplative practice to help us see people as they truly are, starting with the one person we always have with us: ourselves.

However widely our traditions of magic or spiritual paths may differ, they all share in common the most fundamental magical tool and primary instrument of devotional practice: the body. In chapter 3, we'll work and play with various theories and practices of embodiment, and discuss how embodiment can be the single most powerful element of our ritual work. I'll talk about the obstacles of self-esteem and body negativity, issues of ability and disability, and ways to engage with those issues in a ritual setting. I'll also demonstrate how a mindful grounding in our own material bodies can be the first step in becoming the inflection point between spirit and matter, with the help of an unlikely ally: the humble orange.

What is gender, and why are so many people made so very uncomfortable with the term? We'll engage with that oh-so-vexing g-word in chapter 4. It will cover some approaches to gender traditional and modern as well as explore their ramifications for magical praxis, including the concept of gender as a magical tool. It finishes with an exercise in deconstructing the metaphorical symbolic language we use to discuss our lived experiences.

In chapter 5, we'll explore the idea of queerness as a liminality of spirit, identity, and sexuality, including the possibility of magic as a queerness of spirituality. We'll use the power of the magic mirror as a tool for reclaiming our relationships with our own bodies and identities and liberating ourselves from the external forces and influences that would presume to tell us who and what we truly are.

Sex magic is one of the hottest hot-button topics in the Pagan and magical community, something of a testament to its inherent power. In spite of the subject's sensitivity, there's a lot more said about sex magic than is actually done, it seems. In chapter 6, I encourage readers to explore sex magic as one of the easiest, most wholesome, and most enjoyable forms of magic we can do. We'll start by defining and demystifying the terms we're using—sex, magic, and sex magic—and working out what lies underneath them. From there, we'll outline the fundamentals, benefits, and occasional pitfalls of sex magic. The conclusion of the chapter will be a step-by-step walkthrough of a basic solitary sex magic ritual from the beginning stages of design and desire through the completion of the spell.

As the modern Pagan, polytheist, and occult communities have grown and developed, it's become apparent that we have an at best ambivalent relationship with consent and power. This is a product of being ensconced in Western culture, which is deeply flawed in this regard. In chapter 7, we'll examine the ways in which our issues in modern magical and polytheistic communities are a holdover from older paradigms of negotiating power dynamics, and outline ways we can improve those relationships. We'll cover traditional venues of interaction and consent in magical and devotional practice and propose methods to adapt them for a world in which everyone has agency and power. We'll continue this exploration in chapter 8, which focuses on the complex situations which can arise in our interactions with deities.

We'll start bringing all of our theory and ritual practice together in chapter 9. We'll discuss some ways to modify or create our own devotional rituals and magical practices to more closely reflect our own lived experiences of gender, sexuality, agency, and embodiment. We'll conclude with an example of a ritual framework for solo or group practice in which aspirants will invoke the aid of a tutelary spirit to embrace their own agency and power.

By now, we're all on board with the idea that gender, sexuality, and embodiment can be avenues of personal empowerment ... but what does that look like in practice? In chapter 10, we'll cover some of the ways in which our esoteric communities have engaged with—or, sadly, avoided engaging with—issues of power, both magical and mundane. We'll look at some of the common pitfalls our communities encounter when grappling with power dynamics, and I'll suggest some tools for working with those problems when they arise.

Once we've questioned and deconstructed normative ideas about gender and sexuality in relation to our spiritual path, where do we go from here? In the concluding chapter, "An Ending and a Beginning: What Lies Beyond the Circle," I'll suggest some ways that readers can take the lessons they've learned—about themselves, about magic, about spirituality and sexuality and gender—and apply them in the context of their everyday work as magical practitioners, as devotees, and simply as human beings. We'll look at ways this work can be expanded to make our communities more inclusive, accepting, and nurturing places. Finally, we'll end as we began: taking an account of ourselves and seeing how we've changed and grown as a result of the work we've done through the previous chapters.

Who Is This Book For?

The short answer is everyone.

If you're comfortable in the gender ascribed to you at birth, I wrote this for you.

If you've been moved to transition to your truest expression of gender, or to abandon gender altogether, I wrote this for you.

Whether you're straight, gay, bisexual, pansexual, or asexual, whether you're monogamous or polyamorous or aromantic, or something else besides, I wrote this for you.

Whether you're an experienced magical practitioner, an absolute beginner, or somewhere in between those two extremes, I wrote this for you.

Whoever you are, dear reader, and however you identify, I wrote this book with you in mind. If you're a human being, dancing at the inflection point where spirit incarnates as matter, the ideas and issues in this book are key to your very existence, and the practices and suggestions are humbly offered for your consideration and use. Keep what you find helpful, adapt it to your circumstances, and use it with my blessings, discarding anything which doesn't work for you. Alternately, consider it one voice among many, and revisit it when you want to clarify (or complicate) specific points about gender, sexuality, and the places where they intersect with magic.

What Resources Will You Need?

As I mentioned above, there are several practical exercises in this book, ranging from the purely contemplative (where you basically just sit and Think About Stuff) to the analytical (where you spend some time Processing the Stuff you thought about) to the practical (where you get to actually Do Stuff). There are some resources required for a few of these exercises, but none of them should be outside the means of anyone with this book. Other materials may be called for in specific exercises, but the following list will cover most of what you'll need for the exercises in this book:

- *Somewhere to do things.* A space of your own to sit, think, write, and potentially conduct small-scale rituals is essential. While it's not optimal, you could adapt most of these exercises to be done inconspicuously, though a couple of them are emphatically meant to be done only in a private setting.

- *Time to do things.* Spiritual and magical workings require time, both to think through and to actually perform. You'll want to have enough time set aside for the exercise you're doing that you don't feel pressured to get through the exercise on a deadline.

- *Ritual tools.* If you want to ensconce the book's ritual practices within your own established devotional or magical practice, you'll want to have any path-specific tools or items handy.

- *A safe place to keep your stuff.* While you won't necessarily be accumulating a huge trove of ritual implements and sacred writings over the course of this book, there will be a few things that you probably won't want to leave lying about for just anyone to look at. Have a place to put your things that you can lock, or which is unlikely to be discovered.

You'll also want to have a journal and a dedicated writing implement for recording your thoughts and experiences with the exercises which follow, and possibly for taking notes and writing reflections as you read through the text itself. In its simplest and most literal form, this journal would be paper of some sort and a pen or a pencil. You could adapt the practices to other writing media, even to being typed on a computer screen or a mobile device. Whatever medium you choose, make sure it's something that you can keep and reference over time.

A Quick Note about Journaling

Many of us approach the whole idea of keeping a magical journal with a lot of trepidation, so I'd like to take a few moments to speak to that directly. The practice of recording magical and devotional practices is something more than traditional: it's one of the *ur*-practices of spirituality. All grimoires, all religious scriptures, all written records of spiritual practice and experience are attempts at capturing, in words which are all too often insufficient to the task, our explorations and experiences of the numinous.

It's tempting to believe that recording such experiences requires special materials; perhaps not a handmade book of finest vellum bound in calfskin, but at least the sort of fancy leather-bound journal you might find at your Friendly Local Pagan/Occult Bookstore, or even the less-fancy (but more affordable) blank book you can purchase at any decent chain bookstore. All of these choices are perfectly fine, but if you're anything at all like me, you'll soon find yourself with a small library of blank books and journals, all unused. In part, I think it's because they're too nice, and the niceness that originally caught your eye becomes an imposing, foreboding barrier to actually using it. Magical journals can get pretty abused—bounced around in bags, spattered with candle wax and essential oils, occasionally sat upon—but more than that, journals get written in. We do the work, and then we sit down and write some of the most intimate thoughts, feelings, and experiences we have in those journals. Simply doing the writing can be an obstacle in itself, to say nothing of the notion of frantically scribbling in a book you're afraid to damage.

Honestly, my advice is to forgo all of the fancy journals for now, and instead invest in the cheapest spiral-bound notebook you can find at your local drug store, supermarket, or office supply store. Why? Because the best magical journal, bar none, is the one you'll actually use. You're less likely to feel intimidated by a notebook with a featureless texture or cute kittens on the front, or to worry about crumpling or sweat-staining the pages of a three-dollar notebook.

As a final observation, I was once privileged to look over a magical journal kept by one of the most diligent, hardcore magical practitioners I've ever known. This journal contained both records of magical workings and profound meditations on mystical experiences … and was written in varying shades of ballpoint pen, in a spiral-bound notebook (with wide-ruled paper, no less) whose cover bore a truly epic vintage 1980s airbrushed illustration of unicorns galloping across a moonlit pond.

The point is that it's not the paper that matters but what you write on it. If you like, you can see this as a metaphorical illustration of the deeper occult truth that external seemings don't always reflect internal realities, a sentiment sometimes rendered as "never judge a book by its cover." (And hey, cute kittens and unicorns!)

Who Am I?

That's a fair question. Hello! I'm Misha. I was born in central California in the early seventies, and spent the eighties in upstate South Carolina, where I first discovered both modern Paganism and my own queerness. I've since happily transplanted myself to the Pacific Northwest, where I spend a lot of time cuddling with my sweetie and my kid, doing housework to avoid arguing with people on the internet, and listening to really odd music. (If you're curious, "really odd" includes progressive rock, thumpy electronic dance music, avant-garde noise, and the scary kind of heavy metal.)

I've been a practicing witch for over thirty years, first as an eclectic neo-Wiccan Pagan, then later as an initiate of two lines of British Traditional Wicca, Gardnerian and Kingstone. I've practiced ceremonial magic with a Thelemic recension of the Hermetic

Order of the Golden Dawn and worked within the European grimoire tradition. My primary frame of practice these days, however, is as an initiated witch and priest of the Anderson Feri tradition of witchcraft, theurgy, sorcery, and curmudgeonry. (While the gender-neutral term *priestx* would generally be appropriate, given my identity as a person of nonbinary gender, *priest* is the term commonly used within Feri to refer to an initiate of any gender.) I have relationships of varying degrees of intimacy and affection with multiple gods and spirits, with the core of my devotion and love being centered on the Star Goddess and her consort, the Peacock Angel. While my background informs both my magical practice and my approaches to gender and sexuality, it's not necessary to be familiar with Feri, Wicca, or any other magical tradition to read this book. I'll explain any tradition-specific concepts or terminology I use as we go.

I embrace the label *queer* as an umbrella term to encapsulate my own gender and sexual identities: nonbinary, genderqueer, bisexual/pansexual, and so on. I define these terms in the next chapter, so don't worry if you're unfamiliar with any of them. I don't normally front-load references to my sexuality or gender, but since my queerness informs my perspectives and approaches to magical praxis and spirituality, it seems like relevant information to bring up here. (I acknowledge that queer is a contentious term for many people, and I discuss my reasons for using it in the next chapter.)

I have the privilege of holding a bachelor's degree in Gender, Women, and Sexuality Studies from the University of Washington, which also informs my perspective and approach. In fact, the initial concept for this book arose while I was finishing my degree, wrestling with the tensions between gender, sexuality, and spirituality.

Like all of us, I wear a multitude of hats at varying times: spouse, lover, partner, parent, writer, musician, crafter, scholar, sorcerer, and witch. Behind and beyond all of those, I am a child of earth, water, air, fire, and the incandescent spark of divinity. I am flawed and fallible, as are we all, but ever striving toward the ecstasy of union with the numinous infinite.

And, last of all, I'm delighted to make your acquaintance.

As to the issue of how my background informs my approach to gender, sexuality, and magic, the following is a rather personal biographical interlude which might help to establish the groundwork for where I'm coming from with this book, and where I hope to go.

A Personal Reflection on Magic and Queerness

One of the games that witches, magicians, Pagans, polytheists, and other practitioners like to play in the early stages of getting to know one another begins with the question, "So, what was your first book?" This is common enough to be a groan-worthy cliché in some circles, while in others it's the lead-off to a rollicking conversation about our faltering, sometimes cringe-inducing first steps on the Path. Some folks will credit Neopagans like Scott Cunningham, Silver Ravenwolf, or Raymond Buckland, while others will cite ceremonial magicians like Donald Michael Kraig, Dion Fortune, Aleister Crowley, or Israel Regardie. Some might even mention mythologists like Thomas Bulfinch, Edith Hamilton, or my personal favorites, Ingri and Edgar Parin d'Aulaire.

In the past, when it was my turn to play, I usually explained that I first found magic and Paganism in the double-feature of Margot Adler's classic *Drawing Down the Moon* (the 1986 update) and Starhawk's *The Spiral Dance*, which I read simultaneously when I was about fourteen. It's a respectable entry point, though one that dates me pretty precisely; Starhawk's Feri-inflected recension of feminist Wicca and Goddess worship dovetails nicely with Adler's snapshot travelogue of late 1970s/early 1980s Neopaganism, creating a pleasant (if somewhat dated) image redolent of nag champa and Polo by Ralph Lauren, perhaps with a Yes album playing in the background.

The trouble is that it's a false memory. Like so many other modern practitioners of the dark arts, I am forced to confess after all these years that Jack Chick was right: Dungeons & Dragons led me to witchcraft.[1]

A little back story may be appropriate at this point.

In 1981, I was eight years old in the fourth grade. Having gone through the previous two grades in a single year, I was younger and smaller than my classmates. I desperately wanted to fit in with them, of course, and my obvious desperation probably had something to do with my social ostracism. The fact that I was painfully insecure, socially awkward, and used to thinking of myself as the smartest person in the room probably didn't help much.

Some of the cool kids in my gifted class—just let that sink in for a moment—were really into this strange activity that involved shuffling sheets of paper and pencils around, reading from strange-looking books, and rolling polyhedral dice at random intervals. Being the social outcast of the class—yeah, let that one sink in for a moment, too—it was several weeks before I finally got one of them to let me in on the secret: it was a storytelling game, sort of like make-believe, but with rules. I was even allowed to roll up a character of my own ... who died the moment he entered his first dungeon, when the ceiling fell and crushed him into pâté. Despite this less-than-illustrious beginning, this game had opened an entire imaginal realm for me, and I was hooked. I raided the school library for books on mythology and fantasy novels, then

---

1. Jack Chick, *Dark Dungeons* (Ontario, CN: Chick Publications, 1984), 4–5.

moved on to my local town library, all the while moping around my house like a miniature Robert Smith until my mother broke down and surprised me one day with the basic D&D box set and an issue of *Dragon* magazine.

That humble box was more or less the death blow to any chance I might've had for normalcy. Not by itself, of course. Gary Gygax and Dave Arneson's role-playing game of swords, sorcery, and adventure was brilliant, to be sure, but the portrayal of D&D in Chick's hysterical *Dark Dungeons* tract wildly overestimates the extent to which the game draws on real-world occultism. Even in its occasional feinting toward historical magic, D&D tended to get its facts wrong... or, to put it kindly, D&D used bits of historical occultism as window dressing, much as horror films and metal bands do. It created a delightfully atmospheric vibe, equal parts Hammer horror and pulp fantasy à la Robert E. Howard or H. P. Lovecraft, but it was a far cry from anything resembling historical thaumaturgy. Anyone who tried to practice magic as outlined in the *Player's Handbook* and *Dungeon Master's Guide* would find themselves standing in a circle inscribed with meaningless squiggles, holding a handful of tiny balls of bat guano. (For those of you who aren't longtime D&D gamers, bat guano mixed with sulfur is the material component for one of the first truly dangerous magic-user spells, the ever-popular *Fireball*.)

Still, the assembled oeuvre of Gygax, Arneson, and Co. pushed my imagination in directions it might never have otherwise travelled. Through their good offices, I discovered the works of Bulfinch, Hamilton, and the d'Aulaires, as well as a host of fantasists whose books would, for better and for worse, form the basis of my teenaged cosmology: Michael Moorcock, Ursula K. Le Guin, J. R. R. Tolkien, the aforementioned Messrs. Howard and Lovecraft, and a host of others. Again, though, these authors weren't teaching magic and witchcraft in their stories. A great deal of magic can be found in their books, and a careful reader can glean a great deal of spiritual and philosophical truth from their pages (especially from Le Guin's Earthsea novels), but they are fictions, first and foremost. They're no more intended as instructional manuals in the occult than J. K. Rowling's *Harry Potter and the Philosopher's Stone*, despite some excitable Christians' protestations to the contrary. When a child manages to successfully cast *Avada Kedavra*, or even *Wingardium Leviosa*, I'll be forced to revisit my position. In the meantime, I hope we can all agree that the magic of fantasy novels and role-playing games, while entertaining and thought-provoking, is a far cry from the actual practice of magic.

My first exposure to that actual practice came not long afterward from the least likely place I could imagine: my own home library. It was there, as a wee slip of a child in early 1980s California, that I found my mother's copy of *A Treasury of Witchcraft*, Harry E. Wedeck's 1961 classic of sensationalist occultism. Sure, it was an overbaked mishmash of half-understood pieces from a double-dozen unrelated cultures, but the glances I snuck through the leaves of this grim tome sparked my imagination as nothing before, and the terms that danced before my eyes—*osculum infame*, Hand of Glory, *Malleus Maleficarum*, the Black Mass—visited me again in my dreams, rolling from the mouths of robed Inquisitors, chanted by nude devotees streaked with soot and rendered baby fat. That I understood almost none of what I read was not only irrelevant, it was instrumental to the ways in which my imagination ran wild. I pored over his description of the witch's mark and searched my own body for similar markings or scars, desperately hoping to find validation for my occult desires. After all, Wedeck's tome made it clear that something mysterious was happening out there in the world and, with care and perseverance, I could find out what it was ... even become part of it.

Not long after, at my local library, I found the book that sealed the deal for me: Erica Jong's curious 1981 coffee-table book, *Witches*.

An inexplicably unlikely installment in the Harry N. Abrams folklore series (which also included Wil Hugyen's *Gnomes* and Brian Froud and Alan Lee's *Faeries*), Jong's book presented the figure of the witch as both a fairytale monster and a historical reality, part of a hidden tradition of magic and mystery. She added depth, nuance, and a whole host of complications to my nascent understanding of witchcraft. I didn't understand half of what I read at the time, but anything I failed to grasp from her writing, Joseph A. Smith's illustrations to accompany the text rendered as clearly as I could've asked. His evocative, hallucinatory images of witches gathering herbs by moonlight and embracing the Goat of the Sabbat, broken on the wheel and burning at the stake, taught me as much as the written text did, if not more.

It was appealing, poetic stuff—dark, sexual, and powerful—but it was also frustratingly, inextricably tied to a quintessentially seventies, can-do empowerment take on feminism which I knew, even as a late-tweener to early-teen, had little room for someone like ... well, me. This was witchcraft as Women's Wisdom, diametrically opposed to the faux-perfection of glorified toxic masculinity. In all fairness to Jong, she does spend a couple of paragraphs allowing the existence of male witches:

> *Many men were condemned to death for being witches, widowers of witches, fathers of witches. However much we know this to be true historically, the notion of the witch as male never quite sticks. [...] Perhaps this is because we associate woman's creative powers with the manipulation of vast,*

unseen forces. Or perhaps we intuitively understand that during the long centuries when women were the semislaves of society, they were naturally drawn to witchcraft as a cure for their powerlessness, a means of manipulating a world that otherwise painfully manipulated them. In any case, we always imagine the witch as female …[2]

Hers was the classic binary view of gender and sexuality. It was wrapped in feminist Neopaganism and labeled as rebellion but, in many ways, it was as reactionary as a Reagan speech, as mainstream as an upsized combo meal. In *Witches*, Jong danced right up to the edge of something truly transgressive, then backpedaled her Earth Shoes right the hell away from it. Still, her vision had a potency and a poetry which transcended its other limitations, at least for one barely-teenage genderqueer kid lost in the 1980s. I was drawn to the witchcraft she evoked with her words, even as I was barred from it for being a "boy," and that calling—first heard softly, in the pages of role-playing game books and fantasy novels, then amplified by my first confused tastes of what real witchcraft might look like—would haunt me for years after.

My first in-person contact with a real-life Pagan came not long afterward. I was in the fifth grade, the year I injured my left knee in a basketball game as part of a misguided attempt at fitting into my peer group so they would quit beating me up. I was on the playground one day, not playing basketball or getting beaten up, just keeping to myself as usual. My class had a substitute teacher that day: a young woman, blonde and pretty in a vaguely hippie-ish way, though still professional enough to pass muster in a public school in early '80s central California. I don't recall how, but we

---

2. Erica Jong, *Witches* (New York: Harry Abrams, 1981), 69.

wound up in a conversation about Dungeons & Dragons. I may have been walking around reading a D&D book, as was my wont at the time, or she may have struck up a conversation about my interests and drawn out that I was a D&D geek. It may also be that I was somewhat obsessive at that time, and had literally nothing else to talk about with a total stranger. In any event, the subject of druids came up, and I stated, with the iron-clad certainty of the very young, that there were no more druids in the modern world.

"Oh, but there are," she said.

"How do you know?"

"Because I am one," she murmured, softly, for my ears only.

I was floored. If she was telling the truth, if there really were druids—and witches and magicians, perhaps—still kicking around at the tail end of the twentieth century, then everything I thought I knew about history, mythology, and religion was a tower of lies, one she'd just struck with a lightning bolt. (Possibly on loan from Zeus, negotiated through the Dagda.) I felt like I'd just been granted a glimpse behind the veil of a vast, mysterious world, and I wanted in. Oh, how I wanted in. I wanted to ask her so many questions: *How is this possible? What does that even mean? And how do I learn more?*

Sadly, the recess bell rang right at that moment, and I reluctantly filed back into the classroom to reimmerse myself in mundanity … well, as mundane as I could tolerate. After all, I was the weird kid, muddling through the school day as best I could, dodging verbal abuse and the occasional punch thrown my way, and retreating to the refuge of role-playing games and SF/fantasy paperbacks at home. I would wonder idly about that conversation from time to time, but for the most part, I stayed hidden in my own private world.

Music began to factor into that world as well: progressive music, heavy music, music with depth and complexity and a certain inexpressible something to it. I didn't yet have a name for what that something was. I'd first heard hints of it as a child raised on the Beatles, that merry band of psychedelic pop pranksters. Later, I began to pick up that thread in bands like Led Zeppelin, Pink Floyd, Heart, Kansas, and others. As I grew older, I followed that curious thread to other bands: Rush, Marillion, Iron Maiden, Black Sabbath, and more … but those all came later. For now, let's stay nestled in the mid-1980s, cozied up with Gary Gygax and Elric of Melniboné.

A curious thing happened at this point in my life: my family moved from the moderately liberal, left-leaning Central Valley of California to upstate South Carolina.

I spent the first year of my time in South Carolina very, very alone. My multiethnic family were incomprehensibly alien outsiders in a culture whose social hierarchy was overtly based on race, religion, income, and heritage. I found myself dumped into a junior high school environment where I knew no one, and where every facet of my history and experience was irrelevant at best and damning at worst. Faced with a daily gauntlet of mockery, incomprehension, and threats of violence, I withdrew even further into my inner world of fantasy novels and role-playing games. I imagined escaping to some magical land where people like me weren't alien, weren't beaten, weren't mocked and humiliated. I imagined myself with friends. I even dared to imagine myself with a girlfriend, a lover. I imagined myself happy.

And then one day, at a local hobby shop (which doubled as my Friendly Local Game Store), I met a group of People Like Me. They were older—almost all of them adults—but they were nerds, geeks, outsiders. They were fans of Star Trek, watchers of anime, readers of books, players of games. Moreover, they were outsiders in other, deeper ways. Most of them were atheists or agnostics, but a small handful of them were actual, for-realsies Pagans. Similarly, while most of them were straight, some of them were queer in one way or another. Even more remarkable, everyone was accepting of that queerness. It would've been unthinkable to not be. We were, after all, a small band of freaks surrounded by hundreds of miles of reactionary, politically charged Protestant Christianity of the sort that hated the Other, a category which included people of color, queers, agnostics, heretics, non-Christians, and socially awkward nerds like us. All we had to cling to was one another.

And cling we did. It was in that environment—in retrospect unhealthy and unsafe, but far better than the toxic and terrifying experience of being an Other in mainstream culture—that I first traded my sexual innocence for the pleasures of touch, wrapped in a veil of secrecy and shame. The secrecy was a necessity of circumstance: after all, I was fifteen years old, living in one of the notches of the Bible Belt, and my initiators into the mysteries of sexuality—first a biker friend's wife, then a pair of pseudo-sibling Star Trek fans, a straight woman and a gay man—were all legal adults. Each of them seduced me in their own ways, introducing me to the world of adult sexuality at a point when most of my contemporaries were struggling with the clumsiness and terror of adolescent sexuality. By the time I graduated high school, two weeks before my seventeenth birthday, I'd been sexually active with several people in a frankly impressive variety of positions, always accompanied by the pervasive dread of discovery and a crawling sense of shame. I'd had my first STD scare, when my male lover discovered that a former partner of his was HIV+. I'd arranged to spend weekends with my friends, getting drunk enough on Captain Morgan's spiced rum and generic cola that I could slip out of my inhibitions and my jeans, and let them use my body in all the ways I so desperately wanted them to. I went from feeling alone and isolated to feeling seen and known, but I was still a queer teenager in the South with no safe ways to explore my sexuality with my peers. My sense of isolation was still present, if a little less so, and I still felt powerless.

It is, perhaps, little surprise that my first formal introduction to magic came during this same period of my life.

One of the folks in this same circle of friends ran a used bookstore. We'd congregate there sometimes to watch movies, play computer games, and just hang out in a safe space surrounded by books. On my first visit to the bookstore, I noticed a high table in the back room (probably a dresser, come to think of it) covered with a satin cloth, set with a variety of curious objects: candles, a wine glass, a black-hilted Ka-Bar-style knife, and what was clearly a wand of some sort. I knew little about magic beyond the confines of fantasy novels and D&D game books, but even I could put two and two together, so I approached the shopkeeper and asked about it. After a little cagey back-and-forth, the shopkeeper explained that they were a witch, and that the table was an altar. I inquired further, and they left, returning a moment later with a couple of books.

They were, of course, *Drawing Down the Moon* and *The Spiral Dance*.

I read those books with the kind of ravening spiritual hunger only the adolescent can truly muster, an intellectual and emotional craving which consumed me. In those pages, and in the context of my fellow weirdlings, I first found a spirituality which spoke to me, one which embraced both my burgeoning queerness of sexuality and gender and my desperate desire for community, safety, power, and freedom. It wasn't a religion, exactly, but it was something that spoke to that same space in my heart and told me—for, perhaps, the first time in my life—that I was worthy and worthwhile. I was flesh and blood, dust and ashes, but I was filled with sparks of the smokeless fire that lives at the heart of stars. I was both spirit *and* matter: beautiful, messy, sexual, and real. I was queer, and I was magical.

And so it was that I took my first faltering steps along the Path of the Wise, the Crooked Path of witchcraft and sorcery.

The point of this biographical interlude isn't to establish an indelible link between queerness and magic, but to underscore how, in my experience at least, a Pagan worldview and approach to spirituality were uniquely suited to accepting and celebrating my queerness. In a culture where my bodily desires and my ambiguous relationship with gender were seen as antithetical not only to society, but to the sanctity of my very soul, Paganism and magic offered a lifeline, a safe harbor, a way of engaging with my body and identity that was both authentic and empowering, and it's precisely that sense of authentic engagement and empowerment that I hope to encourage in the pages to come.

Whether you're straight or queer, cis or trans, in or out, I want to leave you with one final thought as we set off on our journey into embodiment, gender, sexuality, and magic: it's okay to be queer.

It's okay to be lesbian, gay, bisexual, pansexual, transgender, intersex, asexual, agender, and every other identity, orientation, and lived experience outside the charmed circle of cisgender heterosexuality.

It's okay to be a queer Pagan, a queer witch, a queer polytheist, a queer magician, a queer occultist, a queer magical practitioner.

It's okay to be uncomfortable with heterosexuality as a spiritual metaphor, or to not feel any spiritual or magical resonance with binary gender roles. It's okay to seek the queerness of divinity, and to touch that divinity through your own experiences of gender and sexuality.

In fact, it's more than merely okay: it's beautiful, it's historically valid, and it's utterly essential. What we call queerness has been a part of our devotional and magical praxis as far back as we have records of humans embracing the numinous, because queerness has been a part of human experience as long as there've been humans. Queerness is part and parcel of magic, because magic intrinsically involves stepping beyond the boundaries of the known and circumscribed, and that's the queerest thing I know.

Magic is queer, and queerness is magic.

It's okay to be queer. And anyone who tells you otherwise is wrong.

A Word About Words Before We Start

One of the first principles I learned in university was that just as our ideas change over time, the language we use to express those ideas also changes. The words and ideas we used in the 1970s to discuss gender and sexuality aren't the same words and ideas we use today, as I'm writing this. Where it's been necessary to quote from works which use older, deprecated terminology, I've done my best to indicate how common usage has changed since then. Similarly, the ideas and words I use in this book probably won't all be in accepted use forty years from now, or even ten. So, if you're reading this book ten years down the line, please look as kindly on my language, ideas, and discourse here as you would like others to look upon yours, ten years on from when you write it.

And now, let's get started.

− EXERCISE −
Opening Your Journal

For this exercise, you'll need the following:

- A quiet place to read, write, and think

- Your journal and a writing implement

- About five minutes of undisturbed time

Sit comfortably with your journal and think about reactions and responses to what you've read so far, positive or negative. What are you hoping to find in here? What are you afraid you might find in here, or in the work ahead? What are you looking forward to, or dreading? Think about any words I've been using here that might provoke a strong emotional response, like *queer* or *magic*, and consider both how you define those words and how you feel about them. Whatever your thoughts or feelings are, turn to the first page in your journal and write them down as they come to you, as quickly as you can. You don't have to craft polished, well-reasoned arguments; it's perfectly fine if you only write short declarative statements like "I like _____" or "_____ makes me uncomfortable." The important thing is to keep your pen or pencil moving, and to get your thoughts down in as quick and stream-of-consciousness a manner as possible. Try to keep writing for a few minutes. If you want to go longer or shorter, feel free, but five minutes is about as long as most of us are comfortable free-writing extemporaneously.

The point of this exercise is primarily to get you into the practice of writing in your journal, which can be intimidating, and secondarily to record how you think and feel about the ideas at the heart of this book here at the outset, before you've read any further. We'll revisit this passage later in the book.

Chapter 2
GETTING OUR BEARINGS, KNOWING OUR TERMS

ALL ASPECTS OF HUMAN experience and endeavor are influenced and shaped by gender and sexuality at some level.

This statement is simultaneously so obvious as to be nearly a tautology and so contentious as to start arguments almost instantly. On the one side, the vast majority of humanity got here because two people had sex, the vast majority of us identify with one gender or another, and for most of us, sexuality and gender are all tangled up in one another. Pretty obvious, right? On the other side, though, are the vast array of human endeavors which, at least on their surface, have no relation to gender or sexuality. After all, as conventional wisdom tells us, those issues are rooted in the body, and have no bearing on such cerebral, intellectually detached fields as mathematics, technology, philosophy, economics, and so on. Of course, if you delve into the histories of those endeavors, what you'll find is that they're all deeply rooted in sexual and gender dynamics, and they all have profound implications for how we live out our expressions of sexuality and gender, both personally and culturally.

Spirituality is no different. Whether we're talking about religious belief and praxis or the more active, DIY applications we call mysticism or magic, gender and sexuality inform and influence the ways in which we seek to touch the numinous. Throughout history, spiritual traditions have addressed, and sometimes wrestled with, issues of gender and sexuality as central components of the human experience. In some traditions, gender is seen as a divine binary ordering—"… male and female He created them," as Genesis 5:2 puts it—while in others, gender is a set of polarities, between which exist a wide variety of possibilities. Similarly, some traditions see sexuality is a joyous union, a consecration of oneself and one's chosen partner, while for others it's a necessary evil at best. The connections between gender and sexuality are likewise suffused or imbued with meaning and significance. Many spiritual traditions, ancient and modern, assign explicit social and sexual roles based on gender, rooted in theological justifications that appeal to mythic archetypes.

Outside the Charmed Circle is an exploration of the intersection of gender, sexuality, and spirituality within the context of the modern Western esoteric traditions, those spiritual movements that form a continuation, adaptation, or development from the polytheistic and numinous traditions of the pre-Christian world. This definition includes all of what author and blogger Laura Tempest Zakroff calls "p-words," the various streams of modern magical (or occult) practice and the multiplicity of spiritual traditions falling under the headings of Paganism and polytheism.[3] Practitioners who identify more strongly with one or the other branch of praxis might object to the seemingly cavalier fashion in which I've linked the overtly magical and the devotional, feeling that I'm conflating traditions which have nothing in common. With all respect, I humbly disagree. While on the surface, Golden Dawn–style ceremonial magic or Wicca may seem to have little in common with reconstructionist polytheism or grimoiric sorcery, my contention is that they share far more in common with one another than they do with more mainstream spiritual traditions, or even with other outsider faiths and New Religious Movements, and that a substantial part of that commonality derives from their shared ancestry, which includes shared history and shared cosmological assumptions.

An extensive study of the history of theological and magical views on gender and sexuality isn't really within the purview of this book, but there's a certain amount of historical background that's not only relevant but required as a foundation for the work we're doing here. As an example, it's fairly common knowledge amongst occult scholars that the Hermetic Order of the Golden Dawn was strongly influenced by the Masonic and Rosicrucian background of its three founders, William Robert Woodman, William Wynn Westcott, and Samuel Liddell MacGregor Mathers, as well as by the Victorian fondness for classical Greece and the contemporary Egyptology craze. The Golden Dawn, in turn, was a formative influence on Aleister Crowley, the progenitor and primary source for the religious and magical philosophy of Thelema. The liturgy and poetry Crowley wrote (or, in some cases, channeled), along with a healthy

---

3. Laura Tempest Zakroff, "What's In A P-word?" *A Modern Traditional Witch*, April 5, 2017, http://www.patheos.com/blogs/tempest/2017/04/whats-in-a-pword.html.

dose of magical ritual from a Renaissance-era grimoire called the *Key of Solomon*, were significant influences on the Neopagan witch-cult of Wicca formulated by Gerald Gardner and Doreen Valiente. While Gardner and Valiente were revisioning witchcraft as a kind of magical folk religion, Gardner also introduced his friend Ross Nichols to the indigenous British Isles magio-religious practice of Druidry. Nichols's love for Druidry and Celtic mythology would go on to inspire him to create the Order of Bards, Ovates and Druids, a Druidic organization still in operation today. (The Wheel of the Year so beloved by modern Pagans owes its existence to Nichols and Gardner's friendship, as the two developed the eight-fold schema of solstices, equinoxes, and cross-quarter days together and promulgated it in their separate groups.[4])

For good and for ill, Wicca's rising popularity helped bring the reality of modern Paganism as a spiritual path into public awareness, while groups like the OBOD and other neo-Druidic groups provided a model of what a historically grounded practice of polytheism might look like. Together, these traditions ushered Pagan, polytheist, and magical practice into the modern era, through a doorway formed by Renaissance sorcery, qabalistic Masonry, Egyptian hermeticism, polytheistic recreation, and imaginative extrapolations of folklore and anthropology. Of course, I'm not saying these streams of practice are identical to one another; nothing could be further from the truth. Rather, I want to suggest that all of these traditions share a kind of spiritual and intellectual DNA: a history and a lineage, both figurative and literal.

With that shared history and lineage, all of us p-words within the purview of the Western esoteric traditions are the inheritors

---

4. Ronald Hutton, *The Pagan Religions of the Ancient British Isles* (Oxford, UK: Blackwell, 1991), 337–341.

of a dizzying wealth of lore, wisdom, and techniques for touching the numinous. We're also, sad to say, the inheritors of a dismal tangle of misinformation masquerading as myth, bigotry disguised as truth, and charlatanry claiming to be the one, true, right, and only way to reach God. Sometimes, it's easy to tell fool's gold from true gold, and other times it requires painstaking discernment. In many cases, it's not even as simple as that: the false and the true are found together, seemingly inextricable from one another. In any given spiritual tradition, one can find profound truths and insights of the highest order woven through with faulty logic, outdated science, and cultural biases, as well as with the personal foibles, flaws, and failings of the tradition's founders and promulgators.

Especially in the past century, this dichotomy has led to a great many people becoming disenchanted with spirituality, full stop. As Neal Stephenson wrote in his satirical dystopian cyberpunk novel *Snow Crash*:

> *Ninety-nine percent of everything that goes on in most Christian churches has nothing whatsoever to do with the actual religion. Intelligent people all notice this sooner or later, and they conclude that the entire one hundred percent is bullshit, which is why atheism is connected with being intelligent in people's minds.[5]*

It's easy to look at the misguided parts of a tradition or the hypocrisy of its leaders and conclude that there's nothing of value to be found in the tradition itself. It's much harder, but can also be more rewarding, to discern what there is in a tradition that's

---

5. Neal Stephenson, *Snow Crash* (New York: Bantam, 1992), 63.

good and worthwhile, independent of the logical or moral failings of the human beings within it.

To bring this back around to our point, Western culture has undergone dramatic, tumultuous changes in the past century, and all of its institutions—political, economic, social, religious—have struggled to keep up and adjust to the new realities of life in the modern era. Many of those new realities have revolved around issues of gender and sexuality. Ongoing debates around the acceptance of orientations other than heterosexuality, the changing roles of women and men in society, and the overt interrogation of gender itself—as a paradigm for organizing society, or even as a legitimate psychological reality—are just a few of the arenas in which conventional wisdom has been questioned and, in many cases, found wanting.

So too with the Western esoteric traditions. Magical and devotional spiritual paths have spent much of the past century struggling with the tension between the protean nature of modern life and traditional practices rooted in ancient (and, in some cases, provably outdated) models of reality. For some paths, the challenge of adapting to the modern world has proven too difficult, and their numbers have dwindled, their lore relegated to dusty bookshelves and historical footnotes. Other paths, however, have risen to the challenge, engaging with and adopting new knowledge in a fashion that's both exciting and reassuring. One of my favorite examples of this adaptation is the reframing of the classical Greek elements of earth, water, air, fire, and aether as the states of matter: solid, liquid, gaseous, and plasmatic, incorporating Einstein's mass-energy equivalence to identify aether as energy.

Similarly, the Western esoteric traditions have struggled alongside the broader mainstream Western culture to reconcile their devotional, mythic, and magical traditions with changing sexual mores and concepts of gender, with varying results. Some paths have chosen to double down on their traditional paradigms, viewing those whose sexual lives and gender identities don't fit comfortably into those paradigms as being spiritually sick, "intrinsically disordered," or in some other way innately wrong.[6] Others have engaged with the questions raised by modern understandings of sexuality and gender, entering into larger conversations around the intersection of spiritual praxis, personal identity, sexual and social interaction, and lived experience. As lesbian, gay, bisexual, transgender, queer, intersex, asexual, and other folks become more visibly a part of the Pagan, polytheist, and occult communities, these conversations have become both increasingly common and increasingly necessary.

Of course, this discourse hasn't come without friction. One of the common stumbling blocks is that the terminology we use to describe and define identities and experiences outside of normative cultural institutions can be unfamiliar, and therefore inaccessible, to people outside the communities where those terms originate. In some cases, these terms come from the interlinked communities of people united by their outsider status, based on their sexual or gender identities. In other cases, the terms derive from the work done within the academic world of sexual psychology, feminist studies, or gender theory. In all cases, they're intended to help us grapple with these issues of identity and experience, and to find some way of communicating meaningfully with other people, both those who share our identities and those who don't.

---

6. Congregation for the Doctrine of the Faith, *Persona Humana: Declaration on Certain Questions Concerning Sexual Ethics*, http://www.vatican.va/roman _curia/congregations/cfaith/documents/rc_con_cfaith_doc_19751229 _persona-humana_en.html.

A Handle on My Cup: On Labels and Identity

Let's take a few moments to talk about identity and the labels we use to communicate it. I know that some people are uncomfortable with labels, believing they impose an artificial concrete boundary on the free expression of sexuality, gender, and identity. Some folks will go even further and suggest that codified identities are themselves tools of oppression and division. After all, aren't we all just human beings, no qualifiers needed?

Well, yes … and we're also more complicated. We are indeed all human beings of equal dignity and merit, and the notion that we should be able to exist without boundaries of identity is, I think, a genuinely well-intentioned idea at its core. I would cheerfully embrace this approach if I felt the complexity of lived experience in the day-to-day world were as simple to encapsulate as that. Sadly, and happily, life and identity and behavior are deeply, deliciously complex, and sometimes we need symbols both to help us understand our own experiences and to communicate those experiences to people who might not share our frames of reference.

As an example, I once had a delightful conversation with an eleven-year-old about the power of words to shape our reality, and the labels we use to identify ourselves and others. She'd been talking with her friends at school, and she wanted my help exploring what it meant to "be" something, to identify with some label. I think she was both excited by the power of self-determination that a label can confer and nervous about the responsibility that power incurs. After all, she reasoned, if we define ourselves by some label, isn't that a kind of commitment to *always* be whatever that label designates? Doesn't that make us accountable to some outside authority which adjudicates the boundaries of that label, that identity? What if she identified with a label yesterday, but doesn't today? Does that mean she lied to her friends, many of whom share affinities with her based on those very labels?

All this at the age of eleven, no less. Never let them tell you kids don't think about serious issues.

We talked about labels and identity, and I shared with her my favorite explanation for the utility, power, and limitation of labels, which she seemed to find pretty helpful. Labels, I said, are like the handle on a suitcase or—relevant to my own biases—on a coffee cup: they're things we attach to something much larger, something that's inconvenient to simply hold and carry in our hands. Maybe the thing we're trying to carry is too heavy, or too hot or cold, or simply awkward and unwieldy. Whatever it is, the handle gives us a convenient way to pick it up, hold it, carry it around, and set it down. A handle can be fancy or simple, but ultimately the point isn't the aesthetics. It's the utility. After all, a handle that doesn't help you hold the coffee cup isn't much of a handle, right? At the same time, the handle isn't what's important about the coffee cup. The cup itself isn't even that important. What's important is the coffee itself. You can drink your morning joe from bone china, ceramic, enamelware, or plastic, but none of the materials makes a lick of difference to whether or not you're getting caffeine into your bloodstream.

I trust that most of you can follow this metaphor to its logical conclusion, but just to make it unavoidably clear: those of us in the Pagan, polytheist, and magical communities spend an awful lot of time arguing about labels. As exhibit A, I'll offer the fact that I needed to specify "Pagan, polytheist, and magical communities" in order to circumscribe the subcultural groups I wanted to identify. As exhibit B, I'll point to those communities' extensive histories of infighting and ongoing disputes over what words mean and who has a right to use them, as exemplified by words like Wicca, witch, Pagan, Heathen, and magic. The same holds true in the LGBTQIA+ community, where we savage one another pretty ruthlessly over the increasing granularity of queer and trans identity.

To be clear, I think this granularity of identity is a good thing. I love the power of words to shape the world, and I love how we're developing a language for expressing the shape and nuance of our lived experiences of gender, sexuality, and spirituality. It's fantastic that LGBTQIA+ folks and the Pagan, polytheist, and magical practitioner communities are working through their own self-creation and self-naming, claiming and owning their own experiences and power. What's less fantastic is the tendency for embracing labels to turn into gatekeeping, policing, and ostracizing. After all, the point of a label is to give you a handle on something, a means by which you can carry something much larger, heavier, hotter, more awkward. When you make the cup all about the handle, you miss out on the entire point of the handle in the first place: to hold your cup so you can drink your damn coffee.

The cliché that it's what's inside that matters really is true here, and what's inside is what we're all about. Words like gay, lesbian, bisexual, and asexual are labels we put on a set of lived experiences, as are words like transgender, cisgender, and nonbinary. Similarly, words like witch, magician, druid, and priest are labels for collated sets of actions, practices, beliefs, and experiences. These labels are meant to serve us, to communicate something about our experiences and lives to other people. What they're not meant to do is serve as a choke-chain or a set of handcuffs binding us to some particular interpretation of what those experiences mean. We are the only ones who can interpret the meanings of our experiences with any accuracy, and the only ones who can say which labels are the best handles for those experiences.

I told my tween-age interlocutor that our lives grow and change, that she might grow out of or away from any label she adopts today … and that's okay. The point of life isn't the labels, but the experiences we use those labels to express and share with others.

Words Mean Things: A Quick Lexicon

At the risk of waxing overly academic, I want to define some of the terms I'll be using before we get well and truly under way, terms that many of us use to express our lived experiences. The terms themselves aren't particularly esoteric, but my usage of them might be non-standard, idiosyncratic, or simply unfamiliar to you. These definitions are intended to give you a sense of how *I'm* using these terms, rather than being prescriptive in any way, and other folks will have their own interpretations and definitions for these terms. I don't mind if people disagree with me, but I want to clarify my meanings as much as possible, so they're based on legitimate differences of opinion rather than simple misunderstandings. So, I hope you'll bear with me as I make use of both my gender studies degree and my religious studies background to offer this resource as a starting point for discussions, with the caveat that these are my interpretations of these identifiers, as colored by my experiences, background, and education.

Please note that these definitions have been written for the broadest audience possible, some of whom may be encountering these terms for the first time. Also, some of these definitions refer to deprecated terms and slang words used as slurs, many of which can be deeply hurtful to people against whom those terms are used. These terms are included solely to educate people unfamiliar with the context and nuance surrounding them, so they don't use them carelessly or, in some cases, at all. If you are sensitive to such terms, please exercise caution and self-care.

Gender, Sex, Sexuality, and Magic

So, let's start with the hardest task. After all, we can't really have a conversation about gender, sex, sexuality, or magic if we don't understand what those words mean, right?

Of course, one of the major problems we're going to have in coming up with definitions for those words is that the English language is a hot mess. As the science fiction television show *Babylon 5* accurately summed up the issue, the trouble with English is that we define all our words by reference to other words, which means that none of our words have their own meanings.[7] Gender seems like it would be fairly easy to define, but even the most basic dictionary definition practically constitutes a 1001-level gender studies class syllabus, and will have you wandering off into discussions of biological, social, and cultural notions of sex and behavior in short order. Most definitions of gender make some reference to the concept of non-physical traits which are nevertheless associated with the biological sexes as a category. Of course, sex also refers to things that have little-to-nothing to do with gender or biological sex, which just makes things even more complicated.

Instead of a concrete category, then, what I'll offer you as a working definition is the following set of ideas: cultures have a notion of intangible characteristics—identities, behaviors, and social roles—that exist on a continuum between two poles we call femininity and masculinity. Gender can be conceived as the range of characteristics found between these two poles of categorization, which have been equated in many cultures (in many cases, arbitrarily) with our traditional understandings of the biological sexes found in humans, female and male.

---

7. J. Michael Straczynski, "And the Rock Cried Out, No Hiding Place," *Babylon 5*, original airdate October 14, 1996.

This definition acknowledges the mutable, contextual nature of gender, and delineates both the connections and distinctions between gender and biological sex. For me, it falters a bit with its insistence on defining gender in simple male/female terms. In her groundbreaking 1990 book *Gender Trouble*, philosopher and gender theorist Judith Butler utterly dismantled the notion of *woman* or *man* as concrete categories of lived experience, demonstrating that these words are instead merely labels, socially constructed with the expectation that the people to whom they're affixed will perform the roles demanded of them by the label. In other words, our ideas of what it means to be a woman or a man are defined by the cultures into which we were born, and in which we were raised. We'll delve further into this in chapter 4. For now, let's go with the idea of gender as a range of characteristics and behaviors which tend to be grouped into the binary poles of femininity and masculinity, most (if not all) of the parameters of which are socially constructed.

Having established a working definition of gender, let's take a moment to talk about biological sex as its own distinct category. Human beings are sexually dimorphic, meaning that we tend toward having certain anatomical configurations and characteristics derived from our chromosomal makeup, many of which relate to our particular form of sexual reproduction, which we divide into two categories, male and female. These biological categories are frequently ascribed cultural significance—rights, responsibilities, roles, meanings—which are both conflated with and contribute to the social construction of gender as a role we're expected to play.

Again, though, it behooves us to remember that biological sex is just a schema of categories, invented by humans to help us understand reproductive science. While this schema can be a useful model as far as it goes, it's not an immutable concrete reality even in our own bodies, as recent developments in science have demonstrated. In particular, the increasing awareness of the existence of intersex people and the implications of their lived realities underscores the fact that neither gender nor biological sex are as cut-and-dried, nor as simplistic, as some pundits would like to have us believe.

That brings us, of course, to sexuality. We'll talk a lot more about this in chapter 6, but here's a sneak preview: as far as I'm concerned, sexuality refers to our capacity for experiencing erotic sensation, physically or mentally, and sex includes any activity we undertake for the express purpose of stimulating erotic sensation in ourselves or in others. That includes all kinds of stuff: solitary, coupled, or multi-partnered acts, involving any configuration of bodies who want to be in intimate contact with one another, generating pleasure, generating *eros*.

Last of course, is magic. If you've made it this far in the book, I'm going to assume you have your own definition of magic, and possibly your own forms of practice ... but you wanted to know my definition. So, not to be coy: I define magic as the act of exercising one's will to change reality in a way that isn't easily explained by a clear chain of cause-and-effect. We'll spend much of the rest of the book talking about how that works, most notably in chapter 6.

Queer

I know this word often comes across as confrontational, even offensive, but I'm going to push back on that idea. After all, it's one of the key concepts around which this book was written, and I think it's worth taking a little time to unpack it.

Queer was initially coined as a slur in Victorian England to describe people whose gender performance or sexuality are seen as non-normative, unhealthy, or strange in some other way, and spread throughout Anglophone countries by the early twentieth century. This is especially well documented in *A Very Queer Family Indeed*, Simon Goldhill's biographical overview of one extraordinary Victorian family's literary struggle with the fluidity of their own gendered and sexual identities.[8]

In the 1980s and 1990s, the word was reclaimed by some within what we now call the LGBTQIA+ community as a self-identifying descriptor, a generalized term for a variety of expressions of sexuality and gender which share in common their outsider status in relation to culturally normative gender and sexuality. The exact definition and contents of these sexual and gender norms are a moving target, determined as they are by the mores of a given culture in a given place at a given point in time, all of which change and adapt to the needs of the moment. Queer has also found traction within the academic community, where queer studies and queer theory have developed as fields of study interrogating those cultural norms. Here, queer has come to mean something which challenges the normative assumptions our culture makes about gender and sexuality, and *queering* has come to refer to the act of adapting something—a practice, an artifact, an idea, or a text—to meet the needs of marginalized queer groups.

This can all be pretty confusing. However, we can find a useful lens to view queerness in the work of cultural anthropologist Gayle Rubin. In her seminal 1984 essay "Thinking Sex," Rubin posits that within any given culture, there exists both a set of sexual attributes to which positive values are ascribed, and their antitheses, to which negative values are ascribed. The positively valued attributes form the hegemonic norms or sexual ideals of a culture, which she calls

8. Simon Goldhill, *A Very Queer Family Indeed: Sex, Religion, and the Bensons in Victorian Britain* (Chicago: University of Chicago Press, 2017), 10–15.

the "charmed circle" of sexuality, while their antitheses form what she calls "the outer limits," the shadow-self of culturally normative sexuality. In the post-Christian Western world, the charmed circle encompasses attributes like being heterosexual and cisgender, and practices like monogamy, missionary-position sex, sex solely for reproductive purposes, and non-kinky (or "vanilla") sex. Any alternative to these attributes and practices is excluded from the charmed circle. Homosexuality, bisexuality, asexuality, being transgender, or failing to conform to expected gender norms are all consigned to the outer limits, alongside practices like polyamory, non-missionary sex, sex solely for pleasure, sex work, kinky sex, and so on.

Within the confines of this book, and in my own life, I use queer as an umbrella covering all of us whose gender and sexual identities exist outside the charmed circle of hegemonically normative cisgender heterosexuality, and whose lived experiences challenge those social norms. I'll have a lot more to say about queerness and its relationship with sexuality and magic in later chapters, especially chapter 5. (You'll also note that the title of both the chapter and the book itself references this concept!)

It's worth reiterating that queer is far from being a universally accepted term, one which many LGBTQIA+ people find distasteful or contentious. Some of the word's problematic nature comes from its history as a slur, while others feel the use of queer as an umbrella term erases individual gender and sexual identities. As ever, when dealing with a particular person or institution, it's always best to call them what they wish to be called.

Straight

This generally refers to people of a binary gender, male or female, who are sexually and/or romantically attracted to people they perceive as being of the opposite gender. The technical term is *heterosexual*, sometimes abbreviated as "hetero" or "het" in certain circles.

LGBTQIA+

An acronym for Lesbian, Gay, Bisexual, Transgender, Queer/Questioning, Intersex, and Asexual/Aromantic, with the plus sign standing in for other identities not addressed by those terms. The acronym has changed and grown over the years, from LGBT to LGBTQ to its present state, in response both to the need for an umbrella term covering the whole of the community and to the perception that queer was an undesirable term due to its history as a slur.

Gay

For such a small word, this term covers a lot of ground. Initially, *gay* was a loan word from French, and meant joyful, happy, light-hearted, and carefree. While it still holds on to these meanings in some contexts, gay began to acquire the more lascivious connotation of sexually indulgent roughly around the time Shakespeare was writing plays. By the early twentieth century, gayness had begun to be associated specifically with same-sex liaisons. Today, it commonly refers to people who are primarily or exclusively sexually and/or romantically attracted to people perceived as having the same binary gender, also known as homosexuality. (While "homo" is sometimes used as an abbreviation, be advised that this has highly negative connotations in most circles, equivalent to other homophobic slurs, and should really be avoided unless you yourself are gay.)

Another, perhaps equally common usage refers specifically to men who are primarily or exclusively sexually and/or romantically attracted to other men, though this isn't universal.

Curiously, it's also used as a blanket term to refer to anyone who isn't straight. This usage is both historical (as with the Gay Liberation Front of the late 1960s and 1970s) and contemporary, especially among some younger LGBTQIA+ people. This usage is not dissimilar to "queer," as mentioned earlier.

(I know it's confusing. I wish I could say it gets less so, but... well, let's move on.)

Lesbian

The term *lesbian* refers to women who are primarily or exclusively attracted to other women, sexually and/or romantically. Lesbians are also called gay women at times, though this usage is somewhat less common. The word itself derives from the Greek isle of Lesbos, famously the home of the poet Sappho, whose "Ode to Aphrodite" is a prayer for divine aid in securing the love of another woman. The term *Sapphic*, derived from the poet's name, is sometimes used as an adjective referring to women who love women. (It's worth noting, however, that Sappho wrote love poetry addressed to both women and men; in today's terms, she may have been what we would call bisexual.)

Bisexual and Pansexual

These terms are sometimes seen as interchangeable, and other times as distinct orientations. *Bisexuality* refers to people of any gender who are sexually and/or romantically attracted both to people who share their gender and to those who don't. The term *pansexuality* was coined in response to the perception that bisexual reinforced a binary gender paradigm of being attracted to "both men and women," thus excluding people outside that binary. Many people have strong feelings about one or the other. When in doubt, ask the person how they'd like to be described. (As a personal aside, I refer to myself by both terms, depending on context.)

Asexual, Demisexual, and Aromantic

Simply put, people who are *asexual* don't experience sexual attraction. Some have no sexual inclination or arousal whatsoever, while others may experience arousal, but have no concomitant desire to have partnered sex. A common misconception is that asexuals suffer from some past trauma that has rendered them phobic about sex. In reality, most asexuality has no causal link to trauma, and most asexuals are perfectly well-adjusted people who just happen not to have any interest in sexuality, and in my experience, tend to find the whole thing somewhat amusing or perplexing.

Demisexuality, sometimes seen as a subset of asexuality, refers to folks whose sexuality is only engaged in the context of an emotional bond or relationship. This orientation isn't derived from a save-it-for-marriage sort of morality; demisexuals don't feel sexual attraction to a person unless they feel something emotionally for them first.

Aromantic folks don't experience what we tend to think of as "romantic" love. Mind you, this doesn't mean they don't love! Like asexuality, aromanticism exists on a spectrum, and aromantic people can have a wide range and variety of loving relationships.

I've grouped these folks together in part because their orientations share in common an absence of certain qualities or feelings which some folks seem to believe think are mandatory for esoteric praxis. I've seen it said that it's simply impossible for asexuals to practice sex magic, for instance, a statement which flies in the face of the number of asexual practitioners of sex magic I've known. While I agree that the notion can seem a little contradictory, I can also see how asexuality, demisexuality, and aromanticism could actually be beneficial to the practice of sexual magic. In any event, I find it's best to assume that other people have a better understanding of how their lives and practice work than I do.

Transgender

If you don't identify with the gender you were assigned at birth, you're *transgender*, sometimes abbreviated as *trans*. Some people define transgender in specifically binary terms, i.e., as referring to a transition from male to female or female to male, while others see transgender as a broader umbrella term referring to anyone not of their birth-assigned gender. There's no slur, criticism, or judgment inherent in the term, either in full or abbreviated, but colloquial abbreviations ("tranny," "transie," and so on) are often used as highly offensive slurs and should be avoided by anyone who isn't themselves transgender.

Though less common than in previous years, the term *transsexual* is used by some trans people to reflect their personal experience of being transgender, especially by those who've opted to pursue medical transition. Again, I'd suggest avoiding this term unless either you are trans yourself, or you've been explicitly asked by a particular person to use this term to refer to them.

Cisgender

If, on the other hand, you *do* identify as the gender you were assigned at birth, you're *cisgender*, sometimes abbreviated as *cis*. As with transgender or trans, this is a technical term utterly devoid of inherent criticism, judgment, or insult. (We'll talk more about the meaning of cisgender, and why I give such short shrift to the idea that it's in any way an insult, in chapter 4.)

Nonbinary, Agender, Neutrois, Androgynous, Genderqueer, Gender-Fluidity, Gender-Nonconforming, and More!

All of these terms refer to people whose experiences of gender don't fit neatly within the binary male / female gender paradigm common to Western culture. Some of these folks identify as transgender, while others don't. As ever, it's always a good idea to find out how an individual person identifies before using that term. There's a bit to get a handle on here, so take a deep breath and let's dash through it!

Nonbinary refers to people who don't identify with either of the binary gender options in Western culture, male or female, regardless of what they were assigned at birth. Related terms include *agender* and *neutrois*, which both refer to people who understand themselves as genderless, and *gender-fluid*, which describes people whose experience of gender can be variable, depending on mood, context, and any number of other factors.

Androgynous is a term which is sometimes used for people whose experience and expression of gender incorporates attributes commonly ascribed to both men and women. It's less common than it used to be, and I'd avoid using it unless someone has told you directly that this is the term they use. (Are you spotting a theme here?)

Genderqueer describes people whose identities and expressions of identity play with queer notions of gender, while *gender-nonconforming* describes people whose outward expressions of gender identity don't culturally conform to the gender they were ascribed at birth.

(For personal reference purposes, your humble author identifies as a nonbinary, agender androgyne, all under the transgender umbrella.)

Intersex

The United Nations Office of the High Commissioner for Human Rights defines *intersex* as follows:

> *Intersex people are born with sex characteristics (including genitals, gonads and chromosome patterns) that do not fit typical binary notions of male or female bodies. Intersex is an umbrella term used to describe a wide range of natural bodily variations. In some cases, intersex traits are visible at birth while in others, they are not apparent until puberty. Some chromosomal intersex variations may not be physically apparent at all.*[9]

The term *hermaphrodite*, from the Greek deity Hermaphroditus, has been used in the past to refer to intersex people, but as this term is stigmatizing and often used as something of a slur, I strongly recommend avoiding it unless the person asks you to use it. It's also worth noting that being intersex is not the same as being transgender. While some intersex people may identify as transgender, most do not, and the issues each group faces are distinct, if sometimes related.

– EXERCISE –
A Pin in the Map

For this exercise, you'll need your journal, a writing implement, and a few minutes of undisturbed time.

---

9. United Nations Office of the High Commissioner for Human Rights, *Free & Equal Fact Sheet: Intersex*, www.ohchr.org/Documents/Issues/Discrimination/LGBT/FactSheets/UNFE_FactSheet_Intersex_EN.pdf.

Having just read over this mini-lexicon of sexualities and gender identities, open your journal to a fresh page and free-write for a few minutes about your own gender and sexual identity, and your personal history of engaging with issues of gender and sexuality. Was there a period where you questioned either of those identities, or have you always just known who and what you were? Have you ever moved from one identity to another, or wondered what it would be like to identify as something other than you do? Take as much time as you need to record your thoughts.

Straight, Queer, Cis, Trans: Things We Should Know

With all of these terms and rules around which words to use when, you might be understandably confused about what to say or how to say it. If you're finding yourself a little bewildered at this point, allow me to offer a little advice on how to engage with all of these issues of gender and sexuality. Think of the following as my attempt at being the p-word equivalent of Emily Post or Miss Manners, offering you some high-level suggestions for navigating the sort of thorny social situations that can arise when we work toward making our spaces inclusive and welcoming to people whose experiences we don't necessarily share or understand.

What Straight and Cis People Should Know About Queer and Trans People

Hello, straight and cis readers! To start, I'd like to thank you for being here in the first place and reading what I have to say. It's genuinely heartening to know that there *are* people willing to do this work of inclusion with us, even when it gets uncomfortable … which it often does. That's one of the biggest barriers to allyship, really: the discomfort that straight and cisgender allies feel when confronted with something about queerness or transness they don't understand, and the fear of causing unintentional insult and injury by Doing It Wrong. The reality is that *everybody* does it wrong from time to time, even those of us who've been steeped in queerness and transness our whole lives. Doing it wrong doesn't mean you're a bad person, nor does it mean your mistakes are unforgivable transgressions. These things can be hard, and they're made even harder because our culture rarely talks about them and explicitly says what doing it right looks like. So here are a few things to keep in mind that may help you feel more comfortable about not doing it wrong.

In many important ways, we're just like you. We sleep, wake, eat, drink, bathe, and groom ourselves. We complain about our day jobs (or lack thereof), binge-watch shows on Netflix, and dream of going on vacations. We engage with our faiths, traditions, and magical practices. We work with gods, spirits, and the world around us. We're just people.

However, in many other ways, we're *not* just like you. Our experiences of our identities, our bodies, and the world around us can be fundamentally different from those of cisgender and heterosexual people, rooted in some of the qualities and characteristics that inform our identities and experiences at the deepest levels of selfhood. Those qualities and characteristics—our sexuality, our gender, and the interactions between those two—are shared with straight and cis people in many ways, but the ways they manifest in our bodies, our personalities, and our lived experiences vary widely. Life as a queer and/or trans person has a whole host of challenges that straight and cis people simply don't have to face and of which, consequently, they're often unaware. That statement isn't intended as criticism; it's just an observation of fact. Just as white people can't know what it is to experience racism as black or brown people do, straight and cis people can't really grasp the lived experience of homophobia and transphobia.

So, how can straight and cis people interact with queer and trans people without giving offense or, worse, causing harm? I could offer a list of dos and don'ts, but honestly, most of those rules could be boiled down to a single sentence: listen sympathetically, be friendly, and try not to be too concerned about what's in someone's pants, or what they do in bed.

No, really, I'm serious. Unless you're *extremely* close to someone —for instance, if you're about to have sex with them—don't ask them what's in their pants, or what they do in bed. If they really want you to know, they'll tell you. (And if you're truly dying to know how things work down there, the internet is a treasure trove of information.)

We should also take a few moments to talk about the whole pronoun thing. With the increasing visibility of trans and nonbinary people within our communities, the question of what pronouns to use for a given person has become something of a hot-button topic for a lot of folks. From an etiquette standpoint, it's really quite simple: use the pronouns you're offered, and if you aren't offered any, politely inquire what pronouns the person in question uses … or, better yet, offer your own pronouns: "Hi! My name is Misha, and my pronouns are they/them." This can be a little awkward at first, but it beats guessing wrong and offending or hurting someone. As no less an authority than Miss Manners herself points out,

> *There is a range of gender categories, not just male and female, and a vocabulary that has been proposed to go with*

each, but has not been universally recognized. So guessing is,
if anything, worse than asking.[10]

Another difficulty you might encounter is the use of pronouns other than *he* and *she*. As we've discussed, gender is far more complex than the binary paradigm most of us have grown up with, and linguists and other proponents of gender-neutral language have grappled with the lack of a gender-neutral personal pronoun in English for over a century. As trans and nonbinary people have entered public discourse more visibly, they've contributed their thoughts and lived experiences to the conversation around gender-neutral language. Some folks have responded by coining and proposing nontraditional gender-neutral pronouns, or neo-pronouns, such as *e, ze, xe, thon,* and many others. These gender-neutral neo-pronouns have their proponents, but the clear leader for both casual and formal use as of this writing is the singular *they.*

Part of its advantage is historical precedent: *they* as a singular personal pronoun has been with us since at least the fourteenth century CE, when Geoffrey Chaucer used it in "The Pardoner's Prologue" from *The Canterbury Tales* ("And whoso fyndeth hym out of swich blame, / They wol come up and offre, on Goddes name ..."[11]), and can also be found in the works of William Shakespeare and Jane Austen.

Another advantage is that the singular *they* is already built into how many people already speak. For instance, it doesn't sound par-

---

10. Judith Martin, Nicholas Martin, and Jacobina Martin, "Miss Manners: A simple 'you' avoids any gender confusion," *The Washington Post*, September 27, 2015.

11. Geoffrey Chaucer, *The Complete Works of Geoffrey Chaucer*, ed. Walter W. Skeat (Oxford, UK: Clarendon Press, 1900), http://www.gutenberg.org/ebooks/22120.

ticularly odd to say, "Someone left their phone on the table." We're speaking about an individual, but we don't know who they are, so we don't know their gender. In my experience, we only feel strange using singular *they* about someone when we believe their gender to be something other than the gender (or absence of gender) they've told us they have. Working past that mental hurdle can be challenging, but for folks whose lived experiences are outside the gender binary, the efforts you make to see them as they are can be a profound demonstration of respect and inclusion.

Folks with an essentialist view of gender (see "Defining Gender Essentialism, and Why It's a Problem") may argue that being asked to use the pronouns they've been offered for certain individuals is an imposition on their convictions, that they're being forced to participate in something with which they disagree. At the risk of offending those folks, I want to point out that the putative harm it causes people with gender-essentialist views to refer to trans and nonbinary folks by their correct pronouns is far less than the harm done by imposing gender-essentialist views on people to whom they simply don't apply.

If you've read this far, allow me to encourage you to read the next section as well.

What Queer and Trans People Should Remember About Straight and Cis People

Hello, fellow queer and trans people! You'll notice that I didn't say "Things Queer and Trans People Should *Know* About Straight Cis People," because honestly, most of these are things that queer and trans people already know. After all, cisgender heterosexuality is normative in mainstream culture, and the assumptions built into that culture form the backdrop against which we live our lives. Still, it can be easy to forget these things sometimes and assume that, because someone is spiritually like-minded in certain ways, they'll be sympathetic to our needs, our wishes, and our situations.

In my experience, when it comes to being inclusive of queer and trans people, most straight and cis people really are doing the best they know how. Depending on the individual person and their present context, their best might not be particularly great, but I've found that most people really are trying to be decent. If someone is genuinely treating you in good faith and with best intent, try to give them a break when they screw up and use the wrong words, or say something gauche. Many straight and cis people aren't going to know the language we want them to use, and they might not understand why we feel it's so important to use certain words over others. This stuff is hard, especially when you aren't immersed in it 24/7. It can be hard even for those of us who *are* immersed in it. Yes, it's an unfair burden to place on us, and yes, I wish it were different. Until we live in that different world, though, cutting people slack and being forgiving of their mistakes is not only gracious, but pragmatic.

No matter how nice you are, no matter how carefully you explain things, and no matter how obvious the ethical and practical reasons may seem, some people are fundamentally uninterested in being inclusive or accepting. They may feel that queerness of sexuality or gender is somehow against divine or natural law, or that the kinds of changes they would need to make in order to accept queer people are an imposition on their spiritual freedoms, or that their own conceptions of self, sexuality, and gender would be threatened by inclusivity. Some folks, you won't be able to reach, which is unfortunate, even tragic in some cases.

It's also a reality. All we can really do in those cases is accept that those people are unreachable and walk away. Of course, walking away is easier said than done when the people in question are connected to our lives in some way: our families, our friends, our co-religionists, our coworkers, and so on. Living with and around people who question our identities, our rights, even our existence is one of the realities of queerness that most non-queer people—especially those who are also privileged in other ways—rarely experience and can have difficulty understanding. Sometimes, the best we can do is endure and survive until we can remove ourselves to a better situation.

The following exercise is intended to help you think about the words we use to talk about ourselves—our identities, experiences, and behaviors—and about the ways in which we can use those labels to discover new insights about ourselves.

— EXERCISE —
Taking Measure of Your Self

For this exercise, you'll need your journal, a writing implement, and about half an hour of undisturbed time.

Sit comfortably with your writing things at hand, but don't write anything yet. Instead, take a few minutes to think about yourself. Think about who you are to other people, the identities that make up your persona, and what you do for them, all the different hats you wear that make up the person other people know. What are the various roles you play at work or school? Who are you when you're out with your friends, or when you're with your family of origin? Who are you in the various online spaces you occupy, and how does that differ from who you are in physical spaces? Think about who are you when you're unaccompanied in public. What qualities do you try to display for others? How you want to be seen…or do you want to be seen at all?

Turn to a fresh page in your journal and fold it in half down the middle, so that the right half is tucked behind the left. Now, start writing those roles on the left half. You can use whatever words capture the essential nature of that role. You may find that titles work better for roles related to specific relationships with other people —*spouse, partner, parent, sibling, child, coworker, student, teacher, priest/ess/x, covener, lodge member*—while more general descriptors might better describe roles that are less easily defined—*leader, lover, caretaker, confidant, protector*, and so on. If those roles are gendered, incorporate that language: *mother, father, wife, husband, daughter, son*. In the context of your spiritual life, you might find words like *witch, magician, seeker, mystic, sorcerer,* or *devotee* useful. If you're having trouble coming up with specific terms, you might think about using adjectival phrases: *the smart one, the funny one, the brave one, the strong one, the one who drinks and knows things*. Whatever these words or phrases are, write them down, as many as you can come up with. As you do, you might also find that one term leads you to others.

Once you've got a nice long list of words, set it all aside and think about who you are when you're by yourself, removed from the context of other people. Who are you underneath all the hats, the person beneath the persona? Who are you when you're not being someone else *for* someone else? Who were you before the people around you taught you that you needed to be someone else, someone more suited to their needs or desires? What do you do solely for yourself because it pleases you or fulfills some need within yourself? What qualities do you see in yourself that, as far as you know, only you know about?

Sit with those questions for a few minutes, then pick up your writing implement again. Turn the page so that only the right half is visible, and start writing on that half. This time, write down words or phrases that reflect that sense of who you are independent of other people's expectations, requirements, or demands. Try to avoid words that depend too heavily on outside definitions, or that identify structured institutions or movements: Pagan, Heathen, Wiccan, Thelemite, and so on. Instead, think in simpler, more essential terms: artist, musician, dancer, writer, witch, magician, maker. Because many of us don't spend a lot of time thinking about ourselves in those terms, these words may not come as easily as the first set. Give yourself time to reflect as you write and don't push yourself too hard.

Unfold your paper and look over the two lists you've made. Do any words or phrases appear on both lists or have clear relationships with one another, like *mother* and *caretaker*, or *teacher* and *the smart one*? Conversely, do any of your words or phrases directly contradict others? Are some of the roles and qualities linked, joined by a causal relationship? For instance, do you hide being *scared* under the *brave* face you show the world? Do you play the role of *normal* or *ordinary* to prevent people from knowing that you're *strange*, *queer*, or a *witch*? You can make notes about any connections you draw between these concepts, or your feelings about them as labels and identifiers.

Now read these lists, the external and the internal, and look at them together. Consider them like a personality profile or a character sketch ... because that's what they are. What picture do they draw, and how do you feel about the person they depict? Would you trust them? Is this someone you'd want as a friend? If they came to you afraid or in pain, how would you help them? Where are their strengths, and where could they work to be stronger?

With those thoughts in mind, turn the page and write a brief but honest assessment of the person revealed to you in the traits and roles you identified on the front of the paper. Write about the kind of person you believe them to be, and the kind of person they have the potential to be at their best. When finished, put your journal away in a safe place.

So, was this magic? No … and yes. It's a psychological exercise, akin what Terry Pratchett's iconic witch Granny Weatherwax might call "headology," intended not only to help you see yourself but to help you see *how* you see yourself.[12] It's easy to avoid examining our own self-image, just as it's easy to avoid looking in a mirror. We carry all these components of our identities around with us, sometimes worn for all the world to see, sometimes hidden away in our minds and hearts even from ourselves. Exercises like this are useful tools to ferret out the pieces of our senses of self we've hidden from our conscious minds but which influence how we see and think about ourselves all the same. We can refer to this record of our own self-image over time and see how our perception of our self (or selves) has changed, and where we might yet want to work to change it more, or even just to know ourselves better. As the Delphic priesthood of Apollo reminds us down through the ages, it's crucial that we know ourselves both to live a fulfilled life and to do any kind of meaningful work, including magic. After all, we do magic with our minds.

However, we also do magic with our bodies—or perhaps I should say, in and through our bodies. Let's talk about that, shall we?

---

12. Terry Pratchett, *Maskerade* (London: Victor Gollancz, 1995), 17–21.

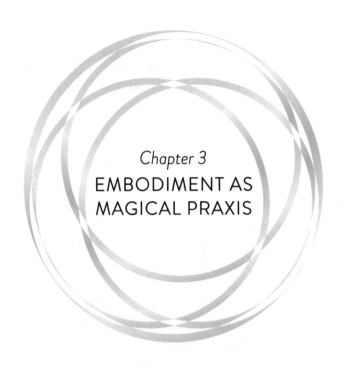

Chapter 3
EMBODIMENT AS MAGICAL PRAXIS

HUMANS ARE AN AMAZINGLY diverse species. We come in a wide array of sizes, shapes, textures, and hues. Humans are tall, short, skinny, fat, and at the midpoint of all of these size ranges. Humans have skin as white as the falling snow, as black as the night sky, and every shade and hue in between. We can no more point to an average human appearance than to an average human voice. The same principle holds true for the cultures we've developed to create meaning from our lives and experiences, and the ways we manifest those cultures in language, art, spirituality, and behavior.

Really, when you come down to it, the only thing that all humans share in common is our bodies: our bruised and beautiful bodies, our flawed and fallible flesh. All of our bodies develop from sperm and egg joined in a zygotic dance of union and division. All of our bodies emerge from within another human body into the world to change and grow, play and work, live and love. And of course, all of our bodies falter, fail, and die. Whatever else may happen beyond that point, death is the end of the line for our bodies. From there, barring artificial processes to detach them from the natural course of events, our bodies will wither and decay, ultimately returning to the elements of which they're composed.

None of these observations is revolutionary, or even notable. After all, mortality is the defining characteristic of the human condition. Countless religions and philosophies have been created for the sole purpose of explaining, denying, or circumventing the reality of death; and an incalculable amount of art, science, industry, and sheer bloody-minded brute force has been committed to the ceaseless struggle to cope with the unalterable final word on life: that it ends.

A somber note on which to begin, perhaps, but it underscores the centrality of the body to human existence and experience. Simply put, embodiment—having the dual nature of both flesh and spirit—is a key component of what it means to be human.

What does it mean to be embodied? In Western culture, we often speak of having a body or a soul, in much the same way that we have a car or brown hair, but there are two kinds of having at work there, and they aren't really the same thing. In one case, we have an object, and having refers to an inventory of our possessions. In the other we have an attribute, and having refers to a quality intrinsic to our being. That quality might change or disappear altogether, or we may divest ourselves of it intentionally. I can see this at work in my own brown hair steadily going gray. I could choose to dye my hair, or to shave it off altogether, but my hair will still and always be my hair. On the other hand, if I sell my car, not only do I no longer *have* it, the car is no longer *mine*; I have, if you will, de-possessed that object. Not only am I divested of physical and legal custody of that vehicle, but—unless I sell it to a personal acquaintance—I will no longer inhabit it.

What does it mean to have a body or a soul? Is a soul an attribute intrinsic to being human, or is it a possession (pardon the pun) to be kept or sold, presumably to some infernal spirit? Is the body a vessel and vehicle, or is it something else, something less reducible to consumerist terminology? And when we speak of *having* a body or *having* a soul, who or what is doing all this having?

Body and Soul, or Body as Soul?

In the Anderson Feri tradition, we are taught that each human being is made up of not a single soul but three, an understanding that can be usefully considered both as interconnected parts of a single entity and as separate entities in their own right. Of course, the concept of a tripartite soul is hardly unique to Feri. The Greek philosopher Plato posits a tripartite soul in his *Republic*, for instance, where he names the three parts as λογιστικόν (*logistykon*, logical), θυμοειδές(*thymoeides*, spirited) and ἐπιθυμητικόν (*epithymetikon*, appetitive).[13] Likewise, the Jewish mystical tradition of Qabalah names three souls (or three parts of a single soul) as the *nephesh*, the *ruach*, and the *neshamah*, which are roughly cognate with the three souls described below.[14] (I should note this is a necessary oversimplification of a vastly complicated subject which a host of highly intelligent, deeply spiritual Jewish scholars have spent their lives studying and writing about.)

---

13. Plato, *Republic*, trans. by Benjamin Jowett (Oxford, UK: Clarendon Press, 1888), 126–139.

14. Rabbi Yitzchak Luria, *Sha'ar ha Gilgulim (Gate of Reincarnations)*, trans. by Yitzchok bar Chaim, http://www.chabad.org/kabbalah/article_cdo/aid/378771/jewish/Gate-of-Reincarnations.htm.

In Feri, these souls are sometimes called the fetch, the talker, and the god-self, though Cora Anderson refers to them in her classic essay *Fifty Years in the Feri Tradition* as the alpha (α), beta (β), and gamma (γ) spirits, respectively. The gamma spirit, or god-self, is that within us which is also a part of God Herself, a spark of brilliance within the curved black mirror of infinite space that is Her all-encompassing body. The beta spirit, or talker, is the soul of the mind, the intellect, and the identity, the part of us which interfaces with the waking world. Last, we have the alpha spirit, or fetch, which is the soul of the body and the senses, the animal soul.[15] The alpha spirit is the part of ourselves that craves physical comforts, the part of us that revels in sensual delights and erotic pleasure. It's also the part of us which transforms those physical, sensual joys into energy or, if you will, into power: raw, untamed, untrammeled sorcerous power. In this book, I call this sensual power *eros*, after the Greek god of sexual love. We'll talk more about *eros* in chapter 6. For now, think of it as the energetic output of the alpha spirit: the shivery thrill of excitement you get from hearing a beautiful piece of music, tasting something delicious, or the feel of a lover's fingertips on your skin. That sensation is powerful—it *is* power—and it's been harnessed for magical purposes by tantrikas, sex magicians, witches, and other practitioners for literally thousands of years.

Sadly, the alpha spirit gets short shrift in Western culture, due in great part to our ongoing struggle with mind-body dualism, in which the body is seen as separable from—and, ultimately lesser in value than—the mind. Some of us indulge our bodies and senses to the point of toxicity, addiction, and ill health. Others deny our

---

15. Cora Anderson, *Fifty Years in the Feri Tradition* (Portland, OR: Acorn Guild Press, 2005), 16–19.

physical needs and desires to the point of mortification, self-abuse, and neurosis. Still others struggle with the perceived need to physically and psychologically master and dominate our own bodies through exercise, diet, cosmetics, even surgery. It's rare for anything between these extremes to be viewed as a happy medium or a desirable compromise. We praise people for their weight loss or critique them for weight gain. We laud or critique changes in personal grooming and styling. We bemoan the loss of ability as we age and fret over wrinkles and gray hair. In all of this, we are upholding a particular set of physical attributes—youthfulness, ability, particular shapes of muscle and fat, particular hues of skin color—as the standards by which physical embodiment should be judged. In doing so, we are literally making judgments about the physical manifestation of someone's soul, specifically the soul through which they interface with the material world. As the body is separated from the whole being and denigrated, so too is the alpha spirit isolated. Our relationships with our own bodies and our own souls become toxic.

The good news is, this is all remediable. We can learn to embrace our embodiment, love our bodies and the souls of our bodies, and thereby reclaim our own power. Even better, a lot of that work is actually quite pleasant.

On Trauma and Embodiment

The slightly less good news is that it *is* work, and some of that work can be tedious and unpleasant, even painful, depending on your background and history. One of the areas in which that work can be both unpleasant and potentially dangerous is the interrelation of trauma, mental health, and embodiment. While embodiment can pose a host of challenges for any of us, particular challenges can arise for survivors of sexual assault, sexual abuse, relationship violence, and/or physical abuse.

I'm sharing the ideas, practices, and exercises in this book with the understanding that many of you reading this have experienced one or more forms of trauma at least once, if not multiple times. There's a spectrum of responses to such experiences; while some survivors might not identify their experiences as traumatic, many others do. This trauma can physically manifest in the survivor's body in a variety of ways, whether or not the violence they experienced was physical in nature: a lack of sexual arousal or an inability to become aroused, reexperiencing the physical sensations of an assault, a physical disconnect or dissociation between the body and the mind, and so on. These sensations and experiences of trauma can be harbored in the body as well as the psyche for years after the initial trauma and may come and go over time.

While the practice of embodiment techniques can be both challenging and potentially hazardous, it can also be empowering, even liberating. Each person's healing process is unique to them and doesn't necessarily run on a cut-and-dried linear pattern. I've done my best to operate in a trauma-informed way to provide every reader, at whatever stage in their healing, with tools for the reclaiming of their own bodies and their own power. With that said, everyone reacts to this work in their own way, and some of the material in this book can be difficult, even for people without trauma. It's entirely possible that some of this material may provoke negative responses for you: you might not be ready to tackle certain parts of this work right now, and I may not have presented the material in the way that's accessible for you.

What I want you to understand is *that's okay*. It's perfectly normal to have your own responses to this work. For some of you, those responses might be wholly positive and empowering, which is marvelous. For others, doing this work may unearth additional traumas or experiences you'll need to process. Whatever your responses, I strongly encourage you to honor those responses, and to engage in self-care.

I call the practices and exercises in this book "work" for a reason. Many of us are working through traumas of one sort or another, and all of us are working in the context of a modern life which has a vested interest in keeping us separated from our bodies, locked into our assigned gender roles, and ashamed of our sexualities. The process of fighting back against those forces and reclaiming our bodies and spirits *is* hard work and can leave us feeling depleted and beaten up.

The following is a list of ways you can nurture yourself, tend your bruises and wounds, and replenish your power, and care for yourself physically, emotionally, and spiritually while doing this work. Fundamentally, these suggestions are what's called self-care, and can be employed at any time, but they can be particularly useful when dealing with traumatic triggers.

Take a Break

I'll start with what is easily the most important suggestion in this list. It's really, truly okay to say to yourself, "This is too much for me to take on right now." The whole point of this work is healing and empowerment rather than retraumatizing ourselves by demonstrating that we can soldier on through anything, even things that are harming us. You can press pause on the work, close this book and set it aside, and come back to it later … and "later" can mean later today, tomorrow, next week, next month, or whenever you're feeling up to it, with no time frame attached. There is no shame whatsoever in choosing your own self-care and well-being over any perceptions of toughness. You have nothing to prove—to me or anyone else. Honestly, that you're here at all is more than enough proof that you're a badass. Honor your own strength and be proud that you have the courage both to take this work on and to give yourself permission to take a rest from it when you need to.

Breathe

Focus on your breathing. If your breathing is fast and shallow, slow it down and take deeper breaths. Get through the next moment, and the one after that. If your heart and mind are racing, calming your breathing can help to bring them down out of the rafters and back into your body. Breathe, and center your awareness on yourself, in yourself. Remember that while you're breathing, you're still alive. That's a victory all in itself. Breathe, and give yourself time to figure out the next step.

Ground and Center

For those who are unfamiliar, "grounding and centering" refers to a category of meditative, energetic practices intended to calm our minds and spirits, reaffirming their connections to our bodies and the Earth, as well as to bleed off any excess energy, which often takes the form of anxiety, jitteriness, and fear. Grounding and centering ourselves is often a useful, even necessary adjunct to getting our breathing under control. If you don't already have a grounding and centering practice, the following is a quick and dirty version you can do while lying in bed at home, riding a crosstown bus, or waiting in line at the bank:

Close your eyes if it's safe to do so, take a deep breath in, and hold it for a moment. As you do so, draw your awareness inward, into the core of your being, and feel the tension and excess energy in your body gather there. Now, release that breath slowly, and let your awareness drop down. If you're standing, let it flow down your spine, through your legs, and into the earth, like a taproot. If you're sitting or lying down, extend your awareness down from your spine directly into the earth. As it does, let the energy you've gathered flow down into the earth and dissipate, like water soaking into the ground. Do this twice more, each time remembering to gather your awareness into your core, then sinking down into the earth. After the third time, take one more deep breath, pull your awareness back into yourself, and exhale, opening your eyes.

Of course, if you already have a grounding and centering practice, the trick is remembering to actually *do* it in the moments you need it. I wish I could tell you there was an easy way to develop the habit of practice, but I'd be lying. I'm just as prone to forgetting to do this in high-stress situations—and then wondering why I feel so agitated, disconnected, and anxious—as the next person. The best suggestion I can make here is to create a mental association between those unpleasant emotional and energetic states and the necessity and desire for grounding and centering, such that over time it becomes second nature to ground and center when you're in those unpleasant states.

Monitor Your Body

Take a few moments to check in with your body. How are you feeling, physically? Are you too warm, too cold, hungry, or thirsty? Do you need a restroom? How's your posture? Are you feeling sleepy, tired, or worn out? Is anything hurting, itchy, achy, or just physically uncomfortable? Are your clothes too tight, or binding you in some other way? When was the last time you stretched or moved around? Whatever you notice, do what you can to alleviate the discomfort or, if it's not something you can remedy in the moment, at least acknowledge the sensation. This practice is an excellent prelude or pendant to grounding and centering, because any of these physical issues can detract from any spiritual work you're doing and can exacerbate any emotional distress you're feeling.

Bathe

Warm baths are a sensual luxury all unto themselves and can be a marvelous technique for regrounding ourselves in our own bodies, physically and emotionally. If you're feeling in need of an additional layer of spiritual protection and grounding, you can include any bath additives you like. This can be as complex as a cleansing bath with oils, tinctures, and candles, or as simple as a sprinkling of salt and an invocation to one of your spiritual allies. If you don't have access to a bathtub, cleansing and grounding showers can be utterly glorious as well, and the additives can be used as a body rinse during or after the shower itself.

Eat and Drink Mindfully

When we're stressed and under strain, it's easy to fall into unhealthy eating habits: eating too little, eating more than we really want, and eating things that are intrinsically unhealthy for us. I'm subject to all three of these, depending on the nature of my stress. When I do, I find it helpful to pay attention to the dietary urges I'm having, and try to sort out what's underneath them, what my body is trying to tell me. If I'm craving sweets, I'm either physically or emotionally worn down and looking for something to pick me up. In those cases, I try to rest and take care of my emotional needs. If I'm overeating, I'm likely insecure and scared, and would benefit from shoring up my security needs, either emotionally or spiritually. If I'm not eating at all, odds are good that I'm either sad or depressed, and if I can push myself to eat something healthy, just a little, I'll have the energy to think about my situation with a little more clarity.

The same goes for drinking, both alcoholic and nonalcoholic beverages. We often use sweet and/or caffeinated beverages to mask our fatigue, or alcoholic beverages to dull our fears and inse-curities. Easing back on those artificial aids is never a bad idea. In any case, I'm rarely drinking enough water, and if you're anything like me, neither are you. According to the Mayo Clinic, that adage about drinking eight 8 oz. glasses of water (which is just under two liters) is still sound advice, and I offer it here as a reminder for all of our benefit.

Spend Time Outdoors

At the risk of sounding far more nature-oriented than I actually am, getting ourselves out of our interior spaces and into the Room with the Big Blue Ceiling can do wonders for our mental and emo-tional states. Fresh air (or fresher air, anyway), natural light, and exposure to plants and wildlife are excellent medicine for stress, and can help us refocus our attention and ground ourselves back in our bodies. It'd be nice if we all had access to beautiful outdoor spaces, but the reality is that many of us live in urban or suburban spaces where hiking and such aren't really an option. There are parks and green spaces to which most of us will have access, and if you do, I highly recommend utilizing them. Going for walks, or even just sitting on a bench or under a tree, can be remarkably restorative. If your access to such spaces is limited or nonexistent, neighborhood walks can offer many of the same benefits. If that's out of your reach, even visiting your own backyard, patio, or front porch can be beneficial. Part of the benefit derives from the change of location and scenery, which disrupts our perceptions enough to get us out of thought processes that reinforce emotional pat-terns of stress and anxiety. Should all else fail, you can open your windows, air out your living space, and remind yourself that your indoor space is still a part of the larger world around you.

Find What Inspires You

Discover, remember, or revisit what feeds your soul. For some of us, that'll be singing along to our favorite singer-songwriter, reading poetry, listening to choral works, or meditating on classical paintings or sculpture. For others, that'll be rocking out to a metal band, going to movies full of explosions and car chases, or binge-watching an entire season of a television show. (My personal go-to for this is sweet, romantic, slice-of-life Japanese *anime*. Your mileage may vary.) The point is, find or remember what works for you, and take refuge in it. It doesn't matter one bit what other people think of it. If that's your safe place, revel in it.

Make Something

One of the most empowering acts we can undertake is to create something from nothing, exercising our will on the material and spiritual planes to make a change for the better. Splash paint on a canvas, string words together, pound on drums, or pick out a melody on a keyboard. Cook a meal, sing a song, bake a loaf of bread, knit a scarf. Even cleaning a room is an act of creation, a production of order from chaos, an expression and extension of your Self into the world around you. In the act of making, we are saying throughout all the worlds, "I am here. I exist. I matter." That's art, that's craft, that's resistance and rebellion. That's magic.

Spend Time with Loved Ones

Our relationships with friends, intimates, lovers, and families—of choice or of blood—can be a balm to our emotional and spiritual wounds. Try to stay in contact with your support networks, and reach out to them when you're in need. That support can look like a sympathetic ear and a soft shoulder, or a night in watching silly movies and eating popcorn. Whatever your support needs are, communicate them to the people in your life, and let them be there for you. Not only does this get you the kind of help you need when you're in a vulnerable place, it allows your loved ones to be helpful, and sends them the message that you're someone to whom they can come when they need a hand, as well.

Seek Professional Counseling

I make this suggestion with some reservations, though not because I have any issue with therapy. On the contrary, I've had marvelous experiences with counselors and therapists, and would cheerfully recommend them to anyone who has access to professional mental health treatment. Unfortunately, as of this writing, many of us—even in the so-called developed world—simply don't have that access, especially those of us in marginalized and disenfranchised groups. Even for those who do have access, the stigma against pursuing treatment can raise social and economic barriers. However, if you can get past those barriers, therapy can be an immensely useful tool for helping you to cope with both past trauma and present fears and patterns.

Give Yourself a Break

Yes, I started with this suggestion, but it's important enough that I'm restating it at the end as well. You are beautiful and brave, dear ones. Take care of yourselves.

When Bodies Fail: Ability, Health, and Embodiment

Another issue around embodiment that we tend to dodge in modern Western culture is the issue of ability. The everyday world in which most of us live is conceived and built around the myth of the average person, a Platonic ideal of the human being. This "average person" is then used as the basis for a host of assumptions about the ability level of its occupants. Some of those assumptions are that we're all sighted, hearing, ambulatory adults within a certain range of bodily dimensions and mass, and that we're all neurotypical. (*Neurotypical* refers to people with typical or normative neurological configuration and functioning, who experience, cognitively process, and interpret their sense-impressions of the world in a similar way. The contrasting term, *neurodivergent*, refers to non-typical neurological configuration or functioning. Common forms of neurodivergence include autism, mood disorders, anxiety, attention deficit disorders, and dyspraxia.)

These assumptions exclude a breathtaking number of people: young people, old people, blind and vision-impaired people, deaf and hearing-impaired people, people with ambulatory impairment, fat people, skinny people, short people, tall people, neurodivergent people, people with mental health issues, and many more.

I've worked to make this book as inclusive as possible toward people with bodies at all levels of ability. However, the reality is that not all experiences are accessible to all people, and that some of those inaccessibilities will be rooted in the body. Rather than dodge this fact, I want to openly acknowledge it and, where it's feasible to do so, offer suggestions for ways that people with disabilities can adapt the ideas, exercises, and practices here to their own experiences of embodiment.

The modern esoteric movement has a curiously paradoxical relationship with the body, depending on which part of it you're occupying at the moment. Some communities are deeply cerebral, while others are openly body-positive and sensual. In my experience, though, an issue where most of our communities falter is in addressing disability. Some of us are born with disabilities, while others become disabled through illness or trauma. Even those of us fortunate enough to avoid misfortune will nonetheless get older, and as we age, our strength will wane, our energy will diminish, our bones will grow brittle. In what ways does our practice help us to deal with our changing relationship with our bodies as our ability diminishes? In other words, what do we do to cope with the reality that our bodies often don't function the way society expects them to?

The most common answer to this conundrum, both in mainstream society and in the subculture of the Western esoteric traditions, is "as little as we can get away with." Even in our ostensibly body-positive traditions, we avoid the subject of disability as much as possible, despite the presence of disabled gods in our pantheons: the club-footed Hephaestus in Greece, Nuada of the Silver Arm in Ireland, the blind Höðr of Norse myth, and so on. Similarly, even in traditions where death is valorized and romanticized as "a necessary part of life" and the so-called gateway to the next realm, there's often little attention paid to what that actually looks like, in practice. We shy away from the awareness that our own terminal approach brings with it infirmity and decrease in ability, both physical and sometimes mental.

Moving past the Western world's avoidance of the reality of disability and death for a moment, we still have a host of body-related issues to contend with. Perhaps we feel that someone's body is too fat, or too thin, or in some other way the wrong shape. Maybe we dislike the things they choose to do (or to not do) with their body: we find the kinds of sex they choose to have distasteful, or we might disapprove of the changes they choose to make (or to not make) in their body. Some of us, deep down, may feel that the way someone else is embodied is intrinsically a danger to our own embodied identities, perhaps even to our safety.

While they may seem disparate, these issues are all related to one another at a fundamental level. For starters, they're all culturally derived, rooted in particular places, times, and demographics. As an example, the benchmarks for what was considered an appropriate body size in Western culture—and, therefore, where the boundaries for too fat and thin are—were radically different even as little as fifty years ago. At that same time in history, tattooing was a marker of belonging to a lower socioeconomic bracket (possibly with a criminal background) or of having served in the military, whereas today it's hardly noteworthy to find elementary school teachers, accountants, computer scientists, and other members of the professional middle class with tattoos. The extent to which we understand and accept sexualities and genders beyond obligatory cisgender heterosexuality have waxed and waned so widely with time and place that it's pretty much impossible to say that any given culture was or wasn't queer phobic without immediately following up with a bunch of disclaimers and explanations, including phrases like "at this point in their history."

In short, like our feelings about sex, our feelings and beliefs about bodies are rooted in our cultures, which are notoriously both intransigent in the short term and mutable in the long term. Because these feelings and beliefs are culturally based, they tend to manifest in ways that shore up our shared cultural identities, to create a clear sense of belonging and to dissuade others from violating these cultural norms. This enforcing of cultural norms around bodies, sometimes called body policing, isn't necessarily a conscious choice. In fact, it's often done unconsciously, triggered by a sense of uneasiness with a body which is clearly not matching the expected norm. Many of our issues around bodies grow out of the conviction that, on some level, we have both the authority and the obligation to tell other people what to do with their bodies.

Most of us carry in our minds a set of standards for what embodiment should look like—how bodies should look, function, and be used—and we find other people's failure to meet our standards of embodiment troubling, distressing, even threatening.

Body-policing is a toxic mechanism, one which does harm to everyone. It's obviously harmful to people whose bodies don't match our cultural standards of beauty, ability, or function, but even those who do fit within those standards are shaped, figuratively and literally, by the toxicity of the belief that we should have power over others' bodies.

A Précis of Body-Positive Esoteric Practice

Our issues around embodiment can be especially pernicious in esoteric, magical, and devotional contexts, where so much of our narrative as a movement is built around notions of body positivity, sex positivity, and valorizing the physical as equally sacred. If we want to live up to our own self-image, we owe it to ourselves to be honest about how we actually think and feel about bodies, our own and others'. Only then can we work through the ramifications of those beliefs and prejudices and embrace a truly body-positive esoteric practice, based in the realities of embodiment.

So, what would such a practice look like?

- *From womb to tomb:* It would openly accept and address both the beginning of life, the alchemical union of the spiritual substance of the soul with the tangible matter of the body, and the end, in which that body returns to its constituent elements and the soul moves on to the next adventure. Dying and death would be as enfolded into our cosmologies and our rites as pregnancy and childbirth, and neither the newborn nor the dying would face their transitions alone.

- *Rooted in reality:* It would enthusiastically incorporate our ever-changing scientific understandings of our own bodies into our theologies, cosmologies, and practices, including the realities of the wide genetic variances within what we think of as biological sex. The biological essentialism of past traditions, based on earlier misunderstandings of biology and psychology, would be replaced with symbolism and rites more closely reflecting our lived experiences.

- *Sex-positive:* It would valorize all forms of healthy sexuality as valid ways of achieving pleasure, expressing intimacy, and approaching the numinous, both within and beyond ourselves. It would likewise support the right of any person to engage—or *not* engage—in any sexual practices they choose, for any reason they choose. As such, it would support sex workers in their vocations and encourage the protection of sex workers' rights to practice their trade free from oppression, shaming, or cultural opprobrium. Likewise, it would support the rights of those who choose not to have any sort of sex, for whatever reasons they choose, for whatever length of time they choose.

- *Consent-positive:* As a necessary corollary of sex positivity, body-positive practice would be intrinsically consent-positive, holding the autonomy and sovereignty of each individual over their own body as one of its highest core values. After all, just as sex without consent is rape, sex positivity without consent positivity is rape culture. This practice would reject every aspect of rape culture, replacing it with a culture of consent. It would overtly and explicitly honor all bodies, in all shapes and states, as the physical, tangible expressions of our souls. When you touch the body, you touch the soul, and our practice would require that we exercise the greatest respect in dealing with other people's souls and bodies.

- *Embodied without shame:* It would embrace and encourage the health of all bodies, of any size or shape, and dispel any notion of shame or judgment targeting bodies which fall outside some arbitrary hegemonic standard of beauty or fitness. Consider the abundant bodies of Silenus, the tutor of Dionysus, or Abundantia, the Roman goddess of plenty later syncretized with the witch-goddess Habondia, or the paleolithic stone figure dubbed the Venus of Willendorf.

- *All abilities welcomed:* Likewise, it would be accessible and relatable to those pushed outside the conventional norms of society by disability or infirmity. Recall again the disabled figures of myth and legend, gods and heroes whose infirmities are as much a part of their persona as their divine might, skill, and power: the lamed Hephaestus, the one-armed Nuada, the blind Tiresias. A truly body-positive practice would embrace and strive to be inclusive of bodies of all levels of ability, and it would work to make that practice as accessible as possible to those with disabilities.

- *Trauma informed:* Our bodies are durable, but they're also vulnerable to injury from both misadventure and violence. Rooted as they are in our bodies, our minds and spirits are also vulnerable to harm stemming from injuries and violations inflicted on the body. The aftereffects of these injuries can linger on in the body, the mind, and the spirit long after the initial physical damage has healed. A body-positive esoteric practice would necessarily be informed by an awareness of and sensitivity to trauma, whether physical, psychological, or spiritual, and would work to foster healing and empowerment for those affected by trauma, both directly and indirectly.

- *Your body is yours:* And, underlying all of these principles, body-positive practice would explicitly acknowledge and support the autonomy and sovereignty of each human being, each human body, as belonging only and solely to themselves. It would reject the imposition of cultural norms onto autonomous bodies: body policing, body shaming, kink shaming, and so on. It would support the right of any person to do with their own body as they will, from body modification to gender transition, without procedural, legal, or social obstacles.

I've occasionally been asked which traditions of practice and devotion I would single out for praise as being especially body-positive. I understand the motivation behind this question, but I think it starts in the wrong place. Any tradition can be body-positive or body-negative, and any tradition can embrace body-positivity as a core value of its praxis. I've met Tantric sex practitioners who used pseudoscientific theories about sexuality and the body to bolster misogynistic ideas about the role of women. I've known ostensibly feminist witches whose body-negativity bordered on the pathological, who felt entitled to judge their acolytes' bodies, sexualities, and abilities. I've seen putative elders of the Craft who treated skyclad ritual as a useful tool for selecting which students they wanted to sleep with. These views aren't an inherent part of any of the traditions in which these individuals expressed them. On the contrary, they're part of those individuals' baggage, smuggled into spiritual traditions and propped up with the authority of doctrine.

Conversely, I've met Pagans, polytheists, magicians, and other esoteric practitioners whose discernment and praxis has led them to embrace the body in all its flawed, fallible beauty, and given them a wealth of tools with which to engage the material world. Nor is this kind of discernment unique to outsider faiths like Paganism and polytheism. I've known devout Christians whose sacramental view of the body led them to a deeply sex-positive, body-positive theology of incarnation and embodiment which puts many modern esoteric practitioners to shame.

Again, it's not about the tradition. It's about where people want to go with it.

Writing Sex and Gender on the Body

Chapter 2 covered the connections and distinctions between biological sex and gender, as well as the habitual conflation of those two categories in most of Western culture. After all, one of the first questions to be asked about a newborn child, or even a developing fetus, is whether the nascent human is a boy or a girl ... a question predicated on the assumption that the biological sex of the child is an indicator of their gender, and that those things somehow determine something useful about the child as a person.

What if that's a false assumption, though? If we accept Judith Butler's assertion that gender is something we *do*, rather than something we *are*, we are forced to question what it even means to be a woman or a man. Of course, there's a host of cultural assumptions, projections, and inheritances in Western culture that go along with the genders we ascribe to people based on their bodies, and our culture is more than happy to supply us with answers to our questions about the value of gender, reinforcing the good and powerful qualities about whatever assignation we've been given. Women are the mothers, the nurturers, the mama bears, the witches, and so on, while men are the fathers, the protectors, the mighty hunters, the sages, and the like. This sort of empowerment through gender-complementarity is incredibly common throughout Western culture and turns up in Paganism and polytheism quite often.

If we look under that mask of empowerment, though, we find our old friends Male Supremacy and Patriarchy. In this paradigm, we are who our culture tells us we are. We write gender and sex on the body and soul, creating a culture based in hierarchy, a societal structure with a place for each person, and each person in their place.

What if we don't accept the gender written on our bodies and souls, though? Who would we be without gender at all … or, phrased another way, who would we be if gender itself were something other than what we've been led to believe? We'll talk more about this in chapter 4.

Embodied Sexuality

While we've spent some time challenging the connection between bodies and gender, the connection between bodies and sexuality is somewhat more obvious. When we think of sex, we tend to think of bodies, frequently naked, doing things with each other, or to each other. Consider popular euphemisms for sex: most of them involve actions and body parts, don't they? It's curious, then, to realize the truth behind the truism that the brain is our most powerful sex organ, the most intense erogenous zone humans have. While our bodies can certainly influence our sex drives, our sexual pleasure, and our sexual desires, none of those things live in our genitals, or in any other external parts of our bodies; they live in our brains. Bodily sensations are just electrical signals firing along our nerves without the brain to interpret them and assign them meaning and value. At the same time, the body is how our brains experience the realm of sensation, the material world of sights and sounds, tastes and scents and, most definitely touches. Experiments with sensory deprivation demonstrate that without the body to give us sensory input, the brain can become unmoored from reality, resulting in hallucinations, panic attacks, depression, even short-term psychosis.

Our sexuality originates within our brains and expresses itself in and through our bodies. Quite literally, it is embodied.

The Body as an Instrument of Magic

All well and good, you might say, but what does that have to do with magic?

That's a reasonable question. The somewhat unreasonable, but entirely accurate answer is, everything. For all of us incarnate beings, our bodies are the inflection point where that spirit meets matter, where spirit *becomes* matter. The sacred mystery of incarnation, of spirit made flesh, doesn't just elevate our bodies above the status of crude matter; it's what empowers us, what enables us to do magic. Our bodies are the first and most powerful instruments of magic we possess, the one with which we have the most immediate and intimate relationship. Bodies are the means by which we experience and interact with manifest reality, and the ground in which our consciousness is rooted to interact with the unmanifest.

We can change the physical realm through our bodies, obviously enough. Perhaps less obviously, we can also use our bodies to raise power which can be employed to make changes in nonphysical, magical realms. This power—the vital, animating force generated by the bodies of living beings—has been interpreted and called by various names in cultures around the world: *prana* in Hindu philosophy and practice, *qi* in traditional Chinese medicine and martial arts, and *mana*, an Austronesian cultural and religious concept appropriated and reinterpreted by Pagans and gamers alike.[16] Modern Europeans have tried to express and engage with

---

16. Matt Tomlinson and Ty P. Kāwika Tengan (ed.), *New Mana: Transformations of a Classic Concept in Pacific Languages and Cultures* (Canberra, AU: ANU Press, 2016), 26–28.

this vital force in scientific terms, such as Carl von Reichenbach's Odic force, the Vril of Edward Bulwer-Lytton's novel *The Coming Race*, and Wilhelm Reich's orgone with varying degrees of success and credibility. Some have even compared it with the Force of George Lucas's *Star Wars*.

Many traditions of modern Western esoteric practice have embraced the raising and use of this power in operant devotional and magical ritual, often in the context of sexual magic. We can also look at the practices of Gerald Gardner's witch-cult of the Wicca, who embraced nude (called "sky clad") working as a means of freeing this power from the confines of both social convention and mid-twentieth-century English clothing. Even without the nakedness, many forms of modern Paganism seek to raise power through dancing, chanting, drumming, music, incense, and other practices that engage both the senses and the physical activity of body itself. One of the best-known examples of this embodied practice is the Spiral Dance used in some traditions to generate a cone of power from or through the bodies of the dancers, which is then used to effect change in both our world and the otherworld.

The body's role as an instrument of magic isn't limited to merely generating power to be manipulated by sheer will. Virtually all magical and religious traditions throughout history have used somatic gestures and poses as a way to channel and direct magical force. Practitioners in Hindu and Buddhist traditions, for instance, use symbolic ritual hand and body gestures called *mudras* to convey meaning and transmit power. Similarly, Western magicians, especially those influenced by Golden Dawn and Thelemic ceremonial magical practice, often employ a variety of signs drawn in the air with a hand or a tool (such as pentagrams, hexagrams, and so on) and bodily poses (such as the Sign of the Enterer, or the Sign of Silence) both for their symbolic value and to project and direct magical power. Many esoteric practitioners also use sympathetic magical practices involving the charging and manipulation of material objects—including one's own body or someone else's—to effect magical change.

What we do with our bodies is every bit as magical as what we do with our minds, or our souls. In many ways, the magic we work with and through our bodies is the easiest to experience, because it's rooted in the immediate, visceral, and tangible world of our senses. And because our senses are intimately connected to our emotional selves and our deepest memories, the magic we do with our bodies reinforces itself and empowers, not only us, but those around us with whom we're connected.

Part of the trouble we encounter is that most of us live in cultures where bodies are either devalued in favor of the mind or valued only for their material function, resulting in the reality that we think too much and work too hard. We spend so much time speculating about the future, daydreaming about the past, and wondering about what's going on somewhere else that we fail to experience our own present moment, rooted in our own bodies.

The following exercise is intended to help get you out of your head and into your body, into the world of sensory experience and feelings. It shifts our focus away from the places most of us spend our time and brings us right back to the here and now. And the best part is, it's delicious.

— EXERCISE —
The Orange

This exercise has been adapted from a mindful eating meditation taught by the Vietnamese Zen Buddhist monk Thich Nhất Hạnh.[17] For this, you'll need your journal and a writing implement,

---

17. Thich Nhất Hạnh, "The Moment is Perfect,"*Lion's Roar*, May 1, 2008, www .lionsroar.com/the-moment-is-perfect/.

as usual. You'll also need a ripe orange, mandarin, or other citrus fruit. You could use another fruit if you're so inclined, but you'll need to adapt the exercise to suit the fruit you've chosen. In any event, it should be one you can open and eat, unadulterated, with your fingers. (Bananas and apples are fine, but I wouldn't recommend lemons, grapefruits, or pineapples. Prickly pears are right out.) It's also nice to have a quiet place, preferably one with a comfortable chair with a table, where you can sit and spend some uninterrupted time in contemplation. A kitchen counter or dining room table would be ideal, but honestly, you could do this exercise on a park bench, or at a bus stop.

Take your orange in hand and feel its weight. Is it light, or is it surprisingly heavy for its size? Run your fingers over the surface of its peel, feeling the shape and texture of the orange. Is it smooth or bumpy, gently curved or knobby? Raise it to your nose: does it have a scent, unpeeled? Hold it up to the light and look at the color of the peel. How bright is the orange hue? Is it a deep orange, or closer to yellow? Are there hints of green near the stem?

Now, start to peel the orange. As you first break into the peel, notice the spray of volatile oils from the skin and the strong orange scent they give off. Observe how the segments emerge from the rind as you continue to peel. Feel the white pith of the orange rind under your fingernails as you peel the orange, both the stringy bits that stick to the segments and the soft, squishy stuff in the empty rind.

When you've finished peeling the orange, hold it in your hands again and notice the difference in weight. Turn it over in your hands, noticing the dark, juice-filled segments peeking out between the lines of pith still adhering to them. Pull the segments apart carefully, noting how they cling to one another, and pluck out any remaining pith in the center of the orange.

Once you've separated all of the segments, focus on one of them. Run your fingers over its smooth, almost velvety inner skin. Is the skin tight against the juice-filled inner cells, or is it looser? Smell the segment, the earthy rawness of the pith set against the hint of citrus suggesting the juiciness of the fruit inside.

Now, put the orange segment in your mouth. Feel the texture of the segment against your tongue and palate, between your teeth. Bite down on it, and taste the zippy tanginess of the juice, sweet and lively, almost electric against your tongue. Continue to chew the orange segment until you've masticated it thoroughly into pulp, then swallow it, juice and skin alike. Sit with it for a moment, letting the taste fade slowly from your mouth.

Continue with the rest of the orange segments, taking the time to eat each one with intention, awareness, and contemplation. Once you've finished the last segment, gather up the orange peel pieces, noting their shape and character now that they're separated from the fruit they once held. Take in their scent one last time, noting how your perception of the scent may have changed now that you've eaten the orange.

Set the peel aside, or dispose of it in your compost or rubbish, then rub your fingers together and notice the sticky residue of juice, oil and pith. Wash your hands to remove this residue, dry them, and rub them together again, feeling how the texture of your own skin has changed.

Once you've finished your orange, take a few minutes to write in your journal. In particular, make note of the emotional and physical responses you may have had to any particular parts of the exercise, and any thoughts, images, or memories which may have surfaced as a result.

So, what was the point of that whole exercise? As delicious as it is, this wasn't just about eating an orange, right?

In fact, there are actually a few points. On one level, it's an exercise in attention, specifically in the Buddhist idea of mindfulness. We spend a truly dismaying amount of time sleepwalking through our lives, our minds focused on everything except where we are and what we're doing in the material world. It would be easy to blame modern technology for this phenomenon—cellphones and tablets and readers, oh my!—but doing so is both facile and fallacious. After all, zoning out and daydreaming are as old as humanity, and anyone who's ever tried to read while walking can attest to the dangerous intransigence of telephone poles and fire hydrants. Our minds *like* to wander off into their own world, especially when we're tired, bored, ill, sad, or in some other way feeling less than optimal. We idle away our moments, and we wind up detached from our physical surroundings, even—or especially—our bodies.

It's endemic to the experience of being a physical being that we're unable to experience and process all of our sensory input all at once. For instance, were you aware of the sensations of your left big toe or your right earlobe before you read these words? If we spent the whole of our mental energy experiencing our physical bodies, we'd be utterly overwhelmed by them, so we spend most of our lives blocking those physical sensations out. By bringing our focus to a specific physical set of interactions between us and an object that engages all of our physical senses, we are reclaiming the connection between our mental and physical selves. We are owning our physical selves and devoting our awareness to them in a way that we rarely do in everyday life.

Chapter 4
GENDER IN THEORY AND PRACTICE

IN CHAPTER 2, I explained why the common understanding of gender is somewhat lacking, and I gave my working definition for gender as a range of characteristics and behaviors, rather than an inherent quality we're born with. I stressed that most of what makes up our ideas about gender is socially constructed, inculcated in us from birth by our culture. I'm going to go a little further now and suggest not only that the common understanding of gender as a quality of how you're born falls short of the full truth, but that it actually harms us, impairing our experience of our own senses of self and hindering our ability to work magic effectively.

That's a pretty bold claim, I know. Nervous? Well, buckle up, dear ones, because this is where we start to go off-roading in the untamed wild country of queerness, identity, and culture, where the GPS doesn't work (and no one carries maps in the glove compartment anymore).

Let's get down to it, then.

Learning at My Grandfather's Knee

I'm going to start by sharing one of my most vivid memories of my childhood, which is also one of my earliest memories of being explicitly confronted with gender and gender roles. It's a memory of an incident at my paternal grandparents' house, when I was perhaps five years old.

Sadly, I have very little in the way of memories of my grandmother, but I remember my grandfather quite well. Born in South Carolina of Scots-Irish and English descent, he served in the Navy during the Korean War and was, as they used to say, something of a salty dog: unabashedly sexist and racist as men of his era and background often were, and prone to bouts of wild anger. An uproariously funny story told in my family recounts him drunkenly chasing my father down the street with a large kitchen knife in hand. Had my grandfather caught him, odds are good that you wouldn't be reading these words now.

Of course, that description wasn't my image of the man I knew as my grandfather. My grandpa was the only male figure at that point in my life who had offered me unconditional love. He was strong, kind, gentle, and funny as hell … except when he was chiding me for whining, crying, or doing anything girly, being anything less than manly. Those two categories, girly and manly, were the only two he knew, into which all aspects and facets of human behavior could be sorted.

The memory I mentioned at the beginning is of returning to the dining room table after a trip to the restroom, and of my grandfather stopping me on my way back to my chair and demanding to know whether I had sat or stood while voiding my bladder. Because, you know, only girls sit to pee. I wasn't a girl, was I?

Even with something as simple, as basic, and as private as bodily functions, I was being educated in what the gender roles were, what the expectations of me were. I was supposed to be a boy. Boys are tough, and strong, and brave. Boys don't cry, don't whine, and don't sit on the pot to urinate.

Of course, I had sat. And then I lied about it. I lied to the one person who ever told me that he loved me unconditionally, because I knew what the actual entrance fee for that supposedly unconditional love was: I had to be what he told me I was. I had to be a boy.

I didn't feel like one then, though. I still don't today, four decades on, and I still hear the voice of my grandfather's chiding when I sit to urinate.

I haven't shared this overly personal (and somewhat depressing) anecdote because I want you to feel bad for me, but because it illustrates something about the ways in which gender identity is inculcated in us from the very beginning, and the profound depths to which that inculcation can affect us throughout our lives. Forty years after this event, which is pretty insignificant in the grand scheme of things, I'm still grappling with questions of gender, the body, and the intimate connections between them. Those questions arise in all aspects of my life: in my personal life as a partner, a parent, and a friend; in my professional life as a writer, a speaker, and a scholar; and in my spiritual life as a witch and a devotional polytheist. After all, gender is one of the tools we use to tell ourselves the story of who and what we are, and our bodies are the vehicles for those stories. Gender is far more than the box on our birth certificate, the restroom we're taught to use, or the clothing department we shop in. Just as our bodies are the first magical tools we learn to use, gender is the first magical persona we adopt, the first mask we learn to wear when presenting ourselves to the world.

Gender as a Schema of Spiritual and Magical Operation

The history of gender in Western esotericism is lengthy, convoluted, and frankly beyond the scope of this humble little volume. For our purposes here, I'm going to summarize it as follows: for the past two and a half millennia, esoteric magical and devotional praxis has largely been framed in terms of binary polarity: active and passive, positive and negative, white and black, and—no prize for guessing this one—male and female. This isn't to say there haven't been other cosmological, theological, philosophical, or magical approaches, of course. It's just that, even in an esoteric context, most of our Western ideas about gender have been framed in gendered terms and concepts which are, for the most part, rooted in theological and cosmological notions derived from Christianity, which has held an effective monopoly on religious, spiritual, and magical discourse in the West for the past 1,700 years or so.

If we want to find the roots of our binary notions of the metaphysics of gender, we should look further back to Plato and Aristotle, the titans of classical Greek philosophy from whom Christianity adapted much of its philosophical and metaphysical underpinnings. It's worth observing that neither philosopher thought very highly of women. Aristotle believed that women were inherently inferior to men as a function of nature, amply demonstrated in chapter V of his *Politics*, where he writes, "…so is it naturally with the male and the female; the one is superior, the other inferior; the one governs, the other is governed; and the same rule must necessarily hold good with respect to all mankind."[18] Later, in chapter XII, he states that "the male is by nature superior to the female, except when something happens contrary to the usual course of nature,"and in chapter XIII, he writes that"a freeman is governed in a different manner from a slave, a male from a female, and a man from a child."[19]

This latter sentiment harmonizes with the Christian apostle Paul, whose letter to the Ephesians offers advice on the proper power dynamic between slaves and their masters which we would rightly find similarly repellent today:

> *Slaves, obey your earthly masters with fear and trembling, in singleness of heart, as you obey Christ; not only while being watched, and in order to please them, but as slaves of Christ, doing the will of God from the heart. Render service with enthusiasm, as to the Lord and not to men and women, knowing that whatever good we do, we will receive the same again from the Lord, whether we are slaves or free.*[20]

Similarly, Aristotle's comment in *Politics* (attributed to Sophocles) that "silence is a woman's ornament" resonates with Paul's infamous comments about the desirability of women's silence in his first letter to the church in Corinth:[21]

> *Women should be silent in the churches. For they are not permitted to speak, but should be subordinate, as the law also*

---

18. Aristotle, *Politics: A Treatise on Government*, trans. William Ellis (New York: E. P. Dutton &. Co., 1912), http://www.gutenberg.org/ebooks/6762.

19. Ibid.

20. Ephesians 6:5–8 (New Revised Standard Version).

21. Aristotle, *Politics*.

says. If there is anything they desire to know, let them ask
their husbands at home. For it is shameful for a woman to
speak in church. Or did the word of God originate with you?
Or are you the only ones it has reached?[22]

By contrast, Plato felt that women's inferiority was not only an issue of biology, contrasting men with "women and other animals," but a spiritual matter as well.[23] In *Laws*, he writes that "A woman's natural potential for virtue is inferior to a man's,"[24] and suggests in *Timaeus* that men who had misbehaved in one life would be reborn as women in the next:

He who lived well would return to his native star, and would
there have a blessed existence; but, if he lived ill, he would
pass into the nature of a woman, and if he did not then alter
his evil ways, into the likeness of some animal, until the rea-
son which was in him reasserted her sway over the elements
of fire, air, earth, water, which had engrossed her, and he
regained his first and better nature.[25]

This superiority attributed to men over women would again find its way into Christianity via Paul, whose views on spiritual authority among the genders were ... well, I'll just give him the mic for a moment:

22. 1 Corinthians 14:34–36 (New Revised Standard Version).

23. Plato, *Timaeus*, trans. Benjamin Jowett (Oxford: Clarendon Press, 1892), http://www.gutenberg.org/ebooks/1572.

24. Plato, *Laws*, trans. Benjamin Jowett (Oxford: Clarendon Press, 1892), http://www.gutenberg.org/ebooks/1750.

25. Plato, *Timaeus*, trans. Benjamin Jowett (Oxford: Clarendon Press, 1892), http://www.gutenberg.org/ebooks/1572.

> *But I want you to understand that the head of every man is Christ, the head of a wife is her husband and the head of Christ is God. [...] For a man ought not to cover his head, since he is the image and glory of God, but woman is the glory of man. For man was not made from woman, but woman from man. Neither was man created for woman, but woman for man.*[26]

This theme of male spiritual authority and supremacy is a consistent thread running from classical Greece through the Christian Bible, but as repellent as we might find this, the point isn't to kick Plato, Aristotle, or Paul for being misogynists. (That's just a bonus.) The point is that these ideas about gender and spiritual authority are part of our inheritance in the esoteric traditions. We can see them at work in the Renaissance grimoires, overwhelmingly written with the assumption that the magus was male, and every single one of which contains spells for the express purpose of compelling a woman to have sex with you.(You'd think that Renaissance gentlemen of leisure with the means to afford the space, tools, and ingredients required for these rituals wouldn't have to resort to the magical equivalent of roofies just to get laid, but I digress.) One can find the occasional bone thrown to the idea that women might have an interest in magic, but even there we find the notion of women's bodies as somehow inferior to men's, and injunctions against a woman even being near consecrated items while in an "unclean" state are reiterated in both mainstream Christian doctrine and its esoteric recension. Consider, for instance, the following passage from Leviticus:

---

26. 1 Corinthians 11:3–9 (English Standard Version).

> *When a woman has a discharge, and the discharge in her*
> *body is blood, she shall be in her menstrual impurity for seven*
> *days, and whoever touches her shall be unclean until the eve-*
> *ning. And everything on which she lies during her menstrual*
> *impurity shall be unclean. Everything also on which she sits*
> *shall be unclean. And whoever touches her bed shall wash*
> *his clothes and bathe himself in water and be unclean until*
> *the evening. And whoever touches anything on which she*
> *sits shall wash his clothes and bathe himself in water and be*
> *unclean until the evening. Whether it is the bed or anything*
> *on which she sits, when he touches it he shall be unclean until*
> *the evening. And if any man lies with her and her menstrual*
> *impurity comes upon him, he shall be unclean seven days,*
> *and every bed on which he lies shall be unclean.*[27]

It's no great leap to connect these notions of ritual purity to this gem of a passage from the parchment consecration in the eighteenth century *Grimorium Verum*: "It is important that this must not be seen by any women, and more especially during certain times of theirs [i.e. having her menses], otherwise it will lose its power."[28]

To reiterate: despite all the invocations of various angels, utterances of the Hebrew appellations of God, even an appeal to the Holy Trinity, the he-man boy-magic being worked here is so fragile that even being *looked at* by a menstruating woman will dispel its enchantment. So much for spiritual authority.

If we roll forward a couple of centuries, we can find an excellent summary of the esoteric doctrines built around this binary

---

27. Leviticus 15:19–24 (English Standard Version).

28. *Grimorium Verum*, ed. and trans. Joseph Peterson (self-pub., CreateSpace, 2007), 29.

notion of gender in *The Kybalion*, a book of Hermetic philosophy written in 1908 and attributed to Three Initiates of unknown identity. The last of the seven Hermetic principles elucidated in the book is that gender, expressed in terms of "Masculine and Feminine Principles," is present in everything throughout all the planes of existence, and that "No creation, physical, mental or spiritual, is possible without this Principle."[29] Mind you, *The Kybalion* is also careful to suggest that gender in the Hermetic understanding isn't the same as Sex, which "is merely a manifestation of Gender on a certain plane of the Great Physical Plane—the plane of organic life," and the anonymous authors make some delightfully snarky comments about "base, pernicious and degrading lustful theories, teachings and practices … which are a prostitution of the great natural principle of Gender," which leads one to wonder if they'd been reading Crowley's then-contemporary work.[30]

The authors go on to espouse a theory of Mental Gender in which the binary Masculine and Feminine Principles are outlined for the reader once again, this time in terms of expression and reception, will and imagination. "The strong men and women of the world," *The Kybalion* tells us, "invariably manifest the Masculine Principle of Will," while the average person is too "polarized in his Feminine Principle of Mind" to be truly effective.[31] Here, at least, gender is somewhat divorced from biological configuration, but nonetheless leans on biology as the central metaphorical language for discussing spiritual authority and magical power, identifying masculinity with power and femininity with weakness.

---

29. Three Initiates, *The Kybalion*, http://www.gutenberg.org/ebooks/14209.

30. Ibid.

31. Ibid.

These gendered spiritual and magical schemas we've been discussing are rooted in gender essentialism, an ideology that insists biology is destiny at every level: physical, mental, emotional, sexual, and spiritual. The discerning reader can probably work out what I think of *that* assertion. We'll delve further into that issue in a little bit, but first, we should talk about gender itself, and look at how we interact with gender in our own lives and self-images.

The following exercise is intended to provoke some thought about the nature of gender and the question of how we ascribe gender to the body. It isn't meant to suggest that you're not who you believe yourself to be or provoke you into questioning your own gender identity. Rather, it's intended to help you interrogate our culture's understanding of gender, to unpack the ways in which we all relate to the idea of gender and the ways in which we've internalized, knowingly or unknowingly, our cultural assumptions about what it means to be masculine or feminine, both, or neither.

— EXERCISE —
An Inventory of the Gendered Body

For this exercise, you'll need your journal, a writing implement, about half an hour of undisturbed time, and possibly a little bit of courage.

Turn to a fresh page in your journal. Down the left side of the page, list of all the parts of your body. You can come up with your own list, or use the following:

• hair	• upper arms	• hips
• eyes	• elbows	• genitals
• cheeks	• forearms	• buttocks

- forehead
- ears
- nose
- lips
- chin
- neck
- shoulders

- wrists
- hands
- fingers
- breast(s)
- ribs
- belly

- thighs
- knees
- calves
- feet
- heels
- toes

Once you have your list written out, set down your writing implement and look at the first word on your list. Read it aloud, feeling the shape of the word on your lips, the resonance of its sound in your mouth, throat, chest. Think about the part of your body that word signifies. Think about the ways other people have related to this part of your body. Think about your own relationship with this part of yourself. If it helps, you can touch that part of yourself as well, feel its shape and texture, feel its connection and relation to the rest of your body.

Now ask yourself: If you had to ascribe a gender to just this part of yourself, independent of whatever gender you identify as, what would it be? Masculine, feminine, a mixture of both, an absence of either, or some other thing altogether? Are there certain qualities about that body part which you feel are more strongly associated with one gender or another? Whatever response you come up with, write it down next to the name for the part of your body.

Continue this process with the next term, and the next, moving through the list you've made, recording the gendered ways in which you identify and relate to your own body. As you do this, note any mental responses you may be having to this process, and physical or emotional sensations that come up. Do you find this inventory interesting, pointless, curious, or silly? Is the act of going through the list making you feel tense, nervous, or threatened? Are you more mentally resistant to ascribing gender to some parts of your body than others?

When you've finished the list, take a moment to recenter yourself, and to let go of any response reactions the inventory may have caused in you. Take a few deep breaths and check in with your body. If you're feeling tense, change the position of your body and shake out the tension. Then, when you're ready, return to your list and look it over. Count up how many of the words you've ascribed to each gender category and compare those categories. Consider, if this is the case, why you've gendered certain parts of your own body as a gender other than your own. For instance, perhaps you have longer hair, which you've identified as more feminine, or maybe you've identified your hands and feet as masculine. Can you identify any trends in how you've gendered your body? Are those associations a function of cultural associations, other people's perspectives, your own history and experiences, or some combination of those factors? Take a few minutes to free-write these associations and any other thoughts or feelings that have come up in the process of doing this exercise.

Why Gender Theory Matters for Us

In everyday life, we tend to use the words "gender" and "sex" interchangeably. We also tend to use "gender" to refer to a few ideas that are related but not identical. This usage isn't generally a problem as long as we all understand what everybody means when they use the word. The trouble is, we don't always understand or agree with how the other person is using the term. For instance, consider the multivalent and much-maligned English word *love*. We can say "I love my life partner," "I love my parents," "I love my cat," "I love music, "and "I love strawberry ice cream," all of which are grammatically and syntactically correct sentences; it should be apparent from context that the word "love" isn't referring to the same emotion in all of those cases. In all cases, it's referring to a positive relationship of affection and high regard, but that's as far as the similarities go. The relationships in question really aren't the same at all, and it would be ridiculous to suggest they were. Not coincidentally, this is why the arguments against same-sex marriage that rely on comparisons to people marrying their pets can and should be dismissed as trivial time-wasters leveraged by people who are arguing in bad faith. Such arguments are attempts to define marriage in a particular way that equates adult humans, who are capable of consent, with animals, who are incapable of consenting relationships with humans. (It makes you wonder about those folks' ideas around consent.)

In the gender studies world, this problem has been worked around to some extent by the development of terminology which helps us to disentangle and identify what we're actually talking about. When we talk about gender and sex, we tend to be referring to specific intersections of identity, behavior, and perception that can be broken down into the following four categories:

Gender Expression

This term refers to how you show yourself to the world, how you are asking the world to see you. Gender expression is made up of a lot of factors, both physical and behavioral, which are derived from the interaction between our identity and the culture in which we live. When we express ourselves and our gender in a particular way, we are making a bid to be seen as the gender we're expressing. These bids can take a lot of forms, from how we dress, style our hair, or make ourselves up to how we speak, move, walk, or express our emotions facially.

Gender Attribution

This term refers to how other people see and think of you in a gendered sense, how they respond to the bid of your gender expression. Again, this relies on a lot of cultural factors around behavior and embodiment and will vary from person to person. One person, for instance, may see me as a man, while another may see me as androgynous or nonbinary, or even as a woman, depending on their perceptions, their personal backgrounds, my gender expression at that moment, and the circumstances of our interaction.

Gender Identity

This term refers to how you see and think of yourself from a gendered standpoint, your gendered self-image. Do you see yourself as a woman, a man, neither, a blend of both, or something else entirely? To consider the question another way, with what aspects of your culture do you identify, and what gender would your culture ascribe to them?

Sex Assigned at Birth

This term refers to what the medical community sees and thinks of you, sometimes referred to as biological sex (or, less commonly, genetic sex). However, biologists and medical professionals are increasingly finding those designations to be insufficient or problematic. We touched on some of the complications wound up in the idea of sex assignment in "Gender, Sex, Sexuality, and Magic." In the meantime, though, the vast majority of us are sorted into one of two bins at birth, female or male, from which we derive the concepts of transgender and cisgender.

Talking Latin Prefixes, and Why "Cis" Isn't a Slur

Let's talk about the c-word, by which I mean cisgender, sometimes abbreviated as cis.

The Latin prefix *cis-* means "on the same side," and can be found in various other words and phrases, such as Cisalpine Gaul ("the part of Gaul on the same side of the Alps as Rome"). Similarly, the Latin prefix *trans-* means "on the other side" or "across," and can be found all over the place: transmission, translate, Transylvania, and so on. No slur, criticism, or judgment is built into cis, any more than into trans. Cisgender and cis are entirely neutral terms to refer to someone's gender identity matching what they were assigned at birth, just as transgender and trans mean that someone's gender identity doesn't match their birth assignation.

That's it. That's all it means. The end.

So why is there so much talk about cis being a slur? I can think of a lot of reasons, but most of it comes back to our ingrained ideas about gender being something natural, essential, and intrinsic to the human person. On some level, a lot of us believe that being cisgender shouldn't require a special term. Identifying your gender as the sex you were assigned at birth is just … normal.

And there's the rub. For many people who see cis as an insult, their preferred term is "normal," with the obvious corollary that being trans is an outlier, an aberration, abnormal. This line of argument is especially popular with certain groups of right-wing Christians and, curiously, certain groups of ostensible feminists, both of whom have an investment in invalidating trans identities. Their arguments are predicated on the idea that women's identities are defined and circumscribed by their anatomy. In other words, they believe that women are defined by having a vagina and a uterus, a textbook example of what we call gender essentialism.

Defining Gender Essentialism, and Why It's a Problem

We should unpack exactly what's entailed by gender essentialism here, beyond that simple definition. Since it's a composite term, I want to approach it in two steps:

- *Essentialism* is the belief or position that any given thing has a fixed, innate "essence," a set of qualities that make it itself and *not* something else. For example, in the category of "fruits," oranges are oranges, rather than apples, because they have the essential nature of "orange": a set of qualities that taken as a whole, we assign to the descriptor "orange," rather than to "apple."

- *Gender essentialism* is the belief that (1) there is some innate essence to the genders we designate "woman" and "man," (2) these essential qualities are identical for all members of these genders, and (3) these genders are biologically determined.

This definition is just the quick-and-dirty version, of course. There's a lot more to it. (For some of that "a lot more," allow me to direct you to Judith Butler's *Gender Trouble: Feminism and the Subversion of Identity*, Elizabeth Grosz's *Space, Time, and Perversion: Essays on the Politics of Bodies*, and Simone de Beauvoir's classic *The Second Sex*.)

One of the big problems with gender essentialism is that because of its claim to universality, it's used to justify a lot of oppressive, dehumanizing, abusive, and just plain awful ideas about people. In order to buy into a gender-essentialist view, you have to believe that there is some inherent non-biological quality—which is somehow still biologically determined, mind you—that intrinsically separates everybody into one of two categories, and that this essence is universal to all cultures throughout history. Predictably, this belief dismisses the lived experiences of people—women, men, and others—who don't fit neatly into those categories, whose experiences don't align with the ostensibly universal experience of gender attributed to persons belonging to a given category.

Gender essentialism is an abusive ideology that imposes oppressive structures on everyone, an ideology which is directly linked to sexism, misogyny, homophobia, and transphobia—and, therefore, to physical and psychological violence. Left unchecked and unexamined, this ideology both constitutes and contributes to toxicity in our communities, a grimy thread woven through the motley tapestry of our traditions, our practices, and our personal spiritual and emotional lives. Nevertheless, this view is shared by a number of folks invested in regressive sociopolitical agendas centered around gender ... to unfortunately include a non-trivial number of Pagans, polytheists, and magical practitioners who use the gender-based cosmological structures we've discussed to justify their views.

Opening a Discourse About Gender Essentialism, and Other Cans of Worms

What does this have to do with Paganism, polytheism, magic, and the like? Let's talk about "masculine" and "feminine" energies, or perhaps we can call them "active" and "passive" energies, or positive and negative polarities. While we're at it, we can talk about the equation of masculinity with active, positive, and projective qualities, and the consequent equation of femininity with passive, negative, and receptive qualities ... but hey, that's not sexist, right? Let's talk about the gendering of the *sephiroth* in the Tree of Life, or the cards in the tarot, or the tools on our altars—athames for boys, chalices for girls! While we're at it, we can talk about the assignation not only of gender but modern gender roles to the gods and spirits with whom we work, play, and worship as well. We can point out the explicit gender roles practitioners in certain traditions are expected to play lest they be cast out as aberrations, abominations, and "not the right kind of people."

Let's talk about the misogyny among certain groups of white, cisgender men who are more than happy to honor the Witch mother but then turn around and treat flesh-and-blood women as servants, relying on the unspoken, unacknowledged labor done by women in so many circles, covens, lodges, houses, sodalities, conventions, conferences, and Pagan Pride Days. Let's talk about the men who make women-only spaces a survival need for all women, cisgender and transgender, and about the cis women who exclude transgender women from those spaces. Let's talk about the ways in which theologies of gender, explicit or implicit, have become a metaphorical tool for excluding anyone who fails to fit into our gender-essentialist definitions of women or men. Let's talk about the extent to which our communities have made themselves not only unwelcoming, but outright hostile to queer and trans people, women and men and others.

Let's talk, in other words, about the interlocking sexism, misogyny, homophobia, and transphobia of our communities, and the ways we justify those forms of hatred by appealing to misinformation, personal histories, spiritual authority, tradition, and gender ideologies dating back to the 1950s—or to the 1550s.

All of these attitudes and approaches have their roots in gender essentialism: the notion that women are *this* way, men are *that* way, and anything which contradicts or transcends that binary is somehow abhorrent. Each of these "let's talk" topics could be a chapter unto itself, if not an entire book.

All the Curses of the Mighty Ones

Some may protest: "Some of those things aren't oppression. They're just how people practice. Those are their traditions you're talking about! Aren't you being unfair, intolerant, and hypocritical?"

Maybe so. Allow me to raise a couple of points before you write me off.

While the primary focus of my practice is within the Anderson Feri tradition of American witchcraft, I'm also an initiate of Gardnerian Wicca, one of the best-known of the English traditions of witchcraft. Wicca is one of the most strongly gendered traditions of witchcraft, as well, which makes it an obvious subject for analysis. If we expand our terms to include all of the traditions of witchcraft informed, influenced, or inspired by the Gardnerian type—and let's be clear, at that point we're talking about anything that calls itself Wicca—it's the biggest target in the Neopagan world. Most forms of Wicca, even neo-Wiccan offshoots with no direct ties to Gardnerian Craft, often come across as *The Witch-Cult in Western Gender Roles*, and it would be a bit obvious to single out Wicca for the gendered symbolism of its theology, cosmology, and practice: the dyadic pantheon of Mother Goddess and Father God, the so-called symbolic Great Rite with athame and chalice, the actual Great Rite with (cis male) penis and (cis female) vagina, the gendering of degree systems in some traditions, the polarity model of magic common to many iterations of Wiccan practice, and so on.

All of these qualities would make Wicca an easy target for someone setting out to disparage the tradition, but that's not what I'm here to do. With a critical eye, I'll examine one element of the Gardnerian tradition as an example of the type of gender bias at work in the larger community of the Western esoteric traditions and consider the historical context of its gendered practice. I'm also going to point toward the magical and interpersonal work modern Gardnerian elders are doing to adapt their traditional practices to modern understandings of gender and sexuality. And in the process, I'll have done my best to respect both my personal commitments to the tradition as an initiate and my oath to the gods and my siblings of the Craft.

In *A Witches' Bible*, Janet and Stewart Farrar's classic exposition of British Traditional Wicca, the authors quote a wealth of material from Gerald Gardner's own Book of Shadows, along with commentary from Doreen Valiente. Of particular interest is this passage from the section titled "To Get the Sight," an instructional document on light bondage and scourging as a means of inducing trance and mystic visions:

> *It has been found that this practice doth often cause a fondness between aspirant and tutor, and it is a cause of better results if this be so. If for any reason it is undesirable there be any great fondness between aspirant and tutor this may easily be avoided by both parties from the onset, by firmly resolving in their minds that if any fondness ensues it shall be that of brother and sister, or parent and child, and it is for this reason that a man may only be taught by a woman and a woman by a man, and that man and man or woman and woman should never attempt these practices together, and may all the curses of the Mighty Ones be on any who make such an attempt.[32]*

---

32. Janet Farrar and Stewart Farrar, *The Witches' Way*, in *A Witches' Bible: The Complete Witches' Handbook* (Blaine, WA: Phoenix Publishing, 1996), 58–59.

To reiterate: the author of this section, likely Gardner himself, is cautioning witches against teaching or practicing this technique with partners of the same gender, on peril of divine and magical opprobrium, because of the possibility of "fondness" arising between two people of the same gender.

Calling this passage homophobic would be denotatively accurate; after all, it literally warns against inducing homosexual feelings. However, the larger historical context is worth examining. Remember that being a witch was still illegal in England at the time Gardner was brought into (or created) Wicca; England's Witchcraft Act, which dated back to 1735, was only replaced by the more lenient Fraudulent Mediums Act in 1951. Gardner published his first book about Wicca, *Witchcraft Today*, in 1954. That same year, the brilliant scientist, mathematician, and WWII code-breaker Alan Turing committed suicide. Two years earlier, an English court convicted Turing of the "gross indecency" of committing homosexual acts and forced him to undergo chemical castration as an alternative to prison.[33] While female homosexuality was legally null and had never been criminalized, consensual homosexual activity between men wasn't decriminalized in England until 1967, three years after Gardner's death. Even then, it was strictly regulated. Among other restrictions, such activities had to be performed in private, which was interpreted by courts to mean that men couldn't have sex with one another in residences where more than two people were present, even in other rooms, as with hotels. These restrictions were eventually overturned in 2000 by the European Court of Human Rights.

---

33. David Leavitt, *The Man Who Knew Too Much: Alan Turing and the Invention of the Computer* (New York: W. W. Norton, 2006), 268.

During Gardner's lifetime, heterosexuality was compulsory, at least for men, and male homosexuality was a prosecutable offense that not even status and prestige could reliably avert. Under those circumstances, it's entirely possible that this custom was at least in part Gardner's attempt to protect his nascent witch-cult from unwanted legal attention. By clearly dissuading any sort of same-gender interactions that could carry even a whiff of male homosexuality, Wicca could avoid running afoul of the law of the land.

Of course the simple fact remains that cisgender heterosexuality was, and is still, the primary religious and magical metaphor within Wicca, and the gender binary is a core component of that metaphor. The depth to which this gender binary is a core spiritual value for some Wiccans was driven home to me in a conversation I had with a Wiccan elder some years ago. I asked about the possibility of transgender seekers being initiated into the Craft, and this elder carefully responded that coven leaders, being autonomous, could initiate anyone they deemed a proper person. This answer seemed a little squirrelly, so I pressed the issue. They elaborated that, while they would never question the validity of a transgender person's initiation, they wouldn't feel right doing so. I asked why and was told that their Craft training insisted that initiations must be cross-gendered—man to woman, woman to man—and to do otherwise was an abomination in the eyes of the Gods. They felt that a transgender person either was the gender with which they identified, in which case the initiation would be valid, or wasn't, in which case it would be invalid and an abomination. They couldn't decide which was the truth, so the thought of such an initiation—regardless of how proper a person they might otherwise be—filled them with anxiety.

I found that interaction heartbreakingly depressing, and if things were still in this dismaying state, I would be inclined to throw my hands into the air in disgust and walk away. Happily, I can report that things have changed a great deal within Wicca. Many priests and priestesses within the British traditions—yes, including the Gardnerians—are engaging with modern understandings of gender and sexuality, having the hard conversations about tradition and innovation, and working to incorporate the lived experiences of queer and trans people into their magical and devotional cosmology and praxis. They are, as the saying goes, doing the Work, and the rest of the Western esoteric community could learn a lot from their progress in this regard.

Wicca and its offshoots and exoteric offspring are hardly the only traditions to have promulgated a gendered, and sometimes gender-essentialist theology, nor are they even the most egregious examples to hand. Notice how little of the "let's talk" list earlier is specific to any one tradition or practice. There are some schools of traditional (i.e., not Wiccan) witchcraft with dismaying ideologies built around gender. Along another axis, we can find self-styled radical feminist witches practicing something that looks suspiciously like eclectic Wicca with the y-chromosomes sanded off, whose theology is built around a monotheistic Goddess as the giant yoni of the Universe.

Moving beyond witchcraft, we could spend several pages discussing misogyny and homophobia in the works of Aleister Crowley, which modern practitioners of Thelema are still working through, or the absurdly constrained gender ideology of Dion Fortune's *Esoteric Philosophy of Love and Marriage*, a bit of a Victorian howler in this regard. If you'd rather take on something a little more modern, we can examine the extent to which some modern magicians seem to be obsessed with their own penises and the fluids they emit (… or we could simply not). If you'd like your sexism, homophobia, and transphobia a little more folkish, we can talk about the misogynist gender ideologies to be found in certain reconstructionist groups. Consider, for instance, the mercifully few (but disproportionately vocal) white supremacists who compound their racism with sexism by advertising their strain of Norse polytheism with photos of white men protectively cradling their white wives, in turn protectively cradling their white babies, all captioned with coded phrasing about "traditional family values."

The point is that gender essentialism isn't just a problem in Wicca nor even a problem with Paganism. It's a human problem, one which plays out in every culture that buys into its assumptions. It's neither unfair nor intolerant to critique those assumptions, or any theologies, cosmologies, and forms of praxis which employ them … especially our own. In fact, I would suggest that it's incumbent upon us to do so. It would be unfair to single out Paganism, polytheism, and the occult for special opprobrium and biased critique, but that's not what I intend here. On the contrary, I want to suggest that all of our traditions exist in a cultural context that virtually guarantees they—and we—will have some deeply toxic ideas about gender and sexuality. Though the critiques I've levied above are admittedly harsh, I submit that they arise from a place of respect. If I didn't think our spiritual traditions were worth careful consideration, analysis, and critique, I wouldn't bother practicing them in the first place. If esoteric spiritual traditions are to have any place in the twenty-first century, we need to be able to approach them with both reverence and rationality, cherishing and developing their strengths while also acknowledging and working on their weaknesses. To do any less would be dishonest and avoidant, neither of which—last I checked—were considered virtues in any tradition of Paganism, polytheism, or magic of which I'm aware.

In other words, I'm not here to abolish gender or polarity. I realize this will surprise some folks (and disappoint others), but I won't presume to deny someone's identity or lived experience, even those folks whose identities and experiences are alien to me. In this, I acknowledge that I part ways with some interlocutors in the discourse around gender. I'm comfortable with that.

I'm here to suggest that we can do better—that we can *be* better, both as practitioners and as human beings—but in order to reach that better place, we have to start by knowing where we are. Some of the specific items listed earlier in the long list of "let's talk about" topics need to be addressed, and we must find some ways to move forward from there. To begin, we need to think about our practices and traditions analytically, even critically, when gender comes into play. What do these things we say and do mean? Why are we assigning gender to these roles within our practices? Who is included, and who is excluded? What messages are we sending— or not sending? And, most importantly, are these the messages we want to send?

One of the ways we can work against these tendencies in our practices, our traditions, and our communities is to examine our metaphorical language and really think about what we're saying with our symbols. The following exercise is intended to help us do just that.

– EXERCISE –
Interrogating Our Symbols

For this exercise, you'll need your journal, a writing implement, and about half an hour of undisturbed time.

I learned this exercise from my partner, who learned the basics of it from her instructors at a poetry intensive. To start with, I suggest using this exercise with mundane, day-to-day concepts rather than spiritual metaphors or symbols, because we tend to be less invested in preserving metaphors to which we're not emotionally connected.

> **Step 1:** Think of a generalized, value-neutral abstract concept for which we have a word: time, movement, age, ownership, awareness, knowledge, relationship, and so on. When I did this exercise for the first time, I used the word *progress*.

> **Step 2:** Turn to a fresh page in your journal and write down your own personal definition for that concept. Mine was, "Progress is the concept of moving in steps from point A to point B."

> **Step 3:** Look over your definition and notice all the places you may have used concrete, physical language to explain or define your concept. Think about how your metaphorical language is rooted in a concrete metaphor, and what that metaphorical basis might be. In mine, I talked about "moving" from one "point" to another in "steps." The concrete metaphorical basis of my definition was travel, as though I were discussing a literal physical change of location from one place to another.

> **Step 4:** Next is the fun part: come up with a concrete metaphorical basis different from the one your definition is based in—sound, speed, color, or anything else—and rewrite your definition using this new metaphorical basis. Whatever you choose, make the choice as arbitrary as possible. Don't try to pick a better metaphorical basis; just grab one and go with it. I used temperature, and rewrote my definition as, "Progress is the concept of shifting state from cold to warm."

Step 5: Now look at your definitions, the old and the new, and notice what emotional associations are built into the terms in question, including any moral value judgments inherent in the words. For instance, I replaced the relatively neutral "point A" and "point B" with "cold," a term that we tend to associate with discomfort and unhappiness, and "warm," a term we associate with comfort and happiness.

The point of this exercise is to show that the ways in which we talk about things have values built into them, and when we change how we talk about these things, we change the values we associate with them. The first part of the exercise (steps 1 through 3) underscores our reliance on metaphorical language with a concrete basis to talk about abstract concepts, while the second part (steps 4 and 5) introduces the idea that using different metaphors changes the way we feel about the things we use the metaphor to describe, even though the abstract concept itself hasn't changed in the slightest. The values we ascribe to otherwise neutral words are in many ways culturally derived and can also contribute to changes in meaning and association. For instance, the metaphorical cultural associations in languages which use an egocentric orientation based on the location of the speaker—left, right, above, beneath, forward, backward—would be lost on speakers of the Guugu Yimithirr language of Australia, which uses geographic orientation based on cardinal directions—north, south, east, and west—or on Sambali speakers in the Philippines, whose language orients the speaker in relation to both cardinal directions and land features, where the literal meanings of their words for east (*baitan*) and west (*libaba*) refer to the mountains in the east and the ocean in the west.

Once you've used this exercise to deconstruct relatively mundane abstract concepts, you can use it to interrogate more esoteric concepts: gender, sexuality, agency, sovereignty, magic, polarity, power, and so on. Look at the ways the language you use to talk about these ideas shape the ways you think about them, suggests the moral values we ascribe to them, and ultimately informs the emotional and spiritual values we invest in them. The goal here isn't necessarily to change how we think but to be *aware* of how we think and why. Once we know what we actually believe and feel, we can then decide if we want those beliefs and feelings to shape our actions, or if we want to find a better way.

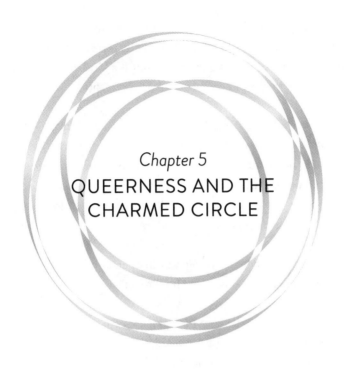

Chapter 5
QUEERNESS AND THE CHARMED CIRCLE

EARLIER, I DEFINED QUEER as an umbrella term for gender and sexual identities outside the charmed circle of hegemonically normative cisgender heterosexuality (chapter 2). A reasonable response to that definition is, "Okay, sure, but what does that *mean*?" Trying to grasp what queerness *is* can be a frustrating experience, intellectually and emotionally, and a reliance on dry, denotative dictionary definitions will only get us so far. It might be useful, instead, to consult with some notable theorists on the subject of queerness and being an outsider, from both the rarified world of academia and the somewhat more immediate world of pop culture.

In his classic text *Cruising Utopia*, Cuban-American cultural theorist José Esteban Muñoz suggests that queerness is something that belongs to the future, rather than something we are or can be in the here and now. He opens the book by throwing the following gauntlet, suggesting that queerness itself is a kind of Platonic ideal to which we may aspire, rather than a lived reality:

> *Queerness is not yet here. Queerness is an ideality. Put another way, we are not yet queer. We may never touch queerness, but we can feel it as the warm illumination of a horizon imbued with potentiality. We have never been queer, yet queerness exists for us as an ideality that can be distilled from the past and used to imagine a future.*

He goes on to describe queerness, in a deeply poetic way, in terms of desire and satiety, longing and fulfillment:

> *Queerness is a longing that propels us onward, beyond romances of the negative and toiling in the present. Queerness is that thing that lets us feel that this world is not enough, that indeed something is missing.*[34]

Writer-directors Lilly and Lana Wachowski captured this feeling in *The Matrix*, an iconic and groundbreaking science fiction film that some commentators have interpreted as a trans coming-out narrative, made by a pair of transgender sisters before they had come out as trans. In the iconic words of Morpheus, the film's psychopomp-*cum*-mentor figure,

> *You're here because you know something. What you know you can't explain, but you feel it. You've felt it your entire life,*

---

34. José Esteban Muñoz, *Cruising Utopia: The Then and There of Queer Futurity* (New York: New York University Press, 2009), 1.

that there's something wrong with the world. You don't know
what it is, but it's there, like a splinter in your mind, driving
you mad.[35]

Queerness is the "splinter in our minds" that pushes us onward, toward that distant, dreamed-of future where our longings are fulfilled, where we are made whole again. In this sense, queerness can be seen as a metaphysical yearning for something beyond the scope of our understanding, an almost Gnostic awareness that the world is broken, or that we ourselves are. Or, to echo the refrain of Leonard Cohen's classic song "Anthem," queerness is the crack in everything, through which we can see the pole star of all possibility, both the light that guides us and the horizon from which it shines. Perhaps we aren't queer *yet*, but the pursuit of our nascent queerness may yet bring us to the promised land, the Eden of our hopes and dreams.

For critical studies theorist Kara Keeling, queerness specifies a way of engaging, not merely with sexuality or gender, but with reality itself and the structures we build to make reality make sense. In "Queer OS," her exploration of the intersections of queer theory, technology, and sociopolitical philosophy, she identifies queerness as an orientation that by its very intrinsic nature, challenges and offers alternatives to our assumed social norms around relationships.[36] Keeling suggests that embracing a normalization of queerness at a societal level could "facilitate and support imaginative, unexpected, and ethical relations between and among living

---

35. Lana Wachowski and Lilly Wachowski, *The Matrix* (Burbank, CA: Warner Bros. Pictures, 1999).

36. Kara Keeling, "Queer OS," *Cinema Journal* 53 no. 2 (2014): 153.

beings and the environment, even when they have perhaps little or nothing in common."[37]

To be queer, then, is to encompass and embrace multiple possibilities and modalities of existence in relation to both oneself and to the Other, giving us access to expressions of our self—of our *selves*—that might otherwise be unavailable to us, even—or especially—modalities and expressions rooted in our ideas about sexuality and gender. In a sense, queerness is best defined as the act of living as one's truest gendered and sexual self in the context of a society and culture where that true self is deemed unacceptable, undesirable, even unreal. To be queer is to be intrinsically Other, standing outside the charmed circle of societal approval for the sake of living an authentic life. Queerness can be isolating, frightening, and dangerous, but it can also be uniquely empowering. Embracing our own queerness as an intrinsic and beautiful component of one's self is a profound, radical act of self-love, self-empowerment, and self-possession.

But if we want all that, we have to be willing to *do* that. We have to be willing to take the first step, to engage, to change, to transform: to shapeshift, as it were, into our truest selves … or, to quote again from *The Matrix*: "I can only show you the door. You're the one that has to walk through it."[38]

The following exercise is intended to provide you with a starting place for walking through that door: a rite of self-possession and self-ownership, an act of claiming your own body … or, more correctly, of reclaiming your own body. Many of us live in a cultural matrix in which our bodies have never truly belonged to us. Perhaps they've belonged to our parents, or to our religious and

---

37. Keeling, "Queer OS," 153.

38. Lana Wachowski and Lilly Wachowski, *The Matrix*.

social institutions, or to our partners and spouses, even to our children. Those of us who queer gender or sexuality often feel that everything about our bodies has been claimed from before we were born, and that the simple act of being who we truly are places us at odds with the institutions and forces of society. In this working, you can set aside a sacred space to shuck off those associations and obligations, and step into your own power. While it may have particular power for those whose identities fall under the aegis of queerness, this exercise is meant for anyone of any identity—queer or straight, cis or trans or nonbinary—at any point along their path.

— EXERCISE —
The Mirror of Reclaiming

For this exercise, you'll need the following:

- A quiet place to work

- A bowl of warm water

- A small dish of salt

- A hand towel or washcloth

- A small dish of anointing oil (see below)

- The largest mirror you have access to (optional)

- About half an hour of undisturbed time

- Your journal and a writing implement

To begin, enter your working space and set your tools somewhere close at hand. If you're using a mirror, it's best to have something in which you can see yourself full-length, but if you don't have one, you can make do with a wall-mounted bathroom mirror, or even a hand mirror. In fact, this rite can be done entirely without the mirror if you're visually impaired, don't have access to a mirror, or would prefer to forgo the visual aspect of this rite.

If you want to formally establish and enclose your working space, feel free to do so by whatever means you deem appropriate. (A sample space-setting can be found on p. 170.) If you don't feel it's necessary, feel free to skip it.

Take a few moments to center yourself in your body. When you're ready to begin, look at yourself, using the mirror or directly with your own eyes and hands. Notice the position of your body, what you're wearing, the expression on your face. Using your hands, feel the texture of your hair, skin, and clothes. As you do so, think about how the ways you dress and wear your hair are shaped by the expectations of the world, and about the ways you portray yourself to the world, how you're asking the world to see you. Feel where there's any tension in your body, beneath your clothes and skin, and think about where that tension comes from: your personal interactions, your work life, your worries about the world, your internal fears.

Now, begin to remove your clothing and jewelry, setting each article aside neatly and deliberately. As you do so, think of the ways in which that article is a layer between you and the rest of the world. Contemplate how the act of setting it aside is a revelation to yourself of both your physical and your internal self.

Once you're fully nude, spend some time looking at yourself, in the mirror or directly. There's a temptation to merely take a quick look to note that we occupy space and reflect light, or to focus solely our faces, with only a cursory glance at the rest of our bodies. I encourage you to resist that temptation, and instead take the time to truly *see* yourself, to look at your body as an artist would: as shapes and shadows, lines and curves, form and color and motion.

Using your hands and eyes, follow those lines and curves, notice the changes in texture and color from one region of your body to the next. Feel the texture of your own skin and hair, and the muscles and tendons and bones beneath. Find where you are soft or firm or callused, dry or moist, smooth or rough. If you find yourself thinking about how you wish you looked or how you'd like to change this or that part of yourself, consciously interrupt that train of thought with a spoken word. That word can be *no*, or *stop*, or whatever word of power you recognize. Do your best to forgo judgment, analysis, or preconception, and to pass over any thoughts about what other people might think of your body. Those thoughts aren't important. What's important isn't what others may think, but what truly *is* in this moment: what you see and feel, right now.

Approach the bowl of water. Sprinkle three pinches of salt into the water, then swirl it with your hand gently, watching as the salt dissolves in the water. Blow three soft breaths over the surface of the water and say, "Water, I cleanse you with salt, and I charge you with breath." This water is now consecrated by your will.

Now, beginning with the top of your head, focus on each part of your body and think about the ways in which that part of your body has been claimed by others for their use or ownership. Once you've thought of that external claim on your body, use your hands to sprinkle or wash that part of your body with the consecrated water, deliberately and with intention. In so doing, you are washing away the energetic connection to that external force and severing its claim on your body. You can envision this as a rush of water sluicing over your skin and washing away lines of force, like threads or cobwebs clinging to your skin. Repeat this process as you move down the length of your entire body, paying special attention to those parts of yourself where you may feel a particular sense of external claim, such as your breasts, genitals, or buttocks, or any other area of your body you feel has been sexualized or exploited by others.

Once you've washed your entire body in consecrated water, take up the dish of anointing oil. This needn't be a fancy magical oil from your friendly local occult store; you can use a massage oil from your local spa/salon or self-care products emporium, an organic coconut oil from the local natural foods co-op, or good old-fashioned plain olive oil. Just be sure to use something body-safe, non-toxic, and hypoallergenic which won't irritate your skin, especially if you intend to anoint your lips, mouth, or other body openings. (If you have any doubts about a particular oil, be sure to test it on some less-sensitive part of your body before applying it to more delicate areas. If you have any sort of reaction, feel free to find and use an alternative, non-allergenic substance.)

Lift the oil dish to your mouth and blow three soft breaths over the surface of the oil. After the first breath, say, "I charge this oil with purpose." After the second say, "I charge this oil for pleasure." After the third, say, "I charge this oil in power." Now set the dish before you, and beginning with your feet, use the oil to anoint each part of yourself that you cleansed with the consecrated water. This anointing can be as simple as a single drop of oil touched to your skin with the tip of your finger, or it can be a self-administered massage, rubbing the oil into your skin and gently working the muscles within. Find what feels good to you, what causes you to feel connected to that part of your body. As you touch the oil to each part of your body, say aloud, "This is my body. This body is mine. This is me." Work your way back up your body, anointing yourself thoroughly, until you reach the top of your head. There, after you make the final anointing, extend your arms outward like wings, as if to embrace someone, then wrap them around yourself.

Speak the following words, or whatever words you are moved to speak in their place:

"I claim this body: its strengths and its weaknesses, its pains and its pleasures. I claim every sensation, every movement, every stillness. This body, my body, belongs to no one but me. No human, no spirit, no god, no institution or force has any claim on my body. This body is a part of me, and I belong only to myself."

Take in a deep breath, hold it for a moment, then tilt your head back and breathe out forcefully, releasing any residual tension or unease along with your breath.

Once you've completed this exercise, take some time to decompress, to sit with the results. The act of declaring that your physical form—the tangible manifestation of your very existence—belongs to you and you alone can provoke a host of reactions. It can feel transgressive, terrifying, exhilarating, arousing, liberating. All these feelings are valid, legitimate responses to the act of taking your body back from the external forces which have declared it to be theirs, under their dominion. No matter how you react, do your best not to shy away from those feelings, unless you believe them to be approaching dangerous levels of distress. Instead, go ahead and feel them, engage with them. Listen to what those emotional responses are telling you about your past, and how they inform your present.

When you're ready, go to your journal and record your experiences. Note those emotional responses and any thoughts, images, or memories that may have surfaced as a result, as well as any particular parts of the exercise that may have provoked those feelings or thoughts.

If you set the space formally, release it at this time. The rite is ended.

Queer Divinities, Queering Divinity

Once we've reclaimed our own queerness, or embraced the queerness of those around us, the obvious next step to look at our spiritual praxis to see how it reflects that element of our selfhood. The Western esoteric movement has a fabulous potential for supporting, sustaining, and embracing queerness as a natural facet of human experience, and we can see that reflected in our mythologies, theologies, and cosmologies.

Of course, cultures throughout history have responded to the diversity of human sexuality and gender in a variety of ways, largely predicated on their own cultural needs and biases. Some cultures have developed social and spiritual roles for individuals who don't fit into the culturally established gender and sexual roles, such as the *hijras* of the Indian subcontinent and the Two-Spirit people of some indigenous North American peoples. Other cultures, in particular the cultures of the West, have worked to quash or ignore expressions of gender and sexuality outside an established binary, or to define such expressions in a way that reinforces the established gender norms.

All of this is to acknowledge that queerness, in the sense I've used the term in this book, is a modern concept...and a largely Western one at that. Some may feel it's a misnomer for devotional polytheists to talk about queer gods, but I obviously disagree. After all, we aren't worshiping Aphrodite (for instance) as the ancients did, because we aren't them: we lack the historical context that being ensconced in the cultural matrix of their era would provide. We are devoted to ancient gods, yes, but we do so as moderns. In that context, it makes complete sense to look to the queerness of ancient gods, because while we are indeed looking to the inspirational mythologies of the past, we're looking through modern eyes.

In the sixth of his Nemean Odes, the Greek lyric poet Pindar of Thebes (c. 522–c. 443 BCE) spoke of the relationship and kinship between humanity and the gods:

> Single is the race, single
> Of men and of gods;
> From a single mother we both draw breath.
> But a difference of power in everything
> Keeps us apart;
> For one is as Nothing, but the brazen sky
> Stays a fixed habituation forever.
> Yet we can in greatness of mind
> Or of body be like the Immortals ...[39]

If the gods exist as independent beings with their own agency, as Pindar and I both believe, then they exist in relationship with us for whatever reasons they choose; to help us become more like them or perhaps more like ourselves. In that case, it can't be an accident that they choose to share their stories with us, nor is it an accident that they have shaped us to be them in body, mind, and spirit. We share with them both form and nature, and that includes our embodied expressions of gender and sexuality.

Alternately, if you believe that human beings created gods to help us understand our own lived experiences, why wouldn't we create and worship queer gods? After all, we crave seeing ourselves and our own stories reflected in the stories we tell ourselves, and most especially in the stories we tell about ourselves.

---

39. Nemean VI, from Pindar, *The Odes*, trans. C. M. Bowra (New York: Penguin, 1969), 206.

Here, then, is a brief look at some deities whose myths and gnosis can have deep resonance for queer and trans devotees, and whose queerness might help straight and cis devotees gain a better understanding and acceptance of queer experience. This list is intended to be suggestive rather than comprehensive, and to provide you with a starting place to explore the complex relationship between gender, sexuality, and polytheist devotion in both the ancient and the modern worlds.

Queer Olympians and Greco-Roman Syncretism

The Sun God

One of the best-known of the Hellenic gods, Apollo has dominion over a wide swath of life: music and poetry, disease and healing, prophecy, the Sun, and light itself. He was commonly depicted in the classical Greek period as a *kouros*, an idealized image of a beautiful man in the prime of his youth … in other words, what would be known in modern gay male culture as a twink. Apollo is not only a canonically queer god, but he is part of one of the first canonical gay love triangles, vying for the love of the divine hero Hyakinthos, who was also desired by Zephyrus, the West Wind. Hyakinthos ultimately returned Apollo's love, but their romance was cut short. During a quoit-throwing contest, a gust of wind from the jealous Zephyrus caused Apollo's quoit to blow off course and strike Hyakinthos, killing him.[40] The grieving Apollo preserved the memory of his slain lover in the hyacinth flower, formed from Hyakinthos's spilled blood.[41]

---

40. Apollodorus, *The Library*, trans. Sir James George Frazer (Cambridge, MA: Harvard University Press, 1921), http://data.perseus.org/citations /urn:cts:greekLit:tlg0548.tlg001.perseus-eng1:Library.

41. Ovid, *Metamorphoses*, trans. Henry T. Riley (London: George Bell & Sons, 1893), http://www.gutenberg.org/ebooks/26073.

The Hunting Girl

The twin sister of Apollo, Artemis is the Hellenic goddess of the moon, the hunt, animals, wild places, childbirth, and virginity, and is especially protective of girls and young women. While there are no recorded myths of Artemis having a female lover (or indeed any lovers at all), Artemis is very much a queer femme goddess and is often revered by lesbians, queer women, and femmes as a goddess for women who love women, an interpretation with some strong resonances for devotees both classical and modern.[42] Arising in a culture that venerated the home, hearth, and family, Artemis a goddess of woman as defined not by man, but by herself: self-contained, self-determining, and self-sufficient. To that end, her myths can speak to anyone who respects and values the agency and dignity of women, girls, and femmes.

The Goddess Beyond Gender

The Greek goddess of love and beauty, Aphrodite is often seen by moderns as a giggling girly-girl goddess, but this is a wild mischaracterization at best. Aphrodite has been worshiped as a warrior goddess, a patron of both mothers and sex workers, and a goddess of queerness who blurs or erases lines of gender with a casual sweep of her hand. For this last matter, we can look to the Roman writer Macrobius, who records in his *Saturnalia* that on the island of Cyprus, she was depicted as "bearded, shaped and dressed like a woman, with scepter and male genitals," and was celebrated as "the nurturing god Venus, whether she is female or male."[43] Aristophanes

---

42. Siobhan Ball, "Artemis Is the Queer Girl Goddess BFF of Your Dreams," *Autostraddle*, May 2, 2017,http://www.autostraddle.com/artemis-is-the-queer-girl-goddess-bff-you-always-dreamt-of-377958/.

43. Macrobius Ambrosius Theodosius, *Saturnalia, Books 3–5*, trans. Robert A. Kaster (Cambridge, MA: Harvard University Press, 2011), 59.

named her Ἀφρόδιτος, *Aphroditos*, and Philochorus identified her with the Moon, stating that "men sacrifice to her in women's dress, women in men's, because she is held to be both male and female."[44] Surviving statues of the time show her as a beautiful woman lifting the front of her skirts, a gesture called *anasyrma* or *anasyromenos*, to display her penis and testicles.

The Androgyne

While Hermaphroditus was originally another name for the androgynous form of Aphrodite mentioned above (the name literally means "Aphrodite in the form of a *herm*," or ritual column), they were later seen as a discrete deity. Ovid describes them in *Metamorphoses* as the beautiful son of Aphrodite and Hermes, who was physically and spiritually united with the nymph Salmacis as a single androgynous being, "a creature of both sexes."[45] Like Aphroditos, Hermaphroditus was depicted in the art of the time as having a beautiful, feminine body with full breasts and a penis.

The Satyr of Arcadia

It would be a gross oversight to discuss sex among the Greek gods without mentioning Pan, the Arcadian god of nature, music, wildness, flocks, and shepherds … and, depending on your source, wild sexuality and fertility. Commonly depicted as a satyr, a man with the legs of a goat and a perpetually erect phallus—"Half a man and half a beast, / Pan is greatest, Pan is least," as Dion Fortune's *The Goat-Foot God* has it—his dual nature suggests his all-encompassing, all-embracing liminality, and it's little surprise that Pan is also depicted

---

44. Theodosius, *Saturnalia*, 59.

45. Ovid, *Metamorphoses*, trans. Henry T. Riley (London: George Bell & Sons, 1893), http://www.gutenberg.org/ebooks/26073.

in artwork through the ages as cheerfully pursuing both women and men for trysts.[46] His status as an iconic queer god was ratified by artists and writers of the Renaissance and later, for whom Pan was the embodiment of natural, healthy sexuality. In Victorian England, he was seen as a desperately necessary corrective to the increasingly prudish, repressive sexual morality of the day, as suggested by the closing lines of Oscar Wilde's "Pan—Double Villanelle":

> *Ah, leave the hills of Arcady!*
> *This modern world hath need of thee![47]*

The God of Ecstasy

From his mythic upbringing disguised as a girl-child to hide him from the wrath of the goddess Hera, to his divine portfolio of wine, theatre, madness, and ecstasy, Dionysus has long been worshiped as a god of transgression against societal norms of gender, sexuality, and propriety. While not as promiscuous as his divine father Zeus, he was classically attested in myth and art as engaging in what we moderns would call queer sexuality, specifically male homosexuality, frequently depicted as an effeminate young man in women's clothing, a gender performance the ancient Greeks would have identified as "unmanly."[48] His devotees, male and female alike, would similarly cross-dress in rituals and processions, with women sometimes also wearing phalluses to emphasize their transgression

46. Dion Fortune, *The Goat-Foot God* (Wellingborough, Northamptonshire, UK: Aquarian Press, 1989), 6.

47. Oscar Wilde, *Charmides and Other Poems* (London: Methuen & Co., 1913), http://www.gutenberg.org/ebooks/1031.

48. Arthur Evans, *The God of Ecstasy: Sex-Roles and the Madness of Dionysos* (New York: St. Martin's Press, 1988), 33–38.

of gender.[49] Those female devotees—*bakkhai* ("women possessed by Bacchus") or *mainades* ("mad women")—were acting well outside the gender roles prescribed for women of the classical Greek era, to both the consternation and the approval of contemporary Greek commentators.[50] In this light, Dionysus can be seen not merely as the god of drunken violation of arbitrary cultural mores, but as a god of liberation from those oppressive mores: an emphatically queer god, in all senses of the word.

The Beautiful Boy

The apotheosized lover of the Roman emperor Hadrian, Antinous is another deific figure who embodies queerness in the form of the *kouros,* or "beautiful boy." Born in the early second century CE to a Greek family in the Roman province of Bithnya (in modern-day Turkey), Antinous became Hadrian's favorite both for his beauty and for his intelligence. When Antinous drowned in the Nile River under mysterious circumstances, he was syncretized with Osiris by the local Egyptian priests, having died in a manner similar to the Egyptian god of the afterlife. The heartbroken Hadrian expanded upon this veneration, proclaiming Antinous's deification throughout the Empire as both an extension of the Imperial cult and a devotional practice in its own right. The cult of Antinous remained vital until the rise of Christianity in the fourth century CE. Even after, Antinous retained his power as a queer icon throughout the ages, resurging in the nineteenth century as writers like Oscar Wilde, Fernando Pessoa, and Victor Hugo upheld him as the pinnacle of male beauty. In the twenty-first century, Antinous's cult

---

49. Evans, *God of Ecstasy*, 19–21.

50. Ibid., 10–18.

has experienced something of a renaissance, as queer polytheists find in his myth a sacralization of divine queer love.

An aspect of Antinous's cult which we have to address here, especially in light of the stress I've placed on consent in this book, is the relationship between the adult Hadrian and the teenaged Antinous. In classical Greek culture, it was considered socially acceptable for an adult man (*erastes*) and an adolescent boy (*eromenos*) to engage in *paiderastía*, a consensual romantic and sexual relationship. While such relationships are emphatically unacceptable by modern standards, at that time and place they were considered unremarkable, even admirable. This observation is not to defend *paiderastía*, nor to give a moral pass on the questions of consent inherent in relationships between individuals of disparate ages, experience levels, and power. Rather, it's to suggest that viewing ancient cultures through a modern lens requires us to engage in a nuanced analysis and to understand how those cultures understood themselves, whether we agree with their self-assessments, or (as in this case) reject their premises and conclusions. For a deeper examination of the socio-cultural issues around classical Greek *paiderastía*, especially from a modern perspective, please see Robin Osborne's *Greek History*, Martha Nussbaum's *The Fragility of Goodness* and "Platonic Love and Colorado Law: The Relevance of Ancient Greek Norms to Modern Sexual Controversies" in *Virginia Law Review*, and Kenneth Dover's *Greek Homosexuality*.

The Mystery of Pales

Somewhat reminiscent of Pan, Pales is a Roman deity of shepherds and sheep who is best remembered today as the patron of the Parilia, a rural festival of purification which came to be observed as the birthday of the Roman Empire. In many ways, Pales is a preeminent example of a truly queer deity. They are female, male, both, and neither. We know next to nothing about them, and we can't even agree on the little we do know. Sources vary in their identification of Pales, who is seen as male and female, as a single deity or as a pair of gods. It's been suggested, most famously by Tom Robbins in his novel *Skinny Legs and All*, that the name identifies an ambiguously-gendered donkey-headed deity worshiped by the ancient Israelites, Philistines, and Canaanites, whose name came to be associated with the region Palestine.[51]

Diana of the Woods, Aradia of the Witches

Diana is commonly understood as the Roman cognate of Artemis, but her history is far more complex than that description would suggest. Her Hellenic origins are as the goddess of hunting and wild animals, but she is also said to have an independent origin as Diana Nemorensis, the patron goddess of Lake Nemi and the nearby city of Nemi, whose power also protected maidens and childbearing women. It was this Diana who was depicted alongside the moon goddess Luna and the witch goddess Hecate[52] as the *diva triformis*, or "three-form goddess."

> *Virgin, goddess, goddess of the groves*
> *And of the hills, goddess to whom the young*
> *Mother in her labor cries out three times*
> *And then again cries out three times O goddess,*
> *Goddess, to hear and rescue her from death,*
> *O goddess triple-formed ...*[53]

---

51. Tom Robbins, *Skinny Legs and All* (New York: Bantam, 1990), 364, 371–372.

52. Andrew Alföldi, "Diana Nemorensis," *American Journal of Archaeology* 64, no. 2 (1960): 140.

53. Horace, *The Odes of Horace*, trans. David Ferry (New York: Farrar, Strauss and Giroux, 2015), 225.

As her cult grew in the Roman Empire, she adopted (or accreted) other titles and portfolios from goddesses in areas assimilated by the Romans, and she came to take on the aspect of a transcendent, celestial Great Mother over time. After the fall of Rome, her influence can be traced through folklore and practice across Europe, influencing or localizing under various names: Nicnevin, Hulda, Dame Habondia, and Perchta.

While she remains known as the Roman Artemis, Diana is also revered in many forms of modern witchcraft as the queen of the witches, the mother of the fair folk, and most especially the fairy / witch / goddess figure at the center of Charles Godfrey Leland's *Aradia, or the Gospel of the Witches*. Here, she is depicted as a unitary, all-encompassing celestial being, "the first created before all creation," who divides herself into two beings: her own self and Lucifer, "her brother and son, herself and her other half,"[54] a syncretic figure conflating the fallen angel of Christianity with the Greco-Roman sun god Apollo:

> *And when Diana saw that the light was so beautiful, the light which was her other half, her brother Lucifer, she yearned for it with exceeding great desire. Wishing to receive the light again into her darkness, to swallow it up in rapture, in delight, she trembled with desire. This desire was the Dawn.*[55]

Through sexual union with Lucifer, Diana became the mother of Aradia, a mysterious salvific figure who offers liberation to her people through magic wielded against the oppressors of the poor:

---

54. Charles Godfrey Leland, *Aradia, or the Gospel of the Witches* (London: David Nutt, 1899), 18.

55. Ibid.

> *And ye shall all be freed from slavery,*
> *And so ye shall be free in everything;*
> *And as the sign that ye are truly free,*
> *Ye shall be naked in your rites, both men*
> *And women also: this shall last until*
> *The last of your oppressors shall be dead.*[56]

The sexuality implied in this verse—freedom equated with ritual nudity—is made explicit in later passages, where Aradia instructs her followers to revel in their sensuality and sexuality, directly under the influence of her mother:

> *And thus shall it be done: all shall sit down to the supper all naked, men and women, and, the feast over, they shall dance, sing, make music, and then love in the darkness, with all the lights extinguished: for it is the Spirit of Diana who extinguishes them, and so they will dance and make music in her praise.*[57]

The provenance of Leland's book is something of an open question. His claim to have received it as a handwritten manuscript from an Italian witch named Maddalena Talenti is essentially unprovable at this date, and modern scholars disagree as to whether the book is a genuine text of a surviving folk religion, a contemporary syncretic text, or an outright forgery. (For an overview of scholarly positions on *Aradia*, see Sabina Magliocco's "Who Was Aradia? The History and Development of a Legend" in the February 2002 issue of *The Pomegranate: The Journal of Pagan*

---

56. Leland, *Aradia*, 6–7.

57. Ibid., 14.

Studies, Robert Mathiesen's "Charles G. Leland and the Witches of Italy: The Origin of Aradia" and Chas S. Clifton's "The Significance of Aradia" in Mario Pazzaglini's *Aradia, or the Gospel of the Witches, A New Translation*, and Ronald Hutton's *The Triumph of the Moon*.)

What can be said without fear of contradiction is that *Aradia* is a significant, even formative influence on modern Pagan and polytheist witchcraft. Simply put, *Aradia*—with its transgressive embrace of sexuality, sensuality, and spiritual power, all derived from a self-sufficient goddess—is unquestionably one of the primary templates for the witchcraft revival of the twentieth century.

Genderqueer Progenitors of the North
The Primordial One
In both the *Poetic Edda* and *Prose Edda* from which most Norse myth derives, Ymir is the primordial ancestor of the *jötnar* (colloquially known as giants), a genderless asexual being who birthed a male and a female *jötunn* from each armpit, and whose legs gave birth to another child. The gods Odin, Vili, and Vé later slew Ymir, and from Ymir's body they formed the Earth itself, as well as the oceans, the clouds, the heavens, and the middle-world (*Midgard*) in which humanity lives.

The All-father
The chieftain of the Æsir, Odin, is revered as the All-father, a figure of manly wisdom and kingly might as well as battle-cunning and trickery, all in service to his people. Much is made of the lengths to which Odin will go to gain knowledge and power; see, for instance, trading one of his eyes for a drink from Mimir's well of wisdom,[58]

---

58. *The Elder or Poetic Edda, Part I—The Mythological Poems*, ed. and trans. Oliver Bray (London: Viking Club, 1908), 287.

or his self-sacrifice hung from the world-tree Yggdrasil to gain the power of the runes.[59] Less well-known, at least among casual readers of Norse mythology, is Odin's practice of the sorcerous art of *seiðr*, which he is said to have learned from the Vanir goddess Freyja. *Seiðr* was widely associated with femininity by Norse culture of the time,[60] which led to Loki's charge of *ergi* (unmanliness or effeminacy) against Odin in the *Poetic Edda*, claiming that the All-father had disguised himself as a woman fortune-teller.[61] Modern Norse polytheists have interpreted Odin's disregard for the gender norms of the day in multiple ways, including simple expediency. After all, if the All-father was willing to tear out his own eye or literally kill himself in the pursuit of knowledge and power, wouldn't he be equally willing to sacrifice his own reputation for manliness? In that disregard, Odin can easily be seen as a god who queers gender, and who suggests to us that the gendered boundaries we draw around practices and power are artificial, arbitrary, and ultimately meaningless.

The Shape-changer

Delving further into the myth-cycle, the Norse god of mischief Loki has seen something of a renaissance in his popularity in the past few decades, due in no small part to his depictions in the recent Marvel Comics film adaptations. Loki's modern devotees are undoubtedly familiar with his shapeshifting abilities, which allowed him to take a variety of forms at key points in the mythology. It's particularly notable, in a culture often deemed to be heav-

---

59. *Edda Sæmundar Hinns Fróða: The Edda of Sæmund the Learned, Part I*, trans. Benjamin Thorpe (London: Trübner & Co., 1866), 51.

60. Jenny Blain, *Nine Worlds of Seid-Magic: Ecstasy and Neo-shamanism in North European Paganism* (London: Routledge, 2002), 18.

61. Ibid., 94.

ily binary in its gender paradigm, that at least two of those forms were female ... and one of those was a mother. The *Poetic Edda* tells us that, while in the form of a mare, Loki was mounted by the stallion Svaðilfari, and later foaled the eight-legged horse Sleipnir.[62] The greatest of all horses, Sleipnir later became Odin's personal steed, whom the chief of the Æsir rode from Asgard through all the worlds, even into Hel, the land of death. Snorri Sturluson's *Prose Edda* book *Gylfaginning* recounts that, after the death of the god Baldr (through one of Loki's machinations, of course), the death-goddess Hel agreed to allow him to return to the land of the living if all living beings would weep in sorrow for him. The Æsir sent out messengers asking the world to grieve for Baldr's death, and all did ... but one. The lone holdout was a female giant named Thǫkk, who refused to shed a tear, saying, "Living or dead, I loved not the churl's son; Let Hel hold to that she hath!" Sturluson concludes this passage, "And men deem that she who was there was Loki Laufeyarson, who hath wrought most ill among the Æsir."[63]

The Queer Craft of the Witches

The Ancient Providence

In many forms of Wicca, especially those derived from Gardnerian Wicca, the Goddess and the God of the Witches are seen as complementary halves of the primordial, monadic godhead, referred to by the Anglo-Saxon term *Dryghtyn* or *Drychton* (meaning "lord"). This divine being, identified in the liturgical piece known as the Blessing Prayer as "the Ancient Providence," is stated to be "the Original Source of all things ... all-knowing, all-pervading, all-powerful,

---

62. Snorri Sturluson, *The Prose Edda*, trans. Arthur Gilchrist Brodeur (New York: The American-Scandinavian Foundation, 1916), 55.

63. Ibid., 75.

changeless, eternal" and is explicitly identified as both male and female.[64] While some Wiccans have made much out of the splitting of Dryghtyn into Goddess and God, citing this as justification for establishing gender-essentialist stances within their practice, others have pointed to the genderless/all-gendered nature of Dryghtyn as justification for the inclusion and celebration of all genders and sexual orientations within Wicca. After all, Wicca's best-known and best-loved contribution to Pagan liturgy is Doreen Valiente's "Charge of the Goddess," where she writes, "Let my worship be within the heart that rejoiceth, for behold: all acts of love and pleasure are my rituals."[65] The "all" in that sentence, as spoken by the Goddess of the Witches, would seem to mandate an enthusiastic embrace of … well, *all* forms of consensual sexuality and pleasure, wouldn't it?

The Old One and the Queen of Elphame

Still, while some forms of modern traditional witchcraft have been leery to embrace queer sexuality and fluidity of gender, others have opted to engage more directly with questions of gender and sexuality, surrendering neither one, but rather widening the circumference of their "charmed circle" to include even those "acts of love and pleasure" considered transgressive or non-normative. Within some lines of traditional witchcraft, sexual initiation and magic are neither unheard-of nor restricted to cisgender heterosexual couplings. In *The Devil's Dozen: Thirteen Craft Rites of the Old One*, British Traditional witch Gemma Gary is explicit about both the sexual nature of the witch's mystical union with "the Old One" and the lack of regard for gender or biological sex of the witch who

---

64. Patricia Crowther, *Witch Blood: The Diary of a Witch High Priestess* (New York: House of Collectibles, 1974), 39.

65. Doreen Valiente, "The Charge of the Goddess," http://www.doreenvaliente .org/Doreen-Valiente-Doreen_Valiente_Poetry-11.php.

undertakes this rite. She allows that, while this initiation is generally "thought of as taking place between female witches and the Devil in full masculine manifestation," the sexual mysteries of the Witches' Sabbat allow for the Old One, manifesting as a woman or a man, to engage in ritual sexual union with male or female witches, or for the Queen of Elphame to join with him in presiding over the sabbat, sexually coupling with witches of whatever gender "in sacred transgression of societal 'normality' [...] no matter how aggressively adverse some modern expressions of the Craft have been to such things."[66]

The Star Goddess

Turning to another line of traditional witchcraft, the heart of Anderson Feri is the super transcendent deity variously known as the Star Goddess, God Herself, and the Black Virgin of the Outer Dark. Similar in many ways to the Dryghtyn of Wiccan theology, the Star Goddess is the all-encompassing, primordial source of all things. While generally referred to as female, the Star Goddess is understood by Feri to encompass all possibilities of gender and sexuality. Victor Anderson referred to her as "the clitorophallic God Herself," and Cora Anderson wrote, "Not only does she have a sex, but she is sex, both male and female."[67] "She is the Holy Virgin because she is complete within herself and needs no other."[68] She is said to have birthed from within herself the Divine Twins, "the divine lovers that created this present universe," variously seen as

---

66. Gemma Gary, *The Devil's Dozen: Thirteen Craft Rites of the Old One* (London: Troy Books, 2015), 109.

67. Valerie Walker, "Feri FAQs, v. 8.3, 11/10," last modified November 2010, http://www.wiggage.com/witch/feriFAQ.8.html.

68. Cora Anderson, *Fifty Years in the Feri Tradition* (Portland, OR: Acorn Guild Press, 2005), 6.

a male/female dyad, a same-gender couple of either gender, or some other coupling beyond gender.[69] The Andersons were notably, delightfully inclusive in their outlook on gender, with Victor opining that "Mere gender, as we think of it here, is always so restrictive."[70]

The Peacock Angel and a Queer Family of Gods

Another of the primary divine beings honored in Feri is Melek Taus (*Tawûsê Melek*, "Peacock Angel"). Adopted from the Yazidi people of Ezidikhan, who praise him as God's chief representative on Earth and the lord of our world, the Peacock Angel has come to be revered by many traditions of modern Paganism and esoteric spirituality. He is seen by some within Feri as the union of the Divine Twins, a being both male and androgynous, the son and lover of the all-encompassing, all-gendered Star Goddess. In this, he is reminiscent of the Apollonian figure of Lucifer from Leland's *Aradia*, an association reinforced in Victor Anderson's poem "Lightbringer," which underscores the fallen, rejected horned god of light and power who offers his devotees the solace of forbidden —and explicitly queer—sexual love.[71]

Other Feri deities can be said to queer gender and sexuality, or to subvert them wholly. Dian-y-Glas, the boyish Blue God who is often said to be connected to (or a mirror of) Melek Taus, is honored as a god of masculine youth and virility, again recalling the figure of Apollo, and is embraced by androphiles of all genders as the embodiment of male sexuality at its peak. At the same time, he

---

69. Cholla Soledad,"Speak of the Devil: *Witch Eye* talks with Victor Anderson," *Witch Eye* 3 (August 2000), 4.

70. Ibid.

71. Victor Anderson,"Lightbringer," *Lilith's Garden* (Portland, OR: Acorn Guild Press, 2001), 39–40.

is frequently depicted as lithe, almost feminine, and emphatically queer in both gender and sexuality. His sister Nimuë is sometimes depicted as a maiden goddess, after the archetype of Artemis and Diana, and at other times as a little girl, albeit one holding all the powers of Creation and Destruction in her sticky little hands. She is seen by some as pre-gender and pre-sexual, in contrast to Dian-y-Glas as the blossoming of gender and sexuality. At the other end of the scale, we find Ana and the Arddhu, the Crone and Old Man Death, who might both be seen as post-gender and post-sexual. Between them, we find Mari and Krom, who are sometimes cast as the archetypal Mother and Father, but even here, the lines of gender and sexuality aren't so clear-cut. Mari wears the crimson cloak and sword of the Battle Goddess as easily as the blue mantle of the Mother and owns the fullness of her sexuality without being defined by it, or letting others define it for her. Similarly, the dying and rising horned lord will hunt with the wild animals in one moment and embrace a playful pansexuality in the next.

Thelema

The Woman Girt with a Sword

While her aspect and imagery derive from the Book of Revelation in the Christian Bible ("... a woman sitting on a scarlet beast ... arrayed in purple and scarlet, and adorned with gold and jewels and pearls, holding in her hand a golden cup full of abominations and the impurities of her sexual immorality"[72]) and were further developed in John Dee's Enochian work, where she is named as the daughter of Fortitude, the goddess Babalon is probably best known today for her depiction within Thelema, the magico-religious and philosophical tradition derived from

---

72. Revelation 17:3–6 (English Standard Version).

Aleister Crowley's writings and practices, where she is identified as the Scarlet Woman, the Mother of Abominations, the Lady of the Night. Babalon is known to her devotees as the manifest embodiment of Nuit, the Queen of Infinite Space, and worshiped as the sacred whore who accepts all lovers, refusing none:

> *This is the Mystery of Babalon, the Mother of Abominations, and this is the mystery of her adulteries, for she hath yielded up herself to everything that liveth, and hath become a partaker in its mystery. And because she hath made her self the servant of each, therefore is she become the mistress of all.*[73]

Christine Hoff Kraemer underscores this intersection of erotic and divine love in her analysis of Alan Moore's depiction of Babalon in the graphic novel *Promethea*: "No one, no matter how poor of body or spirit, no matter how dirty, diseased, or broken, is refused the erotic love of the Goddess, who is the face of Being itself."[74]

Babalon is the keeper of the Mystery of Mastery through Submission and Understanding: by receiving all and comprehending all, she achieves mastery of all. She appears in whatever form her devotee finds most desirable. Through that appearance, she draws them into submission and reveals to them their deepest desires, their innermost selves. For some, she is the woman girt with a sword, Mother Earth, or the Girl Next Door, while for others, she is the Whore of the Book of Revelation, the Daughter of the Night, the Witch-Goddess, even the oft-derided Babalon Barbie cheese-

---

73. From "The Cry of the 12th Æthyr, which is called LOE," in Aleister Crowley, *The Vision and the Voice* (Newburyport, MA: Weiser, 1999), 150.

74. Christine Hoff Kraemer, *Eros and Touch from a Pagan Perspective: Divided for Love's Sake* (London: Routledge, 2013), 50.

cake pinup of some occultists' fantasies. For some devotees, she comes to them as a genderqueer, gender-fluid goddess, a woman girt with another kind of sword. In the rush of her drunken fornications and transgressions against all established norms of gender, sexuality, and propriety, Babalon can rightly be seen as a queer, trans femme goddess *par excellence*.

Queering the Circle

When I defined the word queer in chapter 2, I made reference to Gayle Rubin's charmed circle model of normative sexual mores within culture and suggested that queerness might best be understood as a shorthand term for gender identities and sexual orientations that fall outside the charmed circle of cultural acceptance and societal approval.

Here's the thing: the charmed circle isn't necessarily a bad thing in itself. After all, any tool can be used for good or ill purposes, and a circle is one such tool, a way to circumscribe and set what's within it apart from what's outside it. Just as in magical traditions, circles are used in our culture as protective boundaries, as containers for power, as a formalized way of establishing sacred space. They are, in culture as in magic, a form of discernment: a way of saying, "This, and not that."

The key question, then, is what our criteria for discernment are: what we're using to draw our circle, what it includes, and what it excludes. The classic grimoiric circles were usually drawn physically with chalk, paint, or ink and then filled in with various god-names, magical symbols, and religious scriptures in order to invoke divine spiritual aid in preserving the safety of the practitioner against the forces they were invoking. Some modern witches and Pagans draw circles energetically or symbolically—using their hands or a tool such as an athame or a wand, sometimes with symbols drawn at the four quarters—both to focus their magic and to keep out unwanted influences.

Similarly, the charmed circle of sexuality and gender is intended to include and reinforce cultural norms, and to exclude identities and behaviors which deviate from those norms. In places and times where the dominant culture is influenced by Christianity, these norms are largely derived from Biblical hermeneutics about gender and sexuality. This hermeneutical approach gives rise to a strongly typed essentialist model of binary gender, on which is built a proto-theology of sexual ethics and propriety. This sexual theology posits a man/woman marital and sexual union as both a law of nature established by God ("For their women exchanged natural relations for those that are contrary to nature; and the men likewise gave up natural relations with women and were consumed with passion for one another, men committing shameless acts with men and receiving in themselves the due penalty for their error."[75]) and a metaphor for the relationship between God and the church ("... the head of every man is Christ, the head of a wife is her husband, and the head of Christ is God."[76]), stressing the sacred, secular, and sexual power of men over women. In this construct, homosexuality and other forms of supposed sexual immorality are equated with other forms of vice ("... neither the sexually immoral, nor idolaters, nor adulterers, nor men who practice homosexuality, nor thieves, nor the greedy, nor drunkards, nor revilers, nor swindlers will inherit the kingdom of God."[77]) and prohibited as a perversion of this metaphor worthy of death ("If a man lies with a male as with a woman, both of them have commit-

---

75. Romans 1:26–27 (English Standard Version).

76. 1 Corinthians 11:3 (English Standard Version).

77. 1 Corinthians 6:9–10 (English Standard Version).

ted an abomination; they shall surely be put to death; their blood is upon them."[78]), as well as being contrary to the established primary goal of sexual interaction, which is pregnancy and progeny. Similarly, gender queerness and other forms of gender nonconformity, often expressed as effeminacy or mannishness, are expressly prohibited: "A woman shall not wear a man's garment, nor shall a man put on a woman's cloak, for whoever does these things is an abomination to the Lord your God."[79]

In summary, the underlying assumptions of this Christian-derived charmed circle are that

1. human beings are divided into two biologically determined genders, male and female, and nothing else;

2. some things are for men, some things are for women, and neither gender should have anything to do with the other gender's stuff;

3. women should be subordinate to men in all ways, including sexually; and

4. anyone or anything that violates items 1, 2, or 3 is an abomination.

Some folks are completely comfortable living within that framework, and others are willing to submit their own wills and identities to the dictates of their religion. Those of us who don't fall into either of those categories are left with the non-trivial problem of how to live spiritually, emotionally, and sexually fulfilling lives within a culture whose fundamental assumptions about gender and

---

78. Leviticus 20:13 (English Standard Version).

79. Deuteronomy 22:5 (English Standard Version).

sexuality don't jive with our own experiences, internal lives, or spiritual beliefs.

I don't bring this up to be depressing, or to rail against Christianity. Rather, I start here because the solutions I'm proposing have to start with an acknowledgment of the present situation. Those of us who are queer in some way are metaphorically and literally outside the charmed circle.

Once we have our bearings, where do we go from here? We might be tempted to simply erase the charmed circle and eradicate societal norms altogether, but as I suggested above, the charmed circle isn't intrinsically evil. On the contrary, the reality is that social norms are a good thing, a necessary thing. The charmed circle tells us what behaviors are expected from members of our society, and what penalties we can expect to pay if we should behave in an antisocial fashion. In a society which claims to be humane, ethical, moral, and healthy, we should expect to find norms which discourage or prohibit inhumane, unethical, immoral, and unhealthy behaviors. Similarly, if we want to live in such a society, we should encourage norms which support the behavior we want to see. Note, though, that social norms aren't laws. Laws are a matter of public policy, and in a just society, would serve to support the social norms of that society, which in turn derive from the values of the culture.

Here, we find one of the conflicts at the heart of the American culture war of the late twentieth and early twenty-first centuries. The problem isn't merely an issue of political leanings or economics, but of values and social norms: what behaviors and identities are acceptable, and who gets to decide? Who has the power to act, and what kind of power is it? In her book *Truth or Dare*, ecofeminist activist and witch Starhawk writes that modern culture is built on systems of control, domination, and manipulation rooted in what she calls "power-over," and that one cannot truly change these systems with the same power which created them in the first place. She suggests that we can choose different forms of power, the collaborative "power-with" and the internal "power-from-within," and that doing so enables us to shape our realities and our relationships with other people, both corporeal and otherwise, through cooperation, negotiation, and mutual benefit.[80]

If we want a charmed circle which allows those within it the freedom and the ability to live their truest, most deeply authentic lives, the core of our praxis and the key element in our discernment—the power with which we draw the charmed circle—must be a collaborative, cooperative power achieved through negotiation and mutuality. In other words, it must be rooted in consent. With consent as the core of our praxis, we find that the charmed circle we draw looks quite different indeed.

We'll talk more about this in chapter 7. For now, let's turn to a subject that, for all this talk about queerness, we've been sidestepping for a while: the magic of sex, and the sexuality of magic.

---

80. Starhawk, *Truth or Dare: Encounters with Power, Authority, and Mystery* (San Francisco: HarperSan Francisco, 1988), 9–10.

Chapter 6
SAFER SEX MAGIC FOR BEGINNERS (AND EXPERTS)

SEX MAGIC IS ONE of the more delicate topics one can bring up in a work written for Pagans, polytheists, and magical practitioners, for a whole host of reasons. For some folks, the phrase conjures up lurid images drawn from sleazy B-movies, while for others it brings up all kinds of unwelcome emotions and memories. Sex magic has been used as a pretext for sexual predation and abuse, as the punch line of lewd jokes, and as a justification for deeming certain traditions and practitioners to be sexually and spiritually unwholesome.

This state of affairs is a damned shame; properly understood, sex magic is one of the most wholesome, life-affirming, and joyful practices we have available to us. Sex magic is rooted in the body, the place where spirit meets matter, and it derives from pleasure, the form that joy takes when it manifests in our physical form. It's a form of magic available to anyone with a body and the ability to experience erotic sensation, so it's accessible to almost everyone. There are even asexual people who practice sex magic quite successfully, at that.

What follows is an exploration of sex magic from the ground up. We'll start by deconstructing sex magic as a term, looking at how we're defining our terms, and how those definitions shape our perspectives and our practices. We'll conclude by going through a reconstructed model of what sex magic could be, including a basic ritual frame intended to give any interested practitioner a starting point for their own sex-magical explorations.

Much of what I've written here is geared toward folks who've been practicing some form of magic for a while. If you're new to magic, this might not be the best place to start learning how to do it … but then again, it might be. Sex magic is certainly one of the simplest forms of magic to learn; it's as close to us as our own skin, and it requires no external tools.

Let's Talk About (How We Talk About) Sex, Baby

In order to fruitfully discuss sex magic, we have to talk about what we mean by sex magic, which is kind of a problem because magical practitioners have difficulty agreeing on a definition for it. Part of the problem is that we can't seem to agree on definitions for sex *or* magic, much less for the two words together, a surefire recipe for all kinds of controversy and misunderstanding. In a world with dictionaries and search engines and Wikipedia, you wouldn't think there would be such a problem … and you would be quite wrong. Even a cursory glance at the available definitions drops us into a pile of confusion. We'll start with the myriad definitions for sex itself, which begin as scientifically technical attempts at making biological distinctions between male, female, and intersex organisms and become bewilderingly self-referential in short order, practically requiring a local guide to distinguish between the act of reproduction and the biological categorization of the organisms actually doing the reproduction … and, of course, neither definition addresses all the social, cultural, and emotional aspects of sex.

As for magic, we immediately find ourselves needing to disambiguate the *actual* use of paranormal powers to achieve supernatural feats from the *illusion* of doing the same: the real-magic-versus-stage magic dilemma, in other words.(We also have the problem of defining *paranormal* and *supernatural*, especially within an esoteric paradigm which suggests that such abilities are both normal and natural, but that's more battlefronts than we can really tackle at the moment, so let's pretend we all know what we're talking about.) The engagement with magic as an actual category of phenomena immediately drops us into an academic quagmire in religious studies and social sciences. Scholars in these fields are unable to agree on how to define the term or whether it's even a useful word anymore, to the point where some have suggested that no such umbrella term is useful and instead refer solely to specific cultural practices and beliefs. The topic of magic is an ongoing conversation in the social sciences that is impossible to cover fully here. Interested readers are commended to Dorothy Hammond's "Magic: A Problem in Semantics" in *American Anthropologist* (vol. 72, no. 6, 1970), Bronislaw Malinowski's *Magic, Science, and Religion*, and Owen Davies's *Magic: A Very Short Introduction* as useful entry points for this fascinating subject.

Both sex and magic as categories of experience and practice are bottomless rabbit holes of psychological, philosophical, theological, anthropological, and sociological confusion which are bad enough on their own, and exponentially worse when we combine them. The problem is, we still have to know what both sex and magic actually mean before we get anywhere near sex magic, discursively or practically; coming up with universally accepted definitions for either term is a fool's game. However, if I'm going to talk about sex magic at all, it behooves me to start by sketching out the definitions I'm using for these terms, so, let's have some fun with vocabulary, shall we? (And as ever, please note that these are just my definitions rather than being prescriptive in any way.)

Sex: The First Word in Sex Magic!

I'm far from being the first observer to note that the ways in which we talk about sex are less about what we do sexually and more about how we feel about it. It's worth noting that in English, there are far more euphemisms for sex than there are discrete sexual acts. Either we really, really like getting creative in how we talk about sex, or we really, really don't like just coming out and saying what we're doing with (or to) ourselves and each other ... or, as is so often the case, both. The pressure to preserve social norms of discreet behavior provides a strong impetus for not using obscene language, as with George Carlin's famous "Seven Words You Can Never Say on Television," but social norms have never—I repeat, *never*—stopped people from talking about sex, much less having it. We just learn to hide what we mean, to protect ourselves from social opprobrium.

It's also worth noting what gets lost or hidden when we euphemize our sexual activities and desires. For instance, many of the terms we use to talk about sex as a category refer to sexual intercourse, specifically to cisgender, heterosexual, penetrative, penis-in-vagina (PIV) intercourse. This framing inherently calls into question the validity of any sexual act that doesn't fundamentally reify the characteristics of PIV intercourse as norms: oral sex, manual sex, solo sex, sex using toys, and so on. Of course, that frame might be perfectly fine for folks whose sexuality fits comfortably within the bounds of, say, Pope John Paul II's *Theology of the Body*, but I don't think it's overreaching to suggest that Pagans, polytheists, and practitioners of magic would do well to develop a broader, more inclusive definition of sexuality than the Catholic Church's.

How should we define sex, then? A simple answer might be that sex refers to any activity intended to express sexual feelings. It's an okay definition, but it's pretty mechanical. It also does that annoying trick of defining a thing by itself (the philosophical equivalent of cheating at solitaire), but at least "sexual" is a word for which we can get a halfway-decent definition: related to the physical processes, emotional states, or activities connected with intimate physical contact or attraction. Those of us who take our cues from the polytheist religions of the past might find it useful to think of sexual feelings in terms of *eros*, after the Greek god of the same name. We might likewise consider the value—and the implications—of embracing eroticism, the blending of sensuality and aesthetics with connection and consent, as a core component of our views on sexuality. In so doing, sex can become something more than a vehicle for satisfying mechanical urges: it can be truly generative.

"Whoa, whoa, whoa," I hear some of you cry. "What's all this about sex being 'generative,' huh? I thought you said we were *avoiding* Catholicism! What are you, some kind of hypocrite?"

Calm down, friends, and let me finish. Yes, I said sex is generative, and I meant it. Generative can mean reproductive, but a fuller definition would be something like "having the power of generating, originating, producing, reproducing." The power of creation, in other words.

Sex can do all of those things. Sex can generate pleasure, originate well-being, produce understanding, *and* be the means by which we reproduce as a species. Sex creates, makes manifest new things: new insights, new intimacies, new life, new outlooks on life. Sex is one of the most powerful forces we can access, and it can be terrifying precisely because it's powerful. In the Anderson Feri tradition, sex is the means by which the Star Goddess brought the Universe into being, a supreme act of self-love and sex magic synonymous with creation. Just so for us mere mortals: through our sexuality, we can share in the same power of creation.

An Unavoidably Necessary Detour Through Pre-War England

Having come to a reasonable definition of sex, we should move onto the definition of magic. Of course, this is a serious task, one which demands a modicum of gravitas and other five-dollar words, not to mention a Victorian waistcoat and the demeanor of an Oxford don. However, lacking most of those, we'll just have to proceed as best we can.

Magic is notoriously one of those words such that if you ask any ten practitioners, you'll get thirteen different answers, some of them mutually exclusive, after which the respondents will start arguing about whose definitions are correct, whose are utter tosh, and whose are just reheated Crowley … and since we're talking about both sex and magic in the context of modern Paganism and polytheism, we're going to have to deal with Mr. Crowley sooner or later, so let's just get it over with. Those of you already familiar with Uncle Al may skip the next paragraph, and I won't blame you a bit.

For those of you who aren't familiar, here's the condensed version: Aleister Crowley (1875—1947) was a famous (or infamous)

English occultist, magician, writer, and vocational *bête noire* whose work has for better or worse informed and influenced much of the modern Pagan and magical revival of the twentieth and twenty-first centuries. A full biography of the man is beyond the scope of this book, but there are several in print. I can particularly recommend Lawrence Sutin's *Do What Thou Wilt* (New York: St. Martin's Press, 2000), Martin Booth's *A Magick Life* (London: Coronet Books, 2000), and Richard Kaczynski's *Perdurabo* (Berkeley, CA: North Atlantic Books, 2012) for the reader's own judgment of the man's life and work. The reader may also detect a note of resignation in my discussion of Aleister Crowley. As someone who's been studying and practicing magic for more than thirty years, it would be dishonest of me to ignore Crowley's influence on modern magic, Paganism, and polytheism. It would also be dishonest of me not to suggest that his influence wasn't necessarily a good thing. Crowley's impact during his life and the legacy of his influence have contributed directly and indirectly to a substantial number of the problems our communities face today.

To return to the subject at hand, Crowley defined magick (his preferred spelling, to distinguish it from stage magic) as "the Science and Art of causing Change to occur in conformity with Will."[81] He would further expand on this definition as "the Science of understanding oneself and one's conditions [and] the Art of applying that understanding in action,"[82] suggesting that for Crowley, magic is as psychological as it is parapsychological. (Crowley famously identified the demons of the *Lesser Key of Solomon* as being "portions of the human brain," which may say more about Crowley's brain than anyone else's.) Dion Fortune, the grand

---

81. Aleister Crowley, *Magick in Theory and Practice* (New York: Dover, 1976), xii.

82. Ibid, xx.

dame of pre-WWII English magic, is said to have modified Crowley's definition to refer to changes in consciousness, amplifying the focus on the mind of the mage as a central component of their approach to magic.

So, is magic all in your head? The answer kind of depends on what you mean by "all in your head." Crowley and Fortune both stressed the psychological aspects of magic and also saw magic as a means of changing not only the consciousness of the practitioner, but reality itself. Fortune was expressly concerned with magic's ability to affect the mundane lives of both practitioners and those around them. She discussed the implications of careless or baneful magic in her nonfiction, as in *Psychic Self-Defense*, and explored these themes in her fictional works, notably in *The Secrets of Dr. Taverner*. For his part, Crowley seems to have included both mundane, everyday actions and the more numinous acts of will under the heading of magick, suggesting a lack of distinction between the two. I don't necessarily dispute this, but I don't find it an especially useful definition, either. While the magical and the mundane can (and often should) be interleaved, I find it helpful to make a distinction between the magical act of weaving a spell and the somewhat more mundane act of making a cup of coffee.

This is all well and good, but what is magic?

Dancing in the Space Between Science and Religion

In Western culture, we spend a lot of time talking about science and religion as opposing poles along a single axis. Many people, both the deeply religious and deeply areligious, find that framing to be suitable for their endorphin-rush addictions, but personally, I have a lot of trouble with it. For starters, it ignores the lengthy fraternal relationship between religion and science, past and present. It also, I think, misses the point of both. Science is ultimately about causal relationships, those we can observe and those we can infer. It can't tell us what things mean, only how they behave. Religion is about finding or creating meaning from what we observe. It can't model the physical universe worth a damn, but it can serve as a way of explaining to ourselves why we care, or why we should. Rather than being binary polar opposites, I'd suggest that religion and science operate along separate axes. We can call them x and y, if we like.

Magic is the z axis. It's neither science nor religion but dances between them. It's a doing, one that connects the observable phenomena beloved by science with the myth and meaning inherent to religion. Magic has rules, but they aren't much like the laws of physics or the tenets of faith. They're more akin to the rules of etiquette, or of fairy tales. Those rules may not align with our mundane expectations but, taken on their own terms, they have their own internal logic which is as inevitable and unassailable as the second law of thermodynamics or the Golden Rule.

For our purposes here, I define magic as "changing reality in a manner not constrained by causal proximity." By "causal proximity," I'm referring to the extent to which a relationship between cause and effect is readily apparent. For instance, if I push a glass off the counter and it falls onto a slate floor, in all likelihood the glass will shatter. We can see a straightforward relationship between cause (I push the glass off the counter) and effect (the glass shatters). In other words, the cause is visibly close—in proximity—to the effect. On the other hand, if a friend across the country tells me they've lost an item and I divine its location correctly, we'll have much more difficulty seeing an easily defined cause / effect relationship at work.

At this point, we've left the world of straightforward physics and entered a discursive realm where we're talking about things like healing, remote viewing, clairaudience, prognostication, psycho-kinesis, the structure of the cosmos, the existence of intelligences other than human, angels, demons, spirits, gods, and the things that lie beyond them all. These conversations can make rational, science-minded people really uncomfortable, because either they're having a conversation with a mentally unhinged person or we're question-ing the very nature of reality, and either one gets us into a tangled thicket in short order. (For those of you who *are* interested in ques-tioning the nature of reality, allow me to direct your attention to Dean Radin's *Real Magic: Ancient Wisdom, Modern Science, and a Guide to the Secret Power of the Universe*, an exploration of the scientific sup-port for actual, honest-to-goodness magic as "a natural aspect of reality [which] each of us can tap into … with diligent practice.")

While I truly am sympathetic to the rationalist mindset, I'm not here to reassure anyone about their worldview, nor to advance a particular ideological stance. In the Feri tradition, one of the aphorisms we inherited as verbal lore from our beloved founding teacher Victor Anderson is to "perceive first, believe later"; regard-less of whether or not you're Feri, it's a good bit of advice.

Similarly, I'm not here to convince anyone of the existence or efficacy of magic. Victor also provided us with his own definitions of magic, which never fail to delight me: "White magic is poetry. Black magic is anything that actually works." If you want to know whether magic works, try it and see. Once you've done that, you'll have your own definition of magic, and none of my maundering here will matter one whit. And that's exactly as it should be.

Getting Down to Business, as It Were

We've talked about sex, and I shared the definition I use: "any generative erotic activity—solitary, coupled, or multi-partnered—involving any configuration of bodies who want to be in intimate contact with one another, generating pleasure, generating *eros*." Likewise, we've discussed magic, and I defined it as "changing reality in a manner not constrained by causal proximity," along with some unpacking of what I meant by causal proximity. Now, at long last, we can talk about what sex magic is.

Rather than plowing through another thousand words of philosophizing and moralizing before getting to the definition, let's just cut to the chase: I define sex magic as the use of power generated through sexual activity to change reality in a manner not constrained by causal proximity. We could find a lot of ways to reword that definition and fancy it up, probably using words like *empower* and *charge* and *fluid condenser*, but the simple version actually does the job pretty well. Of course, it'd be pretty lazy of me to just slap my previous two definitions together and call it a day, so we're not stopping there. After all, if my definitions of sex or magic don't work for you, then my definition of "sex magic" likely won't, either…and that's okay! We don't all have to agree on things. What's useful is to know where we disagree and why. Counter to my previous approaches in which I built the case for my definitions before finally getting to them, I wanted to make my usage explicit from the outset, so we can spend the rest of our time together talking about what that definition actually means…by which I mean, how do you actually do sex magic, and why?

Actually, let's take that last question first. Why do sex magic at all? The Pagan, polytheist, practitioner communities are often said to be sex-positive, but the extent to which our communities actually are sex-positive is far more debatable than many of us would like to believe. (For more on this, please refer back to "A Précis of Body-Positive Esoteric Praxis.") Some folks might even wonder why we would sully our spiritual aspirations with something as tawdry, sleazy, and downright gross as sex magic.

My response is that sex magic is a facet of sacred sexuality, one with a long and illustrious history, and it seems a shame to throw the magical baby out with the bathwater. After all, human beings have a marvelous facility for adapting anything we get our hands on (pun intended) to fulfill any need or desire we might have. We shouldn't be surprised that spiritual traditions all around the world—from the erotic aspects of Tantric practice to the *hieros gamos* ("sacred marriage") ritually enacted by mystery cults throughout history to the frankly sexual ecstasies experienced by mystics and saints—conceived of sexuality as a bridge between the material and the spiritual, uniting the quotidian and the numinous. As I wrote before, sex is generative, whether intimacy, peace of mind, magical power, spiritual sustenance, release of tension, an entirely new life, or merely pleasure and good feelings are what's being generated. Sex is literally an embodiment—a tangible manifestation—of the power of creation. It's inherently magical on its own without even the formality of casting a circle first, and it's as close to us as our own skin.

Honestly, why aren't we doing *more* sex magic?

I can think of a few answers; the one I'm going to offer as particularly relevant to our concerns today is that Western culture is *really* messed up where sex and sexuality are concerned. I would haul out some citations to back up this claim, but that seems like trying to convince you that water is wet. Besides, this subject is a bottomless rabbit-hole of study, enough to fill a university degree's worth of study (said the author, whistling innocently).

If you'd still like evidence that we're screwed up about sex, I would first encourage you to visit decent sex education websites, such as Scarleteen (www.scarleteen.com) or Sex, Etc. (sexetc.org). Please note that both sites are aimed at an audience of teenagers and young adults, but don't let that deter you; they're both excellent resources on sex, sexuality, gender, and living as a sexually healthy human being in the modern world. Next, scroll through the headers of posts on Reddit's r/sex and r/sexadvice forums. If you're not feeling quite that masochistic, visit your local supermarket and leaf through an issue of *Cosmopolitan*, though the effect won't be quite as pronounced. What you're going to find is a seemingly endless cavalcade of sad, lonely, hurting people who feel incredibly inadequate as sexual partners, people who are having deeply unsatisfying sex, people who are scared and confused and disconnected from their own sexual lives. Because we're so messed up where sex and sexuality are concerned, we end up having a lot of sex that's uncomfortable, unsatisfying, and just plain bad. This not a simple function of inexperience and ineptitude; the sheer number of people—especially women—who have sex they don't want to have, or who tolerate sex they don't enjoy, is heartbreaking and crosses over into issues of consent. (As you may have noticed, those are kind of a central theme around here.)

I'm not going to point fingers and lay blame about why we're so screwed up about sex, other than to suggest as before that ideologies which treat people as objects don't lead to good outcomes *and* that such ideologies are pervasive in mainstream Western culture. Indeed, some cultural commentators would suggest that these ideologies have come to define Western culture, but I'm not especially interested in figuring out where the blame lies right now. What I'm interested in figuring out is what we can do about this. How do we get to a place where we can engage in powerful, joyful, and ecstatic sex magic, especially when we're so screwed up about sex in the first place?

How to Learn Sex Magic in Three Easy Steps!

Catchy title, right? I was going for a tongue-in-cheek, *Buzzfeed*-meets-*Cosmo* vibe. Yeah, I realize that's not going to be to everyone's tastes, but it amuses me, and if we can't laugh a little, we might as well pack up our ritual gear and go catch a movie or something. Really, though, enough screwing around. (Sorry! I'll stop now.) We've defined sex, magic, and sex magic, and discussed a few tangential-but-relevant issues related to each. It's time to get down to brass tacks.

First, I should apologize in advance for any misapprehensions the title might give. When I say "easy," what I mean is that these steps are easy to outline. In practice, they may be much more difficult, depending on who you are and what your background has been. Sex magic is powerful, empowering, and downright fun, but like all magic, it's also work. Sometimes that work is damned difficult, and sometimes it's simple repetition of things we feel like we should already know by now. As always, practice makes perfect (or at least more proficient).

1. Know what you want to do.

This is likely the easiest step of the three, which makes it a good place to start. If you're reading this, odds are pretty good that you already have a technique (or techniques) of magic you favor, and while not all magical techniques are ideal for every application, most practitioners find that the tools they have on hand can be adapted for most uses. If you're not sure about how to go about that or if the whole subject of magic is still kind of new to you, hang in there. We'll touch on that more in chapter 9.

As in any working, the question comes down to having a clear and unambiguous idea what you want to accomplish. For instance, let's posit a hypothetical situation: you're currently unemployed, or underemployed, and you'd like to change your job fortunes. You may have a specific job in mind, or you may just want a solid job that earns more than you're making now. What I've found in my working is that, just as bakers struggle to balance the light and flaky qualities of their pie crusts, spell craft requires a balance of specificity and simplicity. Aiming for a particular job has the benefit of making your spell quite specific, but this seeming simplicity can actually work against you, as it limits the number of paths by which your will can manifest. On the other hand, declarative statements like "I want a good job" are easy to hold in mind and offer a broader array of paths to manifestation, but "good job" is a pretty vague concept unless you spent a while building up what you mean by those words. As ever, putting in some time discerning what you actually want and need is a solid investment in the success of your working.

2. Know how you like to have sex.

I'm not going to whitewash things: for many of us, this will be the hardest step. Modern culture has invested a considerable amount of energy, time, and money in convincing us we don't actually understand our own sex lives, then selling us solutions or compensations for those perceived failings or shortcomings. I don't mean that in a conspiracy-theorist way, either. As I mentioned previously, the advice columns of women's magazines and internet forums reveal the dizzying extent to which shame, confusion, ignorance, and dysfunction inform the average American's understanding of sex. Pagans, polytheists, and occultists are in no way excluded from this observation, no matter how sex-positive and body-positive we like to think ourselves. Many people simply don't know what good sex is, because they've never learned what they like, what feels good for them.

One possible solution to this problem is to take things back to first principles. You're the one who knows your body best—you've lived every day of your life in it, after all—so you're the most reliable teacher on the subject of what feels good to you. If you don't know what pleases you, stimulates your *eros*, and brings you to orgasm, the obvious answer is to explore the sensations of your body to find out.

Yes, I'm talking about masturbation. (If you need to giggle, go ahead.) Masturbation is often our first exploration of our own sexuality, and the shame associated with it in various cultures is of a piece with the shame around all culturally unsanctioned sexuality. In other words, it's both how we learn about our bodies and how we learn that our culture despises our bodies. This is heartbreaking … but it's also remediable. If, like so many of us, you've spent your adult life not really being in touch with your body and your sexuality, this is an excellent time to spend some time getting to know yourself. Your body is yours: it's the physical manifestation of you. Love yourself, own your own power and form, and treat yourself well.

For those of us interested in sex magic, it's worth noting that masturbation is also a classic, time-honored technique of working, so much so that it's often the first practical technique addressed in books on the subject.

3. Use your sexuality to empower your magic.

Once we know what we want to do and how we want to do it, the logical final step is to do it. Easy, right? Well, yes and no. In theory, the principle of using the erotic energy generated by your sexual activity to bolster the power of your working is pretty straightforward. In practice … well, one of the wonderful things about sex is that it can generate pleasure, even ecstasy, and this can be as much a hindrance to successful magic as it can drive it. Not to put too fine a point on this: a full-tilt, toe-curling orgasm can make it awfully hard to hold a coherent thought in your head, much less to focus your magical will on a predetermined goal. Some folks can manage it with nary a hitch, while others of us may need some practice to get it right. The nice thing is that even failed spell launches can still involve a lot of pleasant sensations ... and might even end with an orgasm.

"That's all well and good," I hear you say, "but how do you actually *do* it?"

Never fear, True Believers. I wasn't planning to bring you this far, only to drop you at the last minute.

— EXERCISE —
A Solitary Sex Magic Working for Absolute Beginners

The following is a bare-bones, quick-and-dirty outline of the steps I go through in any sex magic working, adapted for solitary practice. How you choose to do any of those stages is a matter of taste and efficacy, and the specific methods you use will vary depending on your personality and background. The details aren't as important as the process, and how the process serves to get you to the place where your sexuality and your will can work in tandem.

For this working, all you really need are a comfortable space in which to work and some uninterrupted time. There are a few accessories which can be useful, which I'll discuss as we get to them, but none of them are essential. Similarly, you're welcome to invoke any deities or spirits with whom you're allied or who you feel will be favorable to your working. Doing so isn't an essential part of this working, however, so I've left it out. This ritual frame is essentially an act of thaumaturgy, "wonder-working" through the practitioner's own magical power and will, rather than one of theurgy, in which wonders are worked through the action of divine powers.

I strongly recommend reading through the entire practice a few times before setting out to enact it, rather than reading it as you do it. Not only will the ritual make more sense that way, but you're less likely to knock yourself out of the mood, if you take my meaning. Even better, you can take the further step of writing the ritual down in your journal, including any additions or changes you want to make in the overall practice to truly make it your own.

1. Know your goal.

Depending on how your brain works, this may seem like an odd place to start ... or an obvious one. After all, if you're setting out to do magic, you probably already have an end goal in mind. As I said before, though, it's crucial to know what you want to do before you start doing it. What I've often found in my own workings is that I've put a lot of time into envisioning the end result without giving much thought to whether or not that specific result actually answers the need or desire I have. So, before I undertake any magical working, I give myself time to stop and really think about what it is I want. Do I want *this* job, or do I want a *good* job? Do I want a generalized sense of happiness, however I might define that in the moment, or do I want healing for my injured knee, a better relationship with my partner, a new computer?

Take the time to build the mental image, not of *how* that end might come about, but *what* the desired end is. You can and should build into that image any codicils you wish—i.e., that no one is harmed by the actualization of your goal, that your goal is achieved within a certain time period, and so on—but frame it as something that has already happened rather than to visualize how it will happen.

2. Calm your mind.

If you're anything at all like me, you spend most of your days in what I think of as the ground state of modern life: either a scattered buzz of activity or an unfocused haze of distraction. This is completely understandable—we still have to chop wood and carry water—but it's also not the place from which we can do our most effective or most conscious magic. So, the first step in doing sex magic is the same as in any other kind of magic: getting yourself out of your everyday headspace and into a place of calm, focused self-possession.

Sounds simple, right? Well, yes … and no. Modern life is uniquely geared toward keeping us *out* of that calm, focused headspace, because self-possessed people are much less susceptible to manipulation and intimidation. If you already have a meditative practice you use to calm and focus your mind, feel free to use that. If you don't, the following exercise, adapted from practices within the Anderson Feri tradition, is offered as a way to get yourself started:

Assume a comfortable bodily position, either seated or standing with feet planted firmly. Take in the deepest breath you can and hold it for a moment, gathering all the tension in your mind and body, then blow it out completely, and feel that tension leave with the breath. If you need to do this a few times, do so.

Now, close your eyes and take a slow, deep breath and feel your center radiating a gentle heat. Hold this breath for a moment, then breathe it out slowly. Do this twice more, each time feeling your center grow softer and warmer, spreading a comfortable heat throughout your genitals and belly.

Raise your focus to your chest and take another three breaths, holding and releasing slowly, feeling your lungs expand and the fire of your core strengthen.

Raise your focus to your head and take three more breaths, holding and releasing slowly, feeling the brightness at the core of your own mind radiate light from the center of your skull.

Take one more deep breath and hold it, then exhale slowly, feeling the connection flowing from your center through your core to your mind.

3. Set your space.

The next stage is to establish and occupy the physical and magical space in which you'll be working. As I said above, methods will vary from person to person; some folks want a full formal circle casting with all the trimmings, while others make do with a smooth music playlist and a scented candle. Given my ritual background and personal preferences, I find it helpful to do at least a *pro forma* circle casting using either tools or my own hands and body to create the sacred space within which I'll be working. If you already have a ritual method of setting your space, go with that, but if you don't, feel free to use the following:

Begin by facing the direction in which you wish to start and end your sacred space. I'm being somewhat open-ended here because there isn't any correct direction to start. Some traditions begin circle casting in the east, while others start at north. If you're working in a limited space, you might start your circle casting in the direction of your bedroom door, or toward the bathroom. As with so much else, do what works for you.

Reach out in front of you physically, using your empty hand or a tool. (Some people use athames to cast circles. Others use wands. Again, whatever works for you.) Take a deep breath, then exhale slowly and project your own power before you, envisioned as a coruscating spark of blue-white light about six feet in front of you. Breathe into that spark twice more, seeing it grow brighter with each breath. While continuing to breathe into that spark of light, turn slowly to your right and draw the spark around you clockwise, enclosing yourself in a circle of blue-white light. Bring it to a full revolution, returning to the place you began. Draw the spark above yourself, then below yourself, returning to the beginning of the line of fire where you began. Seal the circle by drawing a penta-gram with the spark of light. See the circle shimmering about you, glowing softly. Now, blow the spark out gently, like a candle. Say:

> *I seal this sacred space*
> *Ringed round by this circle of fire,*
> *And dedicate it to the work ahead.*
> *May it be so, may it be so, may it be so!*

4. Focus your will.

Now that you're enclosed within the sacred space you've created, get comfortable, seated in a reclined position or lying down, and recenter yourself if you need to. Then, focus your mind on the desired result of your working, as discussed in step 1. This is a cru-cial part of the success of the operation and shouldn't be rushed. Spend some time visualizing that result as clearly as possible. Again, you needn't focus on specific details beyond those integral to your image of the goal. The point here is to make that image the single focused point of your consciousness. Let your entire mind become occupied by the image, enough such that no thoughts unrelated to the image can intrude.

5. Raise your power.

This step is the operant portion of your working…or, to put it another way, it's the step that puts the "sex" in sex magic.

While in a relaxed and comfortable position, maintaining the visualization of your goal in mind, begin to touch yourself in whatever ways feel good: gentle caresses along your arms and legs, cradling your belly, teasing your nipples, whatever works for you. The idea is to stimulate erotic sensations—and thus, your *eros*, your erotic power—in a slow, gradual manner. Feel how the sensations you can produce in your own body are filled with their own energetic charge, and as you feel that charge build, move the power of that charge into your visualization.

Continue to touch yourself in whatever ways you find pleasurable, adjusting and increasing the intensity of the erotic stimulation as you see fit, and to imbue your image with the erotic charge. For most people, this will include stimulation of their genitals at some point, building toward orgasm. If that isn't what works for you, though, don't worry. One of the best things about sex magic is that there's no wrong way to have sex with yourself, short of doing yourself harm. If you're enjoying yourself, if you're experiencing pleasure and feeling that erotic charge building, then you're doing it right. Carry on!

6. Release your power.

At a certain point, you'll begin to transition to the next step, that of releasing your power. I can't tell you when that will happen; it's a uniquely, intrinsically personal sensation depending on how your body and your sexuality work. For some, the raising and release of erotic power is a steady, dramatic climb toward orgasmic climax, while for others it's a gentle series of crests and valleys of pleasure, or a steady, humming plateau of *eros* without a specific climax.

Just as there's no wrong way to have sex with yourself, there's no wrong way to finish. What matters is your sense of completion and release, both of the sexual act and the ritual act of using your sexual energy to empower your magic.

If you're orgasmic and are opting to stimulate yourself to orgasm, there will be a fairly clear point at which this transition has begun. Maintaining your focus into and through the peak (or peaks) of orgasm can be tricky, but that's precisely what's called for: holding the image of the desired result of your working with the whole of your awareness while your body triggers all of the physiological, psychological, and energetic reactions that are part of your orgasmic response, to imbue all of that power into the manifestation of your magical will, into seeing your goal as reality. Continue to hold that image in mind as your orgasm subsides.

If you're orgasmic, but you're opting not to trigger an orgasm, you may choose to end the stimulation at the brink of orgasm, halting the raising of your *eros* at that point. This can be an especially useful technique for workings intended to draw something into your life, as the stimulation of *eros* tends to increase the desire for more erotic stimulation, and imbuing your magical image with the sensation of halting that stimulation can create a kind of magnetic pull toward the target of your attraction.

If you're anorgasmic, you may find that there's a clear point at which the energetic intensity of your *eros* drops off, or you may choose to stop at a certain point, either predetermined or intuitively. Either way, you can bring your stimulation to an end, imbuing your image with the residual *eros* of your working before winding things up.

If you intend to use your sexual fluids to charge a talisman or sigil, as is done in certain traditions and practices, be sure to have the material basis you're charging ready when you've reached the conclusion of your working. Likewise, if you're orgasmic and you intend your working to include an orgasmic climax—or even if you don't—and if your orgasms include ejaculation of fluids, it's a good idea to know how you're going to handle those fluids post-climax. (Unplanned things happen sometimes, is all I'm saying.) In any event, it's always a good idea to have warm, damp washcloths on hand for clean-up.

7. Open your space.

The final stage of the ritual, once you've reached a comfortable equilibrium, is to open and release the physical and magical space in which you've been working by whatever means you find appropriate. If your space setting has been done informally, the opening of the space can be equally informal, but if you started with something a little more formal, you'll want the ending to be of an equivalent formality. If you used the ritual space setting provided in step three, feel free to use the following to release the space:

After you've brought your erotic stimulation to a soft landing place, take a deep, conscious breath, hold it for a moment, and breathe it out. As you do so, release both your magical image and any residual tension of your erotic exertions. Give yourself time to cool down physically, energetically, and emotionally, and take whatever care of yourself you need to. Remember that you're in a safe, sacred space, and that you can spend as much time in this space as you need to.

When you're ready, face the direction in which you began and ended the circle around you, and find the pentagram with which you sealed it. Reach out and grab hold of the fiery line, then unwind the pentagram by tracing its line in reverse. As you do so, feel the fire collapsing back into the brilliant spark of light. Once you've unwound the pentagram, trace the line of fire counterclockwise, pulling the fire back into the spark of light. Once you've returned to the beginning, draw the spark back into yourself, reclaiming the power within it. Take a deep breath, hold it for a moment, then breathe it out, releasing any residual tension or energy from the ritual. Clap your hands or stomp your feet three times, as a visceral means of bringing yourself fully back into both your own body and the material world around you.

The rite is ended. Take a few minutes to write about it in your journal, making particular note of any emotional responses you may have had to the working, and any thoughts, images, or memories which may have surfaced as a result.

Winding Things Up

So, there's my introduction to the subject of sex magic, and my suggested "easy steps" for learning how to start doing it yourself. Yes, the exposition is merely a gloss on the full scope of the subject, and yes, the steps are somewhat simplified ... and that's by design. The material above is intended to be a starting point. I encourage you to practice and experiment using this format, but also to do some research on your own. You can find sex-magical practices in virtually every culture and spiritual tradition on the planet (including Christianity and Islam ... yes, really!), and a myriad of resources where you can learn more about them in a respectful, non-appropriative way. This is a topic that could be written about at some length. Hell, you could write a book on the subject of sex magic ... and, as a matter of fact, quite a few people already have! At the end of this book, you'll find some suggestions for books on sex magic and its intersections with esoteric spirituality that I particularly recommend. My intent here has merely been to introduce the topic ... and, maybe, to demystify the process just enough to help a few of you realize your own interest and potential for sex magic.

Chapter 7
FORM FOLLOWS FUNCTION: TOWARD A CONSENT-BASED MAGICAL PRAXIS

IN 1896, AMERICAN ARCHITECT Louis Sullivan published an almost mystically poetic essay on, of all things, the architecture of office buildings. This essay is largely remembered today for its explication of what would become a standard design principle in modern architecture:

> *Whether it be the sweeping eagle in his flight, or the open apple-blossom, the toiling workhorse, the blithe swan, the branching oak, the winding stream at its base, the drifting clouds, over all the coursing sun, form ever follows function, and this is the law. […] It is the pervading law of all things organic and inorganic, of all things physical and metaphysical, of all*

things human and all things superhuman, of all true manifesta-
tions of the head, of the heart, of the soul...[83]

At the risk of mixing metaphors, I submit that the concept of "form follows function" has insights that go far beyond designing buildings. By looking at our magical and devotional practices through the lens of form and function, we can bring our praxis in line with our desired goals and our stated principles.

In chapter 3, I wrote, "just as sex without consent is rape, sex positivity without consent positivity is rape culture." Much of this chapter is about unpacking that statement and pointing a way toward a magical and devotional practice rooted in consent. To do that, we'll have to start by defining what we mean by consent, and by examining some of the problems that the esoteric community has with the idea of consent.

All too often, a chill sweeps the room the moment you bring up consent. Some people freeze up, others get visibly uncomfortable, and still others glaze over and zone out. I'll confess, I find this perplexing and troubling. Consent shouldn't be a boring, conversation-killing topic all knotted up in confusion and accusations of social justice-warriorship, and it *definitely* shouldn't be something we're afraid to discuss. Consent should be as basic a concept as adding two and two to get four, as comforting as a favorite shirt, and at least as conversationally stimulating as an episode of *Game of Thrones*. And yet, we find that people get into raging arguments about consent and express all manner of confusion about what it even means, much less how to negotiate it.

---

83. Louis Sullivan, "The Tall Office Building Artistically Considered," in *Lippin-cott's Magazine*, March 23, 1896: 408.

Let's make this really simple. Consent means assenting, agreeing, saying yes. Why on earth would this ever be a controversial subject? I suspect the answer lies in the issue of power: who has it, who can exercise it, and how we feel about it.

Consent is a funny thing. It has the potential to start or end relationships, to create or ruin lives, to rupture or repair communities. It's a magical word, consent. It has power. Consent *is* power, and human beings have a deeply ambivalent relationship to power. We crave it, usually for ourselves, and we fear it, usually in others. We love the freedom and safety it can provide, and we dread the responsibility and accountability it incurs. Consent is power, and power is complicated.

Unfortunately, there's also power in the inverse of consent, in its absence. That's what rape is, after all: nonconsensual sexual aggression to assert power over someone. One of the most heinous things about sexual assault is that the perpetrator intentionally disregards and violates the will of the victim, stripping them of power at the most intimate level imaginable. It's a violation of another's agency, for the express purpose of the perpetrator getting what they want from the victim. It's the reduction of another person to an object, a commodity to be used. It's an attitude that should have no place in any kind of civilized society, much less in a community that claims to foster spiritual growth and personal empowerment.

Some years ago, I took a leave of absence from magic, witchcraft, and Paganism. One of the main reasons was my growing dissatisfaction with what I perceived as an unresolved, unaddressed set of ethical dilemmas in the communities of which I was part. The dominant discourse in those communities promulgated what I saw as some incredibly ill-informed, unhealthy, and even actively dangerous ideas about power. Power was deemed a moral good in itself with no accountability or honesty around who held power, how it was exercised, and to what end. (It is not much different from mainstream culture, really.)

Rather than engage with those problems, I took a break. To my surprise, when I reengaged with the community, some things had actually changed in the discourse around power, and some of the issues I had found so repellent were being discussed, both privately and publicly. To my horror, it had taken the revelation of some genuinely awful abuses and betrayals of trust to bring those changes into being. (I won't get into any specifics here; they're not the focus of this piece.) To my utter lack of surprise, some things had failed to change. The community still had predators, and people were still making excuses for them. Some people still treated other people as fonts of power to be drained and cast aside: "batteries for their betters," as I once heard it phrased. Some people still believed they were entitled to other people's time, energy, attention, and bodies.

Some of what I've just mentioned is human nature; we have an unfortunate tendency to believe that we should get to have what we want—that we are entitled to the thing we want—merely because we want it. This tendency is understandable in newborn children, whose wants tend to revolve around basic survival needs, or in toddlers, whose brains simply aren't developed enough to understand that other people are just as real as they are and have needs just as much as they do. When children leave the toddler stage, however, we start expecting them to understand that their wants and needs don't automatically trump other people's. By the time they've reached what we call adulthood, we have a general expectation that they'll have grasped this concept well enough at least to get through a day without stealing other people's lunches from the work fridge.

Unfortunately, based on personal experience, this assumption isn't as well founded as we might hope. The reality is that while most people are decent enough, a statistically non-trivial number of people are willing to do things they would themselves define as morally and ethically wrong if there were little to no chance of being caught. Worse, a non-trivial number of people would do things most of us would define as morally and ethically wrong—such as, say, sexually assaulting another person—because they don't see those actions as having a moral and ethical value.

Moral values are not universal, nor are their ethical applications. While many things about what we call civilization merit criticism, one of its great benefits (when done well) is that it allows people with varying sets of moral and ethical frameworks to exist more or less in peace, mostly by demanding that everyone adhere to the same basic set of externally imposed rules—what we call laws—which may or may not have any particular grounding in morals or ethics. The point is, we all get to live in relative harmony because I agree not to punch you in the face and steal your phone, and you agree not to kick me in the stomach and steal my wallet. You respect my right to hold power over myself, I respect your right to hold power over yourself, and we call it civilization.

All of it relies on consent: on respecting other people's autonomy and power, and owning our own. If consent isn't the basis of our interactions with other people, individually or corporately, we have no right to claim to be mature human beings, much less to claim membership in any sort of civilized society. By the same token, if those of us who work with gods, spirits, powers, and our fellow practitioners aren't basing our communities and our praxis in consent, we have no claim to any sort of spiritual advancement or wisdom. We're merely overgrown toddlers who haven't learned that other people, other beings—human or other, corporeal or not, living or dead or something else—don't exist for our convenience, to sate our desires. They have their own agency, just as we do, and understanding that agency should be the core of any interaction, magical or mundane.

This notion does fly somewhat in the face of conventional wisdom in the magical community, which often tends toward what I call the conjure-and-command mentality: if I say the magic words and do the magic dance, the beings I'm summoning are required to show up and do what I tell them to. It's common to think of this as the model on which grimoiric magic operates, where demons are bound with terrible threats before being ordered to find treasure or something, but the most common example of conjure-and-command I know is found in almost every Wicca-influenced Pagan group out there: I say the invocation in the proper direction and draw the appropriate sign with the correct tool, and the Watchtower (or Guardian, or whatever you call it) will show up to protect that quarter because … that's what you do. In both cases, we're assuming that beings we work with will show up when we call them, that they'll do what we tell them to do. We're assuming consent, in other words.

To What End, at What Cost?

It gets complicated quickly, this business of consent, doesn't it? Fortunately, there are ways to work through that complexity.

It may be useful when entering into an interaction—whether with gods, spirits, or our fellow human practitioners—to ask ourselves what we're looking to get out of it, and what we're willing to put into it. My shorthand for these questions is "to what end?" and "at what cost?" It may seem overly transactional or even mercenary, but I find it tends to elicit a much greater degree of honesty in my interactions. That may not be exactly comfortable at times, but if we want to see things as they truly are, we have to be honest about who we truly are to ourselves at the very least. Similarly, if we want to manifest our will, we have to know what we actually want and what we're willing to do to achieve it. Answering "to what end" and "at what cost" shifts us away from treating our interactions as avenues of conflict and dominance, and instead approaches each interaction as a negotiation in which all parties have agency, autonomy, and an opportunity to become invested in the outcome. (For more on answering "to what end," see the exercise "Answering the Grail Question" on page 256.)

Venues of Interaction and Consent in Praxis

Making the transition from dominance to mutuality is fundamentally what consent is about. If we want to get a yes, we have to be willing to accept a no. In fact, the ability to say no is what makes saying yes so meaningful and so powerful. Remember, the definition we're using for consent is "freely-given assent or approval related to a specific action or course of action." Thus, I can give (or withhold) my consent for medical treatment, having my hair cut, or having sex with someone. Similarly, a medical professional, a hairstylist, and a potential sexual partner can all consent (or decline to consent) to interact with me in the aforementioned ways.

Consent doesn't pertain to situations which don't involve action, nor to actions which don't involve my person in some way. I cannot give or withhold consent to how people think of me, for instance, nor to how they speak of me to other people. I cannot consent to being white, having freckles, or having been born in the United States; those aren't things I do, and they don't involve action between myself and another person.

Consent can only exist between two or more parties within an interpersonal interaction, all of whom possess moral agency. This is a key concept, one that some folks might not know by name, so it's worthwhile to take a quick sidebar here. Agency itself simply means the ability to act or effect something. This isn't unique to humans, nor even to living creatures; machines act, as do corporations, weather systems, and other noncorporeal agents. In philosophy, this concept expands into the concept of moral agency, the ability to choose to act or not act based on moral values of right and wrong, which also incorporates notions of responsibility and accountability. So consent exists only as a negotiation between parties that have the ability to make choices and take actions.

It's worth taking a moment here and briefly outlining the different sorts of consent we're likely to encounter in our communities and our practice.

Express consent is an affirmative stated clearly and unambiguously through words or actions. This can be an enthusiastic yes, a signed statement, a nod, or some other action to indicate that the person in question has heard the request, understood it, and is responding in agreement or affirmation.

Informed consent refers to express consent given by someone who has demonstrated a clear understanding of the request, including the surrounding circumstances and possible consequences.

Implied consent is the assumption that consent can be inferred by participation in an activity or situation or is implicit in the circumstances of a given situation. An example of the first sort of implied consent is the assumption of consent to being touched when voluntarily playing a game of tag. As an example of the second sort, medical professionals might provide treatment to an unconscious person under the assumption that, were they able to respond, they would give consent for treatment.

The "freely given" part of our definition of consent is important and shouldn't be glossed over. Consent is agreement, but not all agreements involve consent. Some, in fact, involve coercion, which is just about as far as you can get from consent without crossing into overt physical force. For those who are unfamiliar with the concept (a vanishingly small number, I hope), coercion means forcing someone, overtly or implicitly, to do what you want them to do by threatening them with some unpleasant outcome if they refuse. The nature of the threat can vary widely, from social stigma to actual violence, depending on the context of the coercion. (As I am foursquare in favor of consent in all things, I hope it goes without saying that I find coercion anathematic.)

Unless one is a hermit, most of human existence involves interactions between two or more parties possessed of moral agency. Within the context of magical and polytheist practice, however, there are a number of scenarios particular within our context that merit some consideration, especially in relation to consent. Below are a few, along with some relevant questions we can and should ask ourselves.

Between working partners.
These are the people with whom one shares ritual work: covenmates, circling partners, fellow lodge members, and so on. Is everyone in the ritual space on the same page—figuratively or literally—about what we're doing in the ritual? Does everyone have buy-in to both the outcome and the methods? If there are roles assigned to specific people, are they aware of what's expected of them in that role and freely willing to perform those duties?

Between lay participants.
Here, I mean the people with whom one shares ritual space, perhaps in a public ritual setting without being celebrants or operators in the ritual. This tends to be a pretty flat, even power dynamic, but

there are still issues of consent to consider. Are my actions impinging on other people's ability to have their own ritual experience? Am I attempting to make someone else part of my experience without their consent?

Between caster and receiver.

I'm referring here to the person performing a spell, prayer, or work of some kind, and the one who receives it. Is the receiver aware that the caster is working on them? Are they a willing recipient of the caster's magio-spiritual intent? In cases where the recipient is unaware and unable to respond, as with some circumstances involving healing magic, is the caster relying on the concept of implied consent, as mentioned earlier?

Between summoner and spirit.

I'm using the most generic terms I can to refer to the person who is requesting the attention and effort of a being of some sort and the being they're calling. For the former, we could substitute a number of terms: invoker, evoker, priest/ess, magician, witch, spirit worker, and so on. Similarly, we could identify the latter as demons, angels, ghosts, elementals, guardians, and others. In any case, what is the relationship we're assuming between ourselves and the beings we summon, stir, and call up? Are we superior beings binding them to our will, possibly with threats of immolation or torture? Are we inferior beings supplicating ourselves and submitting our own wills and power to beings we hope will be nice to us? Are we assuming that the beings we summon are willing to be summoned, and to do what we want?

Between devotee and deity.

The issues at work between devotees and their gods are similar to the previous dynamic, but far more complex … enough that it's covered in greater length in the following chapter.

Between initiator and candidate.

The complexity of power dynamics and consent between seekers of mysteries and the gatekeepers of tradition or those who hold the power to grant or deny access to those mysteries are complicated by the secretive nature of many initiatory traditions. Is the candidate aware enough of what may be asked of them, and of any potential risks, that they can give informed consent? Is there an element of coercion in the ritual drama of the initiatory ceremony? If so, is it necessary, and why?

Between teacher and student.

This relationship is one of the oldest in human experience: the one who seeks knowledge, and the one who gives knowledge. This relationship has a hierarchy built into it: the teacher is the one with the power, expressed as possession of knowledge, which they impart or withhold from the student. If I'm a student, am I shouldering my part of the work of learning? Am I honoring myself and my teacher, or am I trying to subvert the boundaries around our roles to advance my position? If I'm the teacher, am I using my power equitably, or am I trying to manipulate my student? Am I teaching my student what they want to know, or what I think they need to know? Am I utilizing the power dynamic between us to inappropriately cross social or sexual boundaries?

Not for Teacher: Addressing Sexual
Power Inequity in Mentorship

Especially in light of this book's subject matter, that last point is worth spending a little time expanding. The inherent hierarchy of the teacher/student relationship derives from a power inequity and consequently creates an inherent kind of dependence; the student trusts and relies on the teacher to educate them, to help them empower themselves. There's a whole body of academic literature discussing the issue of power dynamics between teachers and students. Those dynamics are further complicated by issues of sexuality and gender, and even more so by their intersection with magical and devotional praxis. At a certain point in discussing sexuality and spirituality, it becomes impossible to avoid the subject of sexual relationships between seekers and mentors, students and teachers, disciples and masters, or whatever names you apply to those seeking knowledge and power and those who purport to offer it. Many traditions and teachers explicitly prohibit any kind of sexual contact between students and teachers, citing the inherent power difference between the two roles as an inherently unhealthy dynamic, while others suggest that there is no other way for students to learn sexual techniques of magical or devotional praxis. It'd be one thing if this was a subject about which we could all agree to disagree, but the reality is that this is a topic guaranteed to set fire to your next social gathering of practitioners, largely because no one can agree about the fundamental ethical issues at the heart of the question.

Having been on both sides of the teacher/student power dynamic in the context of traditions with an explicitly sexual component, I've had the opportunity to engage with this issue along multiple axes as well as a front-row seat while others engaged with it, to varying results. It's from that perspective that I'm speaking when I say that it's simply not possible to have an equitable, consensual sexual relationship in that context.

In other words, if you're a teacher, don't have sex with your students, and if you're a student, run from any teacher who says you have to have sex with them.

To offer an illustration by way of pop culture, there are reasons why "Don't Stand So Close to Me" by the Police is objectively a better song than Van Halen's "Hot for Teacher." Regardless of one's feelings about Eddie van Halen's guitar skills, the narratives of these two songs are in completely different artistic galaxies. While they both explore the sexual element of power inequity in teacher/student relationships, the former is a tense, queasy story about a stuffy English teacher's socio-sexual paranoia about being targeted by a *Lolita*-esque schoolgirl with lascivious designs on his body, while the latter is a leering paean to the permanent state of sexual arousal teenage boys are assumed to have over hot young female teachers.

What's curious is that both songs implicitly acknowledge the taboo of those relationships, drawing on an ambivalence that goes back as far as classical Greece, if not further.[84] In the Van Halen song, that taboo is played for naughty humor, whereas the Police mine it for drama. Nevertheless, both songs are underscoring what we all understand on some level to be an inappropriate situation.

Some people reading this may be responding with words to the effect of, "But my situation is different!" Dear reader, I promise you: it's not. It's precisely the same. People concoct all kinds of justifications for sexual relationships between students and teachers—*we're both adults, the student initiated the relationship, we're being open*

---

84. S. Michael Plaut, "Boundary Issues in Teacher-Student Relationships," *Journal of Sex and Marital Therapy* 19 (1993): 210–219.

and honest about everything, it's true love, and so on—but all of those justifications merely underscore the reality that there's an inherent power inequity in such relationships. Any trust-based relationship involves a power dynamic of dependency: therapist and client, doctor and patient, teacher and student. One person is the gatekeeper: the one who holds the keys to the kingdom and provides or denies access to the mysteries. That's power. The other person is dependent on the gatekeeper to hold that power and provide that access: to wellness, for patients and clients, or to wisdom, for students. It's not difficult to see how easily that dynamic complicates questions of consent. We can dance around this as long as we want but the bottom line is that consent isn't possible in a situation where one person has power and the other one doesn't.

If you're in a position of any kind of authority over someone—teacher, mentor, priest/ess, whatever—you have no business being sexually involved with them in any way while in that relationship. If you find that you're having sexual feelings toward a student, you have two honorable choices as their teacher: you can redirect your feelings away from sex or romance, or you can find another teacher for that student. Similarly, if you find that a student has developed sexual feelings for you, you can either gently redirect them, responding to their overtures with nothing more than friendship and professionalism, or you can hand their instruction over to another teacher.

Of course, if you've developed feelings for someone you're teaching, you may want to believe there are other options, that you can find a way to express and explore those sexual feelings with this student without a bad outcome. Many other teachers have felt the same way—and in the vast majority of situations, it doesn't work out well. Even in the best circumstances, you're still engaged in a violation of that student's trust and therefore gambling with their emotional and spiritual well-being.

Likewise, if you're in any sort of subordinate position—student, disciple, coven member, and so on—to someone with authority over your spiritual or magical education, there is no good reason to be in a sexual relationship with them. It's not uncommon for students to develop sexual feelings for a teacher, but it's never a good idea to act on them. If you're in this position, I'd again suggest redirecting your feelings away from sexuality and romance or explaining to your teacher that you're not able to be in relationship with them. If possible, ask for a referral to another teacher. If your teacher expresses sexual interest in you, it's important to remember that they are in a position of power over you, and by asking you to engage with them on a sexual level, they are violating a boundary of trust. This relationship is not viable, and I would encourage you in the strongest possible terms to consider leaving that person's tutelage immediately.

Now, I say "redirect your feelings" as though it's as simple as just deciding not to feel something; emotions don't work quite like that. We can, however, choose how we relate to our emotions and how to express them. In fact, we always do. Unless you're experiencing symptoms of mental illness, the experience of being overwhelmed by our feelings is a lie we tell ourselves, an abdication of responsibility we pretend is a loss of control because it makes us feel better to say we "lost control" than to admit that we consciously chose to do something we knew was unethical. If we're going to work magic and walk with the gods, we don't have the luxury of "losing control," or of lying to ourselves and everyone around us to avoid responsibility for our choices.

Boundaries Are Magic!

Looking back at the venues of interaction and consent described above, one of the key recurring themes is the establishment of boundaries of acceptable behavior and action. These social and emotional boundaries can be established by means as simple as stating unequivocally what you do or don't want, or as complex as negotiation between members of a group. In expression, they can be as explicit as the written code of conduct for a large-scale event or as unspoken as a guest list written to include or exclude certain individuals. Establishing boundaries is as magical an act as the scribing of a circle for sorcerous protection, and, like any magical act, it's important to have a firm grounding in your own sense of self. After all, as flight attendants remind us every time we fly, we have to secure our own oxygen masks before assisting anyone else with theirs.

It's easy to be caught up in the moment, to be swayed by others' emotions or glamour, or to feel persuaded that our own boundaries are somehow restrictive or unfair. In such situations, it's helpful to be able to reestablish and reinforce our own boundaries in the moment both emotionally and magically as well as to remind ourselves of our own power, autonomy, and sovereignty.

The following exercise is a tool I use in those situations, or in any circumstances that call for establishing or bolstering my personal boundaries on the fly.

— EXERCISE —
Expanding Your Sphere

For this exercise, you don't need any tools or even a special place to work. All you need is a couple of minutes, a few deep breaths, and the ability to visualize.

Wherever you are, take a moment to interrupt whatever thought processes are going through your head. I do this by literally halting physically, or by saying or thinking "STOP." Take a slow, deep breath and hold it for a moment, gathering any tension in your body, then exhale slowly and release that tension. Repeat this twice more, each time gathering the tension in your body and releasing it.

While continuing to breathe slowly and evenly, focus on the center of your body, wherever you feel that to be. For some of you, this will be your heart, while for others, this will be your lower belly, a couple of inches below your navel. (Both of these are loci of power known as *dantian* in traditional Chinese medicine, with the lower also known as the *hara* or *tanden* in Japanese martial arts and traditional medicine.) Envision a point of light in your center: white, or blue, or any other color that speaks to you of protection, strength, and safety. This point of light is your own vital power, what I've called *eros*. Breathe into that point of light and see it grow brighter and more brilliant within you as you breathe.

When you're ready, take a deep, deliberate breath, hold it for a moment, then exhale slowly into that coruscating point of light and see it expand in all directions, becoming a hazy sphere or nimbus of light and color surrounding you. It doesn't have to be large; it can be no more than an inch or two beyond the surface of your skin. Nonetheless, the nimbus you've projected around yourself is a clear boundary, a sphere of demarcation between you and not-you, pushing out influences that aren't of your own making or invitation, leaving behind only yourself and what you've chosen to bring into your emotional and spiritual space.

This exercise is what I think of as quick-and-dirty magic meant for practical use in the everyday world to reassert your emotional and magical space. With practice, this technique can become second nature, an almost instantaneous ingrained response to unwanted feelings of incursion or imposition. I've used this technique to good effect while walking through a crowded room, stuck in traffic in my car, or in the middle of a heated conversation. You can also explore ways to strengthen, expand, and contract your boundaries as needed.

As ever, I encourage you to make some notes in your journal about your experiences with this technique. In particular, you might write down how you visualize the spark in your center and any sensations or emotions you felt as you expanded the spark into the sphere or nimbus around you.

Chapter 8

BETWEEN THE MUNDANE AND THE DIVINE: ON NEGOTIATING CONSENT WITH GODS

IT'S NOT UNFAIR TO suggest that most forms of Pagan, polytheist, and magical practice interact in some way with gods. This raises the seemingly obvious question of what exactly these gods are. Are they externalized, anthropomorphic aspects of our own psyche? Are they archetypal figures? Are they cultural artifacts rooted in a specific time, place, and group of people? Are they individual intelligent beings with their own autonomy and moral agency? Or are they something else besides? How we answer that question, consciously or not, shapes the ways we interact with our gods and the issues of consent involved … and if these are beings with their own agency and agenda—in other words, if they're people, for a given value of person—we also have to consider the issue of our own consent to the requests, or demands, that our gods make of us.

Depending on what you think gods and spirits are, those last two issues can overlap quite a bit, and raise some of the same questions around consent. For instance, there's a tendency within some parts of our intertwined communities of practice to simply assume consent from the gods and spirits with whom we work. I would suggest this derives, at least in part, from the previously discussed belief that we're entitled to whatever thing we happen to want at a given moment merely because we want it. This sort of wishing-makes-it-so assumption drives a behavior common within the p-word community in which gods and spirits are treated rather like Victorian servants: come here, do this, take care of that, thank you, that will be all, now off with you. I don't much care for being treated like Mrs. Hughes the housekeeper or Carson the butler, especially if I'm not being paid for my services, so I don't imagine any of the gods and spirits I'm privileged to work with care for it, either.

At the same time, another narrative popular in some Pagan and polytheist circles depicts the relationship between gods and their devotees in a curious, largely unidirectional way: a god will choose a particular person to be their devotee, then proceed to pursue that person until they give in to the deity's advances. The character of this pursuit varies in description, ranging from stalking to coercion to overt assault, but the relationship as described always seems less reminiscent of deity and devotee than of abuser and victim, or possibly of predator and prey. The underlying driver of this narrative is that the devotee ultimately has no say in whether or not to be in relationship with the deity. They don't get to choose, you see, because they've been chosen. Of all the possible devotees in the modern polytheist and Pagan communities, willing or otherwise, this god chose them.

With the exception of folks whose notion of religion or spirituality harming themselves or others, I'm not here to kink-shame anyone or to tell anyone they're doing things the wrong way. Instead, my thought is that once we've embarked on a narrative in which we've cast ourselves as powerless protagonists at the mercy of domineering and socially inept aggressors who control the relationship, it's time to admit to ourselves that we've passed beyond the realm of "differences in practice" and entered into the theological equivalent of a tiresome theme found in romantic fictions from *Rebel Without a Cause* to (gods help us all) *Twilight,* the pseudo-romantic fairytale of the "bad boy." People in this psychologically and spiritually toxic situation derive personal validation from being in an abusive relationship with a deity or some other "ally" spirit who's bad news, relationship-wise. The kicker, though, is that it's precisely this unsuitability which makes the relationship so desirable. The risk of being harmed emotionally, spiritually, or even physically makes the relationship far more exciting and gratifying than being involved with a god who's safe, kind, and… well, boring. The thrill comes from the danger *and* that feeling of being chosen. It makes us feel special, and "feeling special" is incredibly seductive: it can be intoxicating and exhilarating.

As I said, I'm not interested in kink-shaming or relationship-shaming, but if you wouldn't let a romantic partner treat you a certain way, I'd certainly look askance at a god treating you similarly. Any relationship can be abusive, whether it's between two humans or between a human and something other-than-human, and any relationship dynamic that looks skeevy, sketchy, and generally unhealthy between two humans doesn't look any better between a human and a superhuman entity. As I am wholesale against abuse and coercion and in favor of agency and consent, I have some thoughts on how to best handle that dynamic. It all starts with saying no.

Yes, I'm telling you to say no to the gods, and no, it's not as simple as "just say no." But that's where we'll start.

People Are People (and So Are Gods)

In the interest of full disclosure, I should note that I think of gods and spirits as autonomous, ontologically independent beings, rather than as philosophical concepts or psychological constructs which exist only within our imaginations. This assertion isn't meant to say that they're identical to human beings, merely that they share with us the existential idiosyncrasy of having their own agency and agendas. In other words, gods and spirits are what we would call people, for a given value of the term. If this assertion conflicts with your own cosmological views, I encourage you to translate anything I say here into terms you find more comfortable. Before you do that, though, I'll also encourage you to look at these issues through the lens I'm offering, at least for a moment. Not to suggest that you're practicing incorrectly, but some questions look quite a bit different if you think of gods and spirits as people rather than as constructs. If nothing else, doing so could give you some insights you might otherwise have missed.

However, a point we sometimes miss while acknowledging the autonomous agency and power of the gods is that we, too, are autonomous spirits with agency and power. Gods and spirits are people, yes, but so are we.

Is there a difference in power and knowledge? Quite often, yes, especially between gods and humans. Remember what Pindar of Thebes wrote, back in the fifth century BCE: "From a single mother we both draw breath. / But a difference of power in everything / Keeps us apart..."[85] We have reasons for calling them gods, and not elementals or servitors or something; part of the definition of *god* is (or, at least, should be) that they're a being with greater power and knowledge than humans.

Does this superior power and wisdom mean that gods are in a position of authority over us—that they should command, and we should obey? It's an interesting question. Depending on the nature of your relationship, it certainly can mean obedience; it's quite common in both folklore and anecdotal experience for gods to tell devotees to do something the devotees don't initially understand but come to realize later were in their best interests. Similarly, one can find plenty of examples of gods telling devotees *not* to do something, only for the devotees to violate that edict... and suffer the natural consequences. In this dynamic, the god is acting as a figure of authority, power, and wisdom to their devotee, acting as a mentor, a guide, even a parental figure to their human partner.

However, and I cannot state this strongly enough, a mere power differential is not the same as moral authority. Might doesn't make right, no matter how many ancient Greek historians and modern supporters of kratocracy (or kakistocracy) might claim otherwise. Similarly, merely having a greater scope of knowledge isn't any indicator of sound ethical grounding, as the moral and operational collapse of would-be meritocracies in various sectors of modern life suggests.

Whence, then, does authority derive? At what point should we suborn our wills to the will of our gods... and, to come back to my pearl-clutch-inducing statement back at the beginning, when should we say no to them?

---

85. Nemean VI, from Pindar, *The Odes*, trans. C. M. Bowra (New York: Penguin, 1969), 206.

The Life-Changing Magic of Saying No

Despite what some medieval witch-hunting manuals might suggest, magic doesn't teach us to enslave our wills to powerful beings. On the contrary, it encourages us to work in mutually beneficial partnerships with them.

"Mutually beneficial?" I hear from the back of the room. "What could we possibly have to offer the gods?"

Well, lots of things. Hands, for one. Sometimes, a god might want to get something moved from point A to point B, and while it might be entirely possible to arrange a fortuitous string of coincidences, it might be a hell of a lot simpler to just ring up a devotee and say, "Hey, take this across town for me." Yes, I'm being a bit irreverent, but I say this with all reverence: the gods relate to us for their own reasons, just as we relate to them for our own reasons. Making these relationships just and equitable is both an act of basic self-respect and a profound act of respect and honor for the very gods we would seek to work with, serve, worship, or have any kind of relationships with. Note that I said "equitable," not "equal." Remember, we're talking about superhuman entities. Gods are a different order of being, and I would no more presume to enter into an equal relationship with Thor than I would challenge him to an arm-wrestling contest. However, equity—fairness, impartiality, justice—is something to which every being capable of sentience and sapience is entitled, and humans have every right to insist on equitable treatment from the gods as from each other.

Another maxim in the Feri tradition inherited and passed down from our late, much-beloved Victor Anderson is an injunction against giving away your power to anyone or anything. This concept is the logical extension of several Feri principles, and the ground of many of our practices. Giving away your power is an abdication of responsibility, a shying-away from your connection to your personal god-self, which is antithetical to everything Feri teaches. The gods we generally work with want us to be our truest selves, the best versions of ourselves we can be, both for our own benefit and for the world's. Actually, the dichotomy I'm using there is misleading: being the best people we can be is intrinsically, ultimately beneficial to us, both individually and as a part of the greater pattern of gods, spirits, animals, plants, stones, energy, matter, and everything else of which all existence is comprised. Regardless of whether or not you're Feri, or any sort of witch or Pagan for that matter, part of being your true self is owning your own power, being accountable for the things you say and do. Your word is your will, and your actions are the manifestation of that will.

I realize how closely what I'm saying here verges on mealy-mouthed platitudes, so let's bring it back to earth a little: we do what we are, and we become what we do. Saying and doing things that go against who we truly are is a kind of betrayal and blasphemy, and ultimately changes us into people we may not wish to be. If we don't want to become the sort of people who say or do those things, we have to be willing to step into our own power. We have to be willing to say no.

It is, in fact, this ability to say no which makes saying yes have any meaning or value. The act of giving consent—to sexual activity, to divine communion, to anything at all—is meaningless without the ability to withhold that consent, and becomes nothing more than an empty formality, voiced by a depersonalized being without agency.

This principle holds true in every single one of our relationships, including those we have with gods. Remember, not all gods are benevolent or beneficent, and not all spirits are who or what they claim to be. Our desire to connect with something greater than ourselves can lead us to make questionable relationship choices in both the quotidian and the numinous realms. It can also lead us to accept and excuse behaviors from divine beings that we wouldn't accept from humans. Don't accept them. Don't excuse them. You belong to yourself, and you get to decide who has access to you, to your body or mind or spirit. You have the right to say no. You have the right to consent and withhold it. You have the right to set the terms of your relationships, and to renegotiate those relationships over time.

And any being who can't respect that—human, spirit, or god—can go to hell. Metaphorically or literally.

#NotAllGods: Some Rules of Thumb for Working with Gods

Let's now cover some of the challenges of establishing those firm boundaries and maintaining them when the gods come knocking on your door. After all, exercising your will is obviously going to have consequences. It may well be necessary to say no to a god but doing so can lead to us being in situations that are unpleasant to live through, difficult to navigate, and impossible to explain to someone unfamiliar with polytheistic spirituality. While I understand that some belief systems disagree with me on this point, I maintain quite firmly that human beings are inherently possessed of the autonomy and agency necessary to say no to anyone, from humans to animals to spirits, even to gods.

How you do that is a matter of context. Sometimes it's as easy as simply not doing something, while at other times it's a matter of closing your eyes for a moment and saying, "I understand that you want something from me, but I can't give you that," or even "…but I'm not going to give you that." On rare occasions, it can even require a formal abjuration, a renunciation of that being and anything to do with them with all the ritual trimmings. I recommend starting at the shallow end of the pool and only going as deep as you need to. Gods are generally quite able to hear a no when it's delivered clearly.

Unfortunately, hearing that no doesn't necessarily mean they're going to listen. After all, we're talking about gods: ancient, immortal beings with superhuman power and perspective who are not (and mostly never have been) human, whose agendas and values may be inscrutable, and whose very conception of the nature of reality is fundamentally, unfathomably alien to ours. To put it bluntly, gods may cherish certain qualities and values in human beings, but that doesn't mean they share them. A cursory glance through any halfway-decent collection of myths will provide us with multiple examples of forced transformation, abduction, seduction, rape, outright murder, and other instances of nonconsensual divine interference in human lives. If human practitioners of theurgy and thaumaturgy choose to place ourselves in proximity to such beings and mingle in their affairs, we are by definition placing ourselves at risk of having our lives disrupted, even against our will.

In the hopes of making it a little easier, I'm going to posit a few basic principles to keep in mind when interacting with gods. Some of these may seem obvious, especially to folks who've been working with deities for a while. Nevertheless, I think they bear repeating from time to time, especially when people are in the middle of dealing with such interactions.

Not all spirits are gods.

It might go without saying, but not every being that claims to be a god actually is one. Sometimes, a mischievous or malevolent being of some kind—a demon, ghost, or spirit—will put on a god mask and try to fool humans into worshiping, serving, and feeding them.

Some of them are ridiculously transparent, while others can be dismayingly successful. This principle is one of the reasons why I'm a big proponent of doing lots of research before metaphorically jumping into bed with a new god. Research can take the form of lots and lots of reading, preferably texts with some historical legitimacy, or consulting experts on the subject, either academic or practical. I'm also strongly in favor of consulting an appropriate oracle or using a preferred method of divination to get a sense of who and what you're dealing with.

Not all gods are nice.

Pantheons around the world and throughout history are filled with gods of decay and death, gods of mischief and mayhem, gods of slaughter and sacrifice. Some gods you wouldn't invite into your home for a social event, much less into your head. Some gods who are rude and boorish, gods who are outright *evil*, and gods who are, from a human perspective, just kind of ... well, assholes. I won't go so far as to suggest that gods get into moods, exactly, but a particular god may show different faces to different people or to the same person at different times, just like any other sentient being. The point is that they're not all benevolent or beneficent, and even the nice ones aren't always nice.

Most gods don't care.

Not to put too sharp an edge on it, but the reality is that gods are just too busy with their own affairs—you know, that whole keeping-the-universe-functioning thing—to spend much time hounding and harassing humans. If a particular human isn't willing, it's vanishingly rare that a god will do anything other than shrug and move along. And the reason for this is ...

Most gods want willing devotees.

Devotees who are cheerfully, enthusiastically engaged with acts of service and devotion are much better than grudging devotees who've been forced into the role against their will. I mean, duh, right? Whenever I hear someone complaining about being a devotee of a particular god, I'm reminded of nothing so much as that one person who complains about what an oaf their spouse is but still claims to love them ... and I wonder why that god keeps this devotee around. (It's not my relationship to manage, though.)

Gods are smarter than you.

If you don't care for the word "smarter," please feel free to substitute any or all of the following terms: older, wiser, cleverer, more knowledgeable, more aware, more perceptive, more experienced, and so on. Simply put, in any interaction with divine powers, humans are at a marked disadvantage in the realm of knowing and understanding how things work on a cosmic level. Gods have perspectives, modes, and levels of awareness unavailable to us other than in extraordinarily limited circumstances; that's the whole superhuman-intelligence part of being a god.

Gods Behaving Badly: Managing Outcomes When Things Get Complicated

Working with divinity is a little more complicated than saying some pretty words and trusting in the good will of the gods. After all, sometimes the gods don't *have* good will, while at other times they're happy to work with us, but what they want is complicated. There may well be occasions when gods will tap you on the shoulder or ring your doorbell and for whatever reason, you simply aren't willing to answer the call and give them what they want. Maybe you're a pacifist who doesn't want to be a devotee of the goddess of battle. Maybe you don't have the space in your monogamous, married life to serve the goddess of lust and sexuality in the fashion she requires. Maybe you just don't like the god of mischief. The point is, you're not interested.

That's where the ability to say no to gods becomes important, as does having a plan for managing the outcome of saying no to a being responsible for at least some part of how the universe itself functions. The possible outcomes of that refusal can vary widely, depending on a number of factors: who you are, who the god is, what the nature of the interaction is, how they ask, how you respond, and so on. It is, however, possible to group these outcomes—benevolent, malevolent, or simply apathetic—into five general categories. I've listed these categories below, in order of increasing consternation, along with some suggestions on how to respond to them.

Nothing

Exactly what it says on the tin. You're hanging out at home, perhaps cooking dinner and listening to music, when a god rings your doorbell and asks you for something or offers you something: a relationship, a boon, power, glory, whatever. You decline—politely, one hopes—and they go on about their merry way, leaving you to finish making dinner.

Suggestions: Nothing! Proceed as normal. Enjoy your dinner.

Negotiating

A god rings your doorbell and offers you something. You say, "No, thank you," and they respond with, "Well, how about I sweeten the deal?" What now?

Suggestions: Well, consider the situation: a being of power is offering to negotiate with you. How you respond will vary, depending on a number of factors. Is your refusal a soft no or a hard pass? Are they a being with whom you would be willing to have a business relationship, or something more? Do you believe they're trustworthy? Are they offering you something meaningful or valuable to you? Also, consider the question of why this deity wishes to be in a relationship with you. What are they looking to get from this negotiation? Consulting your preferred oracle or divinatory system is an excellent idea at this point. I also recommend researching the god negotiating with you, either through reading or (if you can) conversing with devotees of that god, as they may be able to help you interpret and understand what's going on.

Nudging

They ring the doorbell, you decline politely, and they go away. They turn up again, every couple of weeks or months, just to see if your no is still a no. As with Negotiating, this is a pretty clear indicator that the god in question is interested in you, specifically. Where it differs is that rather than an immediate offer to make a deal, the god steps back a bit, gives you some space, and taps you on the shoulder periodically to remind you that they're still around.

Suggestions: Some of the questions above also pertain here: why are they focused on you, what are they asking of you, and what are they offering you? Just like negotiation, oracular queries are a good idea, as is consulting with one of their devotees. Moreover, I recommend doing some internal work to sound out if you're more open to the contact than you may have initially thought. This is *in no way* intended to justify unwanted contact, but to point out that gods can respond to our subconscious and unconscious desires and impulses as readily as to those we feel and express consciously. It's entirely possible to want things we know aren't good for us, or to have desires which conflict with one another. A call we're refusing on the conscious level may be appealing to something we're feeling but of which we aren't fully conscious. (Note: This concept refers to interactions between humans and gods, not between humans and other humans. If you're thinking of conflating the two, don't.)

Nagging

The god called, you declined, and now they just. Won't. Stop. Bugging. You. They're constantly just *there*: tapping you on the shoulder, popping up in your rituals, dropping little hints of synchronicity that they'd *really* like to have a relationship of some kind with you.

This category of contact is where things start to cross the line from persistent to predatory. It can seem similar to the Nudging I just described, but where Nudging is more of a periodic check-in, Nagging is a near-constant phenomenon reminiscent of a whiny child requesting a cookie … or, worse, the creepy petulance of a guy who keeps asking for your number and demanding to know why you've friend-zoned him. While some instances of this behavior are actually a desperate attempt to get a message across to you ("No, seriously, *don't get involved with that coven!*"), this behavior is far more commonly a mischievous or malicious entity trying to get your attention. Remember, not everything that calls itself a god actually *is* one … and even if it is, not all gods are nice. Some beings, divine or otherwise, simply enjoy messing with people, and some beings thrive on our attention … and consequently our energy.

Suggestions: The aforementioned methods of oracular investigation and diligent research can help verify whether or not this being is who it says it is. If it's something masquerading as a god, you have a variety of options for ridding yourself of unwanted contact ranging from an increasingly firm No to a very firm no backed by magical (or divine) efforts. Many traditions of praxis employ banishing rituals, self-purifications, and summoning of allies to underscore the very firm No. If your best efforts suggest this being *is* who they say they are, a firm No followed by some overt negotiation can be a useful strategy. Sit down with them and ask what they want and why— what it would take to mollify them, essentially—that you're willing to give. This can be a sticky negotiation, and I encourage anyone pursuing this course to do so with outside assistance, human and otherwise.

Nasty

Hoo, boy. This category is the nightmare scenario … figuratively and literally. The god called, you declined, and they responded by getting nasty with you. You're having synchronicities and weird happenings all over the place, but they're inconvenient, even unpleasant. Devices and machines go on the fritz or just die outright. Weather patterns turn ugly but only in your general vicinity. Your personal relationships take sharp left turns into miscommunication, and you become mysteriously ill or accident-prone. You're having nightmares, and they all seem to point in the same direction: someone is displeased with you for not responding to them the way they want you to. They've *chosen* you, and they're not willing to take no for an answer.

I'm going to say something here that's sure to be unpopular in some circles: this scenario is *really* uncommon. Not unheard-of, mind you; I know a few people I legitimately believe to have been touched, god-haunted, or god-bothered … and by a few, I mean I could fit them all in my car for a road trip. I've also known a number of folks who've claimed to be god-bothered but whose experiences consisted of what I'd consider some mild coincidental unluckiness coupled with a strong desire to feel wanted or claimed by something larger than themselves. While that's a legitimate desire, I don't think it's unfair to suggest it's not the same thing as being genuinely hounded by a superhuman alien intelligence.

Suggestions: As before, my first suggestion is to verify that what you're dealing with actually is a god and not a malicious spirit of some kind. If it's an impostor, my personal go-to response is the very firm No with optional banishing.

If it's not an impostor, things get a lot more complicated. Whatever you choose to do, *don't* do it alone. What I suggest at this point is reaching out to your community. Talk with people close to you, let them know what's going on, and let them know that you'll need more support than usual. Touch base with any spiritual allies you have and ask them for their assistance and advice. On a mundane level, remember to take care of yourself physically and emotionally, and do what you need to do to bolster your mental health.

If a god is leaning on you, they tend to have a reason for it, and ascertaining that reason is key to resolving the situation in an amicable way. If you choose this route, I strongly suggest reaching out to devotees of this god to ask for their insight, advice, and their intercession, if it comes to that. Once you've done that, sitting down and engaging with the deity in question may be your best option. In the next chapter, we'll discuss some ways you might go about having that sit-down meeting.

Chapter 9

QUEERING YOUR PRAXIS: DEVELOPING AND ADAPTING MAGICAL PRACTICES

LET'S SAY THAT YOU'RE new to the whole world of esoteric spiritual practice. Perhaps you're excited by what you've read and are eager to get started but also want to avoid getting invested in a form of spiritual practice weighted down with exactly the kind of gendered or sexual baggage you came here to get away from. Alternately, maybe you've been around the block a few times and have a solid grounding in a particular system. Perhaps your heart's gone out of certain elements of it—the gendered metaphors, the conjure-and-command model, the cerebral nature of the whole thing—and you're interested in working toward creating a practice that's more in line with your values of consent and embodiment.

The Western esoteric community is made up of numerous traditions, paths, and practices, and the vast majority of them have their own built-in cosmologies that tend to include built-in assumptions about gender, sexuality, power dynamics, and consent. With the wealth of magical and devotional practices available to us within and outside the context of established traditions, one of the questions facing would-be practitioners of esoteric spirituality is what to do: should they modify the practices of existing traditions to suit their needs, assemble their own paths from publicly available bodies of lore and practices, or develop their own systems of practice? Each of these approaches has its own benefits and drawbacks that complicate the question even further. Let's break into that and see if we can't make some sense of things.

The Modified Traditionalist

The first approach is to adapt an existing tradition to your needs, what I call the Modified Traditionalist model. The primary benefit of this approach is that there are fewer time costs up front. If you start with a practice whose underlying structure and symbolic language work for you, it won't be necessary for you to reinvent the wheel. You can modify the language to be gender-neutral, you can tweak the sexual or gendered metaphors, you can adjust the practices to be a little more holistic and grounded (or less all up in your own head), and so on.

For many people, this is easy. It gets you on the road quicker, certainly, and can give you access to a wealth of magical lore and techniques for working with power. You can develop deeply meaningful relationships with gods, spirits, and fellow practitioners, some that may last a lifetime or longer.

The primary drawback is that you're working with a system that already has its own identity: its own personality, if you will, made up in part of a history, a symbolic language, and a current of power that have been in operation for longer than you've been around... in some cases, *much* longer. Such traditions can be highly resistant to change, which is both a strength which keeps them vital and a hindrance for anyone whose lived experiences don't mesh with their cosmology, theology, or psychology. As an example from my personal history, my early training experiences within British Traditional Wicca were hugely influential on my practice as a Witch and sorcerer. I learned techniques for working magic, divinatory methods, and devotional practices that still serve me in good stead, and I have the utmost respect for the gods and the tradition. However, as I came to a deeper understanding of my own gender and sexuality, I came to realize that I couldn't express my own lived experiences using the symbolic language at the heart of Wicca's cosmology, and my practice no longer comfortably fit within the binary gender polarity model wired into the model of the traditional Craft as I learned it.

The happy news is that many living traditions today are considerably more open to including and embracing all genders and sexual orientations than they were even twenty years ago, and even within traditions which are less so, there are individual practitioners and groups which are actively working to effect positive change from within. If you're called to that kind of work, you may experience pushback from the more hardline traditionalists, but you also won't be alone in doing it.

The Magpie

The eclectic, dim sum approach of assembling your own system of practice from whatever parts you find work for you, which I think of as being a magpie, gives you the ability to choose and adapt practices that work for you rather than trying to work within the strictures of an established tradition. This approach allows you the freedom to work with those practices and beliefs which most strongly resonate with your lived experiences of gender, sexuality, and embodiment, and can grow organically from those lived experiences. It also allows you to avoid the pieces of a system that are factually outdated, culturally irrelevant, not effective or resonant for you, or simply not to your tastes. You can, in a sense, custom-build your own path to attain whatever goals you set for yourself and work with or serve whichever deities call to you.

As before, the Magpie approach has some drawbacks that bear some consideration. One problem is that for the most part, spiritual paths tend to evolve internally consistent symbolic languages in which everything is connected to everything else and interdependent. The cosmology, theology, ritual structure, practices, and techniques of a given tradition are grounded in its metaphysical assumptions, which is great when you're working within the context of that tradition. However, if you're attempting to utilize a piece of that tradition outside its context, you may find it doesn't work in the way you expect, or at all. Perhaps its efficacy relies on having a connection to the culture in which the tradition is rooted, an initiatory link to the tradition, or a mediated relationship with certain gods and spirits. Living spiritual traditions are rather like ecosystems; removing something from its native habitat without considering the interconnections and impact tends not to end well.

This invokes the principle of Chesterton's fence, an axiom against making changes to any part of an institution—like, say, a seemingly abandoned fence standing alone in a field—without first studying it carefully to determine what it does, why it was built, and what else might be changed by changing it: "If you don't see the use of it, I certainly won't let you clear it away. Go away and think. Then, when you can come back and tell me that you do see the use of it, I may allow you to destroy it."[86] One way to avoid the Chesterton's fence dilemma is doing the work to understand the practices you adopt in the way the people who created them understood them as best you can. Doing so will involve a lot of research and study, preferably with people who already understand the practices you're adopting, or from sources created by the people with whom the practices originate. Without this work and respect, you're all too likely to slip into spiritual tourism and theft, committing violence against the very traditions whose practices inspire you. This kind of cultural appropriation is especially common among white esoteric practitioners adopting the practices and spiritual lore of cultures of which they are not a part, especially marginalized and oppressed cultures. Don't do this, okay? It's a bad look.

Another thing to consider is that whether you're talking about information science, mechanical engineering, social institutions, or spiritual traditions, the structures we build reflect the minds of their builders and have our perspectives and modes of thinking built into them. Present even in large-scale institutions, we tend to think this kind of built-in bias (e.g., the well-documented phenomenon of researcher bias) will ameliorate other types of bias and average out any individual prejudices to a happy medium. Built-in bias is especially, emphatically true of structures that are the product of a solitary intellect. What this means in practice is that building a system to fit your individual spiritual and emotional needs can also mean building a system that caters to your intellectual and emotional biases or, worse, one which coddles and reinforces your personal weaknesses. This personalized echo chamber can foster and magnify inherent blind spots in the practitioner, places where

---

86. G. K. Chesterton, *The Thing* (London: Sheed & Ward, 1929), 29.

your own biases and weaknesses are wired into the practices and ignored or, worse, reinforced, leading to amplified prejudices, spiritual stagnation and morbidity, and other unhealthy states.

The best way I know to circumvent this tendency is to get outside perspectives on both the practices you use and the effects they have on you. Consulting with fellow practitioners, diligent journaling, working with a therapist, and talking with friends who know you well enough to be honest with you are all excellent hedges against the possibility of creating a spiritually regressive practice. Devotional spirit work, especially divination, can also help to guide your practice away from negative outcomes if—and this is key—you can be honest with yourself about the responses you get from your gods and spirit allies.

The Innovator

The straightforward method of creating your own spiritual path from scratch without using any outside material whatsoever is always available to you. This is the path of the Innovator, the solitary mystic who's willing and able to develop useful spiritual practices based solely on their own needs, experiences, and perceptions. For those who can pursue this route, it can be the most uniquely transformative path to take; it can lead to insights and understandings no other path could provide.

Of course, this approach may also be the hardest of them all. In fact, most of us might find it impossible. After all, there's nothing new under the sun. Virtually every form of spiritual practice humanity can devise—meditation, prayer, mysticism, and magic of all sorts—has already been created. Coming up with your own guided meditation visualization is pretty easy, but the meditative techniques on which it's based have been around for thousands of years. As with the Magpie approach, carving your own spiritual path can lead to the same sort of built-in blind spots, without even the mitigating influence of outside traditions.

Another challenge the Innovator faces is the problem of communicating their experiences and insights to anyone who doesn't understand their personal system. My magical and life partner illustrates this dilemma with a story told by theoretical physicist and all-around brilliant human Richard Feynman. While teaching himself advanced mathematics at the age of fifteen, Feynman decided that the established mathematical notation was insufficient to his needs, so he developed his own notation. All was well and good ... until he had to discuss math with other people, including his instructors, who obviously didn't understand his personal system. To his chagrin, Feynman had to go back and learn the traditional notation system in order to get through his classes.[87] So it is with the spiritual trailblazer. Unless you intend to found your own religious tradition or live as hermit, the lack of a language and frame of reference shared with other people can be both frustrating and spiritually limiting. The workaround for this latter drawback is simply a willingness to compromise. Committed solitary mystics and magicians who still want to be able to hold a conversation with other practitioners may need to learn their language, purely out of necessity. They can still do incredible, innovative work within their own systems, of course, but it's nice to be able to chat with like-minded folks over the beverages of your choice from time to time.

---

87. Richard Feynman, "He Fixes Radios by Thinking!" in *Classic Feynman: All the Adventures of a Curious Character* (New York: W. W. Norton & Company, 2006), 26–28.

Bringing It All Together

What's the best approach? The answer, my friend, depends entirely on you. Ultimately, the best approach is the one which helps you fulfill your spiritual and psychological needs. If you're someone who craves structure and educated verification of your experiences, the Modified Traditionalist approach may be best. If you resonate with established practices but are averse to outside influences on your own experience of the numinous, you may be more suited for the Magpie approach. If you find any externally derived impositions on your magical or spiritual life to be a hindrance, the Innovator approach might be your thing.

The reality is that very few people subscribe solely to a single approach, especially over the course of their lives. Some practitioners begin as Innovators, possibly with a touch of the Magpie, then bring their unique insights and experiences into the context of extant traditions to revitalize or, in rare cases, redefine those traditions. Similarly, some Traditionalists use their early training as the base from which they launch into Innovation, or modify their tradition with practices adopted, Magpie-like, from other spiritual paths. It's worth noting that most of the luminaries of the Western esoteric world, from Dion Fortune and Aleister Crowley to Gerald Gardner and Doreen Valiente, utilized all three approaches in their own spiritual practices, and in creating the traditions they passed on to us.

Many of you reading this will already have a spiritual practice in which you're working, but for those of you who don't, I humbly offer the following ritual as a starting point for getting a practice going, for either solo or group work.

– EXERCISE –
An Invocation of Aradia as Tutelary Goddess

For this exercise, you'll need the following:

- A quiet, undisturbed place to work

- A bowl of warm water

- A small dish of salt

- A small dish of anointing oil

- About an hour of undisturbed time

This ritual follows a framework which probably accounts for more than 90 percent of the ritual work done in modern Western esotericism: the creation of a sacred microcosm in which to work, the magical or devotional working proper, and the opening of the microcosm and return to everyday reality. Being the somewhat irreverent creature I am, I refer to these three components by the less-than-awe-inspiring names of Setting the Space, Doing the Thing, and Releasing the Space.

Now, I'll tell you a little secret: I've actually hidden most of the pieces of this ritual throughout the book. If you've read all the previous chapters, you've already encountered most of them, and if you've done the exercises and rituals included in those chapters, you've already done many of the practices that make up this ritual. In the ritual script below, you'll find page references for the practices we've already covered, in case you'd like to revisit them.

As discussed previously in chapter 6, a key factor in the success of your ritual work is knowing what you're actually trying to accomplish with your ritual. While this ritual is intended to be a framework in which you can fit any working you desire, I've included an actual working in the Doing the Thing section of the script, to give you one example of the kind of devotional and magical praxis you can pursue with these practices. In this case, I've included an invocation of the powers of embodied material existence (represented as the four classical elements of air, fire, water, and earth), as well as the celestial and chthonic powers above and below us, as the setting for the central work of this rite: an invocation of and communion with a deity for the explicit purpose of asking for their aid and guidance. The figure at the heart of the ritual as written is the witch-goddess Aradia, a deity dear to my own heart, in her aspect as a tutelary spirit. I've found her to be a sympathetic guide to working in queer-inclusive spaces, as well as a gentle introduction to working with gods generally, for those who are unfamiliar with the practice. Before working this invocation, I encourage you to reread "Diana of the Woods, Aradia of the Witches" (p. 136) and to familiarize yourself with C. G. Leland's *Aradia, or the Gospel of the Witches* as a preliminary introduction to the goddess.

This ritual really is intended to be a frame for your own work, though, and I encourage you to experiment with it and adapt it for your own purposes. If you already have a relationship with a deity and would rather work with them, or you don't feel any particular draw to Aradia and would prefer to approach another deity, feel free to do so! If you're interested in exploring other queer divinities, read over "Queer Divinities, Queering Divinity" in chapter 5 and explore their myths. Do some outside research into the cultures and the places where those gods' worship arose; see if any of them call to you. If so, consider writing your own invocation to that deity and incorporating it into this framework.

Setting the Space

This can be done by whatever means you feel appropriate. I recommend starting by grounding and centering oneself (p. 68). Once you've done this, consecrate the water with salt (p. 125), then lightly sprinkle the consecrated water around your working space, holding in your mind the idea of banishing or driving away any undue outside influences. After you've done this, use this same water to sprinkle yourself, again with the intent of removing any unwanted external influences. Then, take up the dish of oil and charge it, then use that oil to anoint your body in whatever places you feel are significant to the work you're doing. For general ritual purposes, I usually anoint in the following places: forehead, lips, nape of throat, insides of wrists, and ankles. (If I'm nude while doing ritual, I'll also anoint over my heart and above my pubic bone.) This anointing is a way of sealing yourself to yourself after the cleansing, and a callback to "The Mirror of Reclaiming" in chapter 5 in which the ritualist anoints their own body as an act of self-possession.

With your body and your space made clean and consecrated, enclose your working space within a circle of power, either by using the circle-scribing method from chapter 6 or some other method of your choosing. After sealing your circle, you can move on to the actual magical and devotional working part of the ritual.

Doing the Thing

Facing the east, use your fingers or a magical tool (such as a wand or athame) to draw a point-up triangle with a line across it at the periphery of your circle and say, "From the east I call to you, powers of Air, and ask that you guide me with your discernment and clarity of thought."

Turning to the south, draw a hollow point-up triangle at the periphery of the circle and say, "From the south I call to you, powers of Fire, and ask that you warm me with your passion and strength of will."

Turning to the west, draw a hollow point-down triangle at the periphery of the circle and say, "From the west I call to you, powers of Water, and ask that you embrace me with your fluidity and depth of feeling."

Turning to the north, draw a point-down triangle with a line across it at the periphery of the circle and say, "From the north I call to you, powers of Earth, and ask that you support me with your stability and fortitude."

Move to the center of the circle. Lift one hand to the heavens, point the other to the center of the earth, and say, "I call to the stars above me and the fire beneath me: let me hold the space where your twin flames entwine, and be the bridge between." Bring your hands together and clasp them, saying, "As above, so below."

Turn to face the north, and assume whatever bodily position bespeaks reverence for you: standing, kneeling, or sitting, with your hands clasped or lifted. Close your eyes and, with your mind's eye, envision the goddess Aradia. Remember that Aradia is the divine daughter of Diana and Lucifer and also had a mortal life as a witch-priestess in Tuscany; envision her as a young woman from that region. If you want a visual cue to work from, picture her with olive skin flushed with youth, long black hair cascading past her shoulders, eyes filled with the light of a thousand stars dancing like fireflies. See her as wearing a simple, sleeveless Greek-style tunic dress that falls to her feet, and a diadem of stars in her hair, mirroring the stars in her eyes.

When you have her image formed in your mind, speak the following invocation or one from your heart:

Aradia, Scion of Diana.
Aradia, Daughter of the Moon.
Aradia, Queen of the Fireflies.
Aradia, Saviour of the Witches.
Aradia, comforter of the lost and dispossessed.
Aradia, teacher of the hidden ways.
This, and only this, do I pray of you,
Most holy Aradia,
If it be your will:
Lend me your favor, Secret Queen,
and guide me through the days ahead.
Teach me your cunning arts,
and help me find my own way:
Alone or accompanied,
In broadest daylight,
Shadowed in twilight,
Or mantled in night.
With my own voice do I sing
your praises, most holy Aradia,
And through my own will do I pray
you grant my petition and prayer.
May it be so.
May it be so.
May it be so.

You may feel moved to repeat your invocation multiple times, or you may find that a single iteration is enough. When you've finished, remain in silence and listen for any response you may receive from the goddess. This may come as an audible or internal voice, or a series of images, or a sense of presence. If you aren't having any of those experiences after performing your invocation, once or multiple times, there are a few possibilities in play. The ritual may not be working, at least in the way you hoped; after all, gods have agency too, and the deity you're invoking may simply not want to answer your call. Alternately, your ritual may be working just fine, but you might not be on the deity's wavelength yet. It's also possible that the deity isn't planning to speak to you during the ritual but will visit you later: perhaps in your dreams, or less conveniently, while you're stuck in traffic.

If and when they do respond, however, pay attention. Listen and observe. If they enter into a dialogue with you, respond with respect, but don't plead or grovel. Own your power, be honest, and remember the recommended principles for working with deities (see chapter 8).

Releasing the Space

Once your ritual work is complete, you're free to just hang out in the sacred space you've created, but eventually we all have to get back to the business of daily living. In some traditions, a circle isn't formally dispelled or banished, but is instead left either to dissipate on its own or, if the work is being done in a dedicated ritual space, to infuse and reinforce the previous dedications of that space. As time goes on, you'll figure out what works best for you, but to begin, I would recommend actually dispelling the circle. If you used the circle-scribing method in chapter 6, you'll find its companion circle-opening method there as well.

After you've released the ritual space, take some time to write about your experiences in your journal. Make particular note of your interactions with the deity you invoked as well as any messages or guidance you received from them if you feel it appropriate. Also make note of your emotional responses to the rite, including any thoughts, images, or memories that may have surfaced.

Chapter 10
GREATER THAN ONE: THOUGHTS ON POLITICS, POWER, AND COMMUNITY

UP TO THIS POINT, we've discussed embodiment, gender, and sexuality, but our focus has mostly been on those qualities individually in relation to our magical and devotional praxis. However, we're not merely our bodies, nor our genders or sexualities, and our practice doesn't end at the edge of the circle. We encompass all of those distinct but related qualities; for our spirituality to truly reflect who we are, it must incorporate all aspects of our being into the larger context of our lives. For most of us, that larger context means other people. We define ourselves and enact our identities through our relationships with others, in both mainstream culture and the smaller subcultures of polytheist spirituality and magical practice. And to discuss all of that in a useful way, we have to talk about politics.

Now, before you throw this book away, give me a little time to talk about what I mean when I use the word *politics*. I promise that it's relevant, not just to gender and sexuality but also to magic and devotional work, and to existing in community with one another as devotees and practitioners.

I've participated in the interlocking worlds of witchcraft, polytheism, Paganism, magic, and related fringe communities and subcultures long enough that I've noticed a recurring pattern whenever politics comes up in conversation, in person or on the internet. One person will say something relating magic or polytheistic practice to world affairs, and another will respond with some variation on the theme of, "Oh, I don't pay attention to any of that. My practice (or craft or tradition) is apolitical."

As much as I believe in letting people define their spirituality as they choose, I would be doing a grave disservice to both the community at large and you, dear reader, if I let that notion go unchallenged. If you live in any kind of contact with other human beings—if you're a citizen of a nation-state, if you have a job, if you talk to other people, if you use the internet—you are engaging with politics. You're political.

The problem here may well be in how we define our terms. I won't presume to speak for other countries, but in the U.S., many people define politics solely as a turf war between rival political parties, an arcane drama transpiring in some mythic land far removed from the daily doings and goings-on of everyday folk like you and me. It's an understandable belief to hold, and I'm genuinely not denigrating people whose understanding of politics starts and ends there. However, when I get stuck on complex concepts, I sometimes find it helps to go back to etymology. As I'm sure you're all aware, the word *politics* derives from the Greek word *polis*. A *polis* was a city-state of classical Greece, but more broadly, the term refers to any society or state and the sense of community fostered by belonging to such a society. In other words, the *polis* is you and me. Once we strip all of the parochial partisanship away from our terminology, politics really just means the process of negotiating the daily doings and goings-on of some specific group of people … again, like you and me.

Politics doesn't merely mean the shady dealings in the hall of power in Washington, DC, nor even in your local state capital or city hall. Politics also means knowing how to navigate the bureaucratic systems that encompass our own survival in modern civilization. It means knowing how to conduct the everyday business that gets us through the next few hours at work, or the next social occasion. Politics means knowing how to placate your racist uncle before he ruins Thanksgiving with yet another rant about the Mexicans next door, and it means choosing not to placate him, but instead calling out his racism, and thereby ruining Thanksgiving in a completely different way. Politics means choosing to laugh uncomfortably at the sexist jokes your supervisor tells over Friday night beers, and it means telling your supervisor that such jokes are gross and uncalled-for, and to expect a Monday morning phone call from the Human Resources department. Politics means not having to notice when women, people of color, transgender people, queer people, and religious minorities are being systematically beaten down and screwed over … and it means choosing to notice anyway, choosing to care, and choosing to work against those oppressions.

Politics is, in short, another word for talking about and negotiating power … and if I've learned anything at all about the p-word communities in the past couple decades, it's that a lot of us are really uncomfortable with power. Yes, we like the *idea* of power:

witchy woo-woo, sorcerous might, all that kind of thing. Where we start to get uncomfortable is when we're asked to be accountable *as well as* powerful ... when we're asked to be responsible for what we do with that power, and when told there's a cost for how we wield it, or how we fail to wield it. After all, if our power can't make the world a better place, what exactly is it for? And if it can actually make the world better but we're not using it to do so, what does that say about us?

In the face of such questions, the apolitical stance begins to sound a lot like another name for avoidance. It begins to exude the sour reek of fear, and the spoiled-milk stench of complacency and complicity.

What would our ancestors say to such an attitude, or our gods?

I've agitated against this mindset for some years now and have been criticized in return for attempting to "smuggle" politics into spirituality, for pushing an agenda, for being a cultural Marxist. Nevertheless, I'm afraid I must insist that everything—*everything*—about human nature and endeavor is political. Sweet summer kisses, fancy dresses and snappy suits, the prayers we whisper, the spells we cast, the gods we invoke and worship: all of these are interwoven with politics, the negotiation of power. If you doubt me, let's have a look at the subjects at the heart of this book.

Gender is political. Consider the power disparity between the binary genders in politics, or the yawning abyss that is the gender pay gap in the developed world. Contemplate, if you will, the number of laws whose entire purpose is to establish, regulate, and control the performance of gender norms in both public and private spaces, and especially those which police the bodies and behaviors of women, queer people, and transgender people.

Sexuality is political. While we're at it, let's talk about those bodies and behaviors, the ways in which they're legislated, and the social and political capital attached to the correct performance. It's worth mentioning that the last of the United States' laws prohibiting various kinds of sexual activity (including oral and anal sex) between consenting adults—homosexual or heterosexual, married or unmarried—were only repealed or struck down in 2003, the same year that *Pirates of the Caribbean* and *Finding Nemo* were released. Many forms of sex work are still illegal, and those which aren't are often covertly punished or regulated by laws intended to make their practice difficult or impossible.

Okay, fine, you may think, but what about spirituality? Spirituality is surely devoid of politics, right? Not religion, perhaps, but magic, Paganism, polytheism, witchcraft?

Magic is political. Against the notion that magic as a practice is somehow inherently apolitical, allow me to point to the language of political titles in the Western esoteric corpus to express the celestial, infernal, or terrestrial hierarchies of gods, angels, demons, and other spirits. Allow me to gesture vaguely at the language of power dynamics: beseeching and pleading, summoning and commanding, all by appeal to power and authority ensconced within an established structure. Permit me to point out all the charms and spells intended to curry favor with temporal powers. As examples of this, the *Greek Magical Papyri* offers us a prayer to the sun god Helios (PGM XXXVI: 211–230) to obtain and receive, among many other boons, "reputation, wealth, influence, strength, success, charm, / favor with all men and all women, victory over all men and all women,"[88] while *The Magical Treatise of Solomon* suggests the proper planetary days and hours for making talismans for appearing before, addressing, avoiding, or securing the love of

---

88. Hans Dieter Betz (editor), *The Greek Magical Papyri in Translation, Including the Demotic Spells, Volume 1* (Chicago: University of Chicago Press, 1986), 274.

any lords you might happen to have in your social circle.[89] Note the assumption here that you associate with nobility often enough to need such talismans!

Speaking of assumptions, let's also consider the temporal needs for most magical operations in the classical grimoires: apartments, terraces, servants, exotic ingredients, tools made from precious materials, and simply the spare time and privacy to goof around doing something that wasn't related to work, and which would likely get you into serious trouble with the religious and political authorities of the day. These are books which assume that you belong to a particular socioeconomic class, one with both access to disposable income and some immunity to social opprobrium. When you're rich enough and connected enough that you can safely practice black magic in a society whose laws are partly determined by the church, that's political power, friends. But what about worshiping the Old Gods?

Polytheism is political. I'm going to be frank: the notion that polytheism has ever been apolitical is an ahistorical innovation unique to the past hundred years, or less. If polytheistic religious practices were apolitical, the Gods of Olympus would never have been the core of the Greek state. The Pharaohs of Egypt and the Emperors of China and Japan wouldn't have derived their authority from lineages linking them directly to the Gods. The fates of entire peoples wouldn't have turned on the struggles of deific figures, as in the Irish myth historical chronicle *Lebor Gabála Érenn*. Divinity and rulership have been intertwined as long as humans have spoken with gods and followed rulers, which makes politics as much a natural part of the polytheist worldview as believing in

---

89. Ioannis Marathakis (translator and editor), *The Magical Treatise of Solomon, or Hygromanteia* (Singapore: Golden Hoard Press, 2011), 40–41.

the sovereignty and agency of the gods. But perhaps you meant Paganism, as in modern Neopaganism?

Paganism is political. Consider the books by Reclaiming founder and activist Starhawk, particularly *Dreaming the Dark: Magic, Sex and Politics*, as well as the works of druid and eco-spiritual pundit John Michael Greer, such as *The Blood of the Earth* and *Dark Age America*. Consider the leftist Pagan blog Gods & Radicals (abeautifulresistance.org) or David Salisbury's *Witchcraft Activism*, or the work of Michael Hughes, author of *Magic for the Resistance* and the now-famous Spell to Bind Donald Trump and All Those Who Abet Him. Consider Crystal Blanton's anthologies *Shades of Faith* and *Shades of Ritual*, which uplift minority voices in Pagan practice, as well as her book *Bringing Race to the Table: Exploring Racism in the Pagan Community* (with Taylor Ellwood and Brandy Williams).You may or may not find any of these authors' books to your tastes, and you may or may not agree with their politics. What you *cannot* say is that their work is apolitical, nor that it isn't inherently rooted in a Pagan worldview. Indeed, in each case their politics are a natural outgrowth of their spirituality and are woven throughout their spiritual work. To suggest otherwise is to engage in patent denial. As for witchcraft…

Witchcraft is political. Don't believe me? If it weren't political, would we be greeted in the opening lines of *Aradia, or the Gospel of the Witches* by these images…

> *In those days there were on earth many rich and many poor. The rich made slaves of all the poor. In those days were many slaves who were cruelly treated; in every palace tortures, in every castle prisoners. Many slaves escaped. They fled to the country; thus they became thieves and evil folk. Instead of sleeping by night, they plotted escape and robbed their masters,*

> *and then slew them. So they dwelt in the mountains and forests*
> *as robbers and assassins, all to avoid slavery.*[90]

… or with this explicit directive to Aradia, from no less an authority than her mother Diana, the Goddess of Witches?

> *And thou shalt teach the art of poisoning,*
> *Of poisoning those who are great lords of all;*
> *Yea, thou shalt make them die in their palaces;*
> *And thou shalt bind the oppressor's soul …*[91]

If someone wants to argue that *Aradia* isn't their kind of witchcraft, I won't insist on its universal applicability, but the point stands that it *is* a witchcraft text, and its political leanings are impossible to overlook. It's not difficult to find similar instances of witchcraft and politics being linked throughout history. After all, the Spanish Inquisition may have been styled a religious pogrom intended to eradicate witchcraft, but there's substantial evidence that many of the accusations of witchcraft, and even the Inquisition itself, were politically motivated.[92] Of course, you'd be hard pressed to squeeze a sheet of parchment between church and state at that point in history. As a positive modern example, I'll offer the Operation Cone of Power ritual performed by the New Forest Coven of English witches, including Wicca's founding father Gerald Gardner, which sought to plant in the minds of military leaders in Nazi Germany

---

90. Leland, *Aradia, or the Gospel of the Witches*, 1–2.

91. Ibid, 4.

92. Henry Kamen, *The Spanish Inquisition: A Historical Revision* (London and New Haven,, CT: Yale University Press, 1997), 170.

the suggestion that they would not be able to cross the English Channel and invade Great Britain.[93]

Here's the thing: I'm not telling you to change your practices or beliefs, nor suggesting that you need to start going to protests, donating money to causes, or marching in the streets. What I *am* saying is that this thing we call politics is, like any other realm of human endeavor, a way in which power is negotiated and exercised. Claiming that our lives are removed from that one sphere of power is an attempt to intentionally sever ourselves from it, and from our own power in that space. In the Anderson Feri tradition, we call this giving away your power, and it's one of the greatest mistakes we can make.

Part of the problem is that, as the myth of Spider-Man teaches us, with great power there must also come great responsibility.[94] We look around us and see what a trash fire we've made of the world, and we can feel a powerful desire to find someone, anyone to blame for it, as long as it's not us: "Hey, it's not my fault, this place was a mess when I got here!" We can wash our hands of any responsibility—and, therefore, of any accountability—for the mess. If I don't have any power to influence the outcome of elections, then it's not my fault that corrupt politicians are elected or that bad policies are enacted. It's not my fault when people of color or transgender people are legally disenfranchised and murdered or when our government refuses to help its own people during natural disasters. That's wasn't me, after all. I had nothing to do with any of that. I'm not political.

---

93. Philip Heselton, *Wiccan Roots: Gerald Gardner and the Modern Witchcraft Revival* (Berkshire, UK: Capall Bann, 2000), 244–250.

94. Stan Lee, *Amazing Fantasy #15* (New York: Marvel Comics, 1962).

The trouble is, compartmentalizing our lives so we can claim to be apolitical is a privilege, one afforded to those whose lives aren't endangered by politics. Like politics, *privilege* is a loaded term in today's America, and many people—in my experience, mostly white Americans of European descent—have strongly negative associations with it. Given those negative associations, it's understandable that some people would reject or distance themselves from the idea of privilege, but understanding the actual meaning of the term is essential to comprehending how power works. Privilege is simply power which is available to some people and not others, based on whether or not they're part of some particular group. While we can debate the ethics or morality of systems of privilege, there's *no* moral judgment inherent in simply having privilege.

As an example of how this works, I belong to some groups which are marginalized in American culture: I'm a multiply queer, nonbinary survivor of child abuse who grew up poor, and I belong to a minority religious group with a dubious reputation in much of American culture. However, I also belong to some highly privileged groups: I'm a white, mostly able-bodied, university-educated American who can pass for a cisgender heterosexual male, semi-comfortably ensconced in the United States' dwindling middle class. I am directly subjected to some political developments and largely insulated from others. Political movements targeting queer and trans people and legislation enforcing Christian religious doctrine in the public sphere have a direct impact on me, while political movements targeting people of color and legislation disempowering people with disabilities have less of an impact.

To put it more viscerally: America might hate some aspects of me, but for the most part I'm as safe as houses. That's privilege.

I want to encourage us all to think about power, privilege, and the ways we interact with one another, both individually and in larger group settings. Specifically, I want to discuss four concepts we all understand on some level, but which we may not have examined in the context of queerness, esoteric spirituality, and power: community, diversity, inclusivity, and leadership. A solid grasp of these principles and their ramifications is essential not only to queer magical and devotional practice but to all esoteric work that isn't conducted in an isolated hermitage. I realize some readers may be approaching these terms with prior associations, both positive and negative, so I'll begin each section with my definition for the term to get us on the same page, conceptually speaking. After that, I'll discuss the qualities inherent in that principle and offer an argument for why that principle is a key component of a healthy, grounded spirituality. Finally, we'll talk about how each of these principles can be actualized. Along the way, I'll outline exercise for learning how to put these principles to use in a practical way.

So, let's jump into the deep end of the metaphorical pool, shall we?

Community

For our purposes here, I use community to refer a group of people larger than one's immediate circle of intimates who share a relationship of mutuality—a common identity, a continuity of history and experience—with one another. Communities define themselves by a number of factors, individually or in conjunction, including region, age, ethnicity, gender, sexuality, spiritual/religious praxis, vocation, and so on. As examples, we can talk about the community of Pagans in the Dallas/Fort Worth area, the community of New Orleans Tarot readers, and so on. Communities can also be centered around specific identities and experiences. For instance, we can usefully refer to the communities of particular traditions, such as the Thelemic or Gardnerian Wiccan communities, or to communities of shared experience, such as queer polytheists or Pagans of color. While communities are often thought of as existing in physical space, the internet has become an increasingly standard venue from both the facilitation of community in the material world to the fostering of virtual communities whose members only interact online.

I'm going to lean into the topic of community in a most unprofessional manner, dear reader, by admitting that I often find the concept intensely anxiety-inducing. My anxiety stems from my lifelong associations with community, stemming from growing up weird and queer, which have equated the word with a large group of people who don't like me, don't accept me, don't understand me, and want to either control me, drive me away, or hurt me. Of course, I'm not alone in those associations, either as a queer person or as a practitioner of esoteric spirituality. After all, the charmed circle often functions as a kind of social boundary separating us from them, and by their very nature, queer people and p-words exist outside the charmed circle. In a world where our relationships, livelihoods, and even lives can be put at risk by a failure to pass comfortably within the larger populace, perhaps it's not terribly surprising that many of us would be a trifle gun-shy about community.

Still, I have to own that it's an irrational set of associations. After all, both queer folks and p-words have communities of their own. The LGBTQIA+ community is a sprawling network of interlocking sub-communities built around shared experiences of sexuality and gender, some of which have maintained consistent identities over time, and others that have shifted and morphed as both their understandings of identity and society itself have changed and grown. Similarly, the Western esoteric movement is made up of a dizzying array of communities of belief, practice, and circumstance. Many of us practice with others, or in the context of a regional community, but even those of us who are committed solitary practitioners are still part of a community of praxis. Whether in person, over the internet, or from books, most of us learn our paths from others, and we identify those paths by reference to what others before us or around us have done: Pagan, Heathen, Wiccan, Thelemic, and so on.

As such, whether or not we like it, we're all connected to communities of devotees and practitioners. After all, what community really means is *us*, as in "all of us." If you do the things we do, if you feel the things we feel, if you've experienced the things we've experienced, then you're one of us.

That *us* can be a marvelous, magical thing. At their best, regardless of the identity or experience which serves at their center, communities nurture and support us in all areas of our lives: emotional, physical, spiritual, and more. In the context of esoteric spirituality, our communities are ideally the places where we can be most wholly ourselves, where we can express and explore those aspects of our lives that don't fit neatly into the sorting matrices of the overculture. Our connection to community doesn't merely provide us with a social circle of cheerleaders and confidants, though. Community connects us to other people, the living and the dead, and places us in a continuity of knowledge, practice, and belief stretching back into the past and moving into the future. Our devotional and magical practice is deepened and broadened through that connection, and the work we do as part of our community gives back to the community, furthering the continuity of practice and belief for the people who follow us.

There are catches, of course. The first is all the conditional phrases I used in that paragraph: "can be," "at their best," "ideally," and so on. After all, communities reflect the people within them, and people are notable for being people—flawed, fallible, and possessed of their own agency and agendas—rather than ideal constructs. Not every community is healthy, and not every person in a given community abides by the shared values of that community at all times.

Another catch, as mentioned in my introduction to this section, is that not everyone is going to feel welcome. By their very nature, communities distinguish between *us* and *not-us*, which isn't inherently a bad thing but can feel exclusionary for folks in the not-us category. Moreover, communities inherently have rules and standards which outline the behavior expected from members, sometimes overt and explicit, sometimes unspoken and implicit. These expectations are another way that communities establish belonging; if you're part of the community, you abide by the social contract of the community, and vice versa. However, outsiders and newcomers to a given community may find these rules, standards, and expectations intimidating, restrictive, off-putting, even oppressive.

The workaround for both of these catches is everybody's favorite social-systems buzzword: transparency. This term gets bandied about quite a bit, but in this context, transparency just means that everyone knows how everything works. This transparency doesn't have to be enforced by anything as formal as constitutional bylaws, but it does need to be a community standard in itself. Communities need to make it a core value to be open, honest, and explicit about the contents of their social contracts: the standards that community members are expected to meet, the rules by which everyone is expected to abide, and the mechanisms by which people who violate the contract are held accountable. In return, individual members and prospective members of the community have to be honest with themselves and others about what they expect from the community, and about whether or not they're comfortable with the community's expectations.

A Visit from the Ghost of Community Past

In all of this, you may note that I haven't referred to the Pagan Community as such. My reason for eschewing the term is that while I can easily point to plural and specific Pagan communities, I've yet to identify any sort of monolithic Pagan Community. Not only do I doubt the existence of such an entity, I suspect the concept promotes a vision of Pagan, polytheist, and magical practice that is both misleading and, in the long term, actively harmful.

I haven't always felt that way, of course. Having been a Pagan for about thirty years on and off, I'm part of the last generation of folks to come to magic, witchcraft, Paganism, and polytheism prior to the widespread adoption of the internet. To be sure, the internet did exist then; p-words were posting in various spots on Usenet and private message boards prior to my discovery of Paganism, but those venues were very much a niche phenomenon. My discovery of magic and devotional polytheism was mediated and facilitated entirely through books, magazines, and interpersonal contact. (How very twentieth-century, right?) I'm not suggesting that my experience was better or more valid than that of the folks who came before or after me; merely it was *different*. And a key part of that difference is that my generational cohort are among the last folks to come into this world with an unexamined belief in that nebulous, vaguely defined universalist notion called the Pagan Community (or just "the Community").

So, what is the Community? Was there ever really such a thing? We can see something of it in the books and zines of the sixties and seventies, at least in retrospect. For some, it means the articles and letter-columns of magazines like *Green Egg*, *Nemeton*, and *The Cauldron*, but my image of the Community derives almost entirely from *Drawing Down the Moon*, Margot Adler's oft-mentioned collection of textual snapshots of the Pagans and polytheists she knew and met in the United States of the 1970s and early 1980s. It was from *Drawing Down the Moon* that I adopted a definition of Paganism as a polytheist spiritual movement that saw the numinous as being present in the manifest world, a collection of faiths and practices drawn largely from the pre-Christian world. Alongside that definition, I internalized my idea of the Community as the collective body of practitioners who practice one form or another of Paganism: "Witches, Druids, Goddess-Worshippers, and Other Pagans," as the book's subtitle would have it. Whatever their differences in practices and even belief, there was the subtle assumption that these folks all shared a commonality of identity, and all belonged together in the same bucket.

I still nurture a rueful fondness for idea of the Pagan Community, but I've come to accept that what I still sometimes think of as the Community is actually an amorphous, interlinked, and interrelated conglomeration of communities of faith, practices, social bonds, common interests, and historical association, all of whom have reached for an increasing degree of granularity in the early twenty-first century. We don't really have the Community as such. What we have instead is something like a Venn diagram of traditional Wiccans, eclectic Wiccans, traditional witches, druids, Goddess-worshipers, various other flavors of Neopagan, practitioners of living indigenous or diasporic religions, reconstructionist polytheists from damn near every traditional culture known, Hermetic magicians, grimoiric magicians, and many other folks, all of whom might attend the same events but don't hold in common the shared beliefs, experiences, or identities we associate with the concept of community. Even the articles of faith so beloved of many p-word folks—the sacredness of nature, the mysteries of existence, and so on—aren't universal within the umbrella of the Community, nor even within the individual communities of praxis and belief I used to put beneath that umbrella.

Where am I going with this? Some years ago, I took an art class to learn the basics of drawing and found myself grappling with one of the hurdles most beginner artists hit sooner or later: creating images with values and shading, rather than with lines the way a comics artist does. The technical shift was hard enough, but the real problem was that I'd never really learned to *see*. I looked at things all the time, but there's a world of difference between looking at something and actually seeing it for what it is. I spent much of that class learning how to see what was right in front of my face and draw what I was seeing, rather than drawing something I'd only looked at from memory.

We need to accept that the concept of a monolithic Pagan Community has always been a myth, an assumption of universality papering over a wide array of smaller communities, many of which have little in common with the others. We don't have to be the Community to recognize our similarities and our differences, and to value them both. We just have to be willing see what's actually in front of us. Without that true sight, real transparency is impossible, and our dream of community is just another universalist myth papering over real differences. We have to see what's in front of us, and to express that openly.

The following exercise is intended to help us do just that.

— EXERCISE —
Seeing Ourselves as We Want to Be

For this exercise, you'll need your journal, a writing implement, and about ten minutes of undisturbed time.

Begin by imagining your ideal community. You can imagine any sort of community, but for our purposes here, let's focus on spiritual community, however you want to define that. Perhaps the community you envision is a coven or a circle, a magical lodge, a convention, or some other configuration of like-minded folks. Think about all of the qualities that community would have. How many people make up your community, and how often does it meet? Once a week, once a month, once a year, whenever you feel like it? Where does your community meet? Do you have a physical space that belongs to you? Are you all outdoorsy types who like to go camping, or is your community made up of city mice who prefer air conditioning and flush toilets? What beliefs, practices, or values do you share? What do you do when you get together? Do you talk, teach, do ritual, play music, all of the above? How do art, music, and other cultural artifacts feature in your community? Do you have drum circles, bardic circles, or drinking circles? How does your community feel about drinking, or other recreational intoxicants? What is your community culture around sexuality?

Write down a description of this ideal community you've imagined, with all of the details you imagined. Read over it and add any details you may have missed. Once you're satisfied you have a reasonably complete sketch, set it aside. We'll come back to it shortly.

Diversity

While community does means all of us, diversity reminds us that we're all different. To be diverse is to be comprised of things whose natures or backgrounds vary from one another. In a cultural context, diversity usually refers to the sociocultural elements of people's backgrounds: race, ethnicity, age, sex, gender, sexual orientation, economic class, spiritual or religious affiliation (or lack thereof), and so on. That definition is pretty straightforward on the surface, but diversity has become a politically and socially loaded term these days, one imbued with both positive and negative value. Some folks see diversity as a cultural weapon or a tactic to disempower one group of folks in favor of another, while others see it as a necessary first step toward acknowledging the reality of our communities, both the secular and the spiritual.

The easy out would be to tell you that neither of those associations are inherent to the real, apolitical meaning of diversity, which is just about variety and heterogeneity ... but I'm not going to do that, because it would be a lie. Diversity does indeed have an inherent social and political value, because all the components which make up diversity are politicized in our culture ... and, despite what some commentators might suggest, it's emphatically a good thing with a net positive value, especially if—and this is crucial—we embrace it rather than fear it.

At the end of the previous section on community, I mentioned valuing the differences in communities of devotional and magical practice as much as we value the similarities and suggested that difference is just another word for diversity. Our aggregated cluster of communities thrives in great part because of its diversity of practice and belief, tradition and innovation, background and vision. That diversity is one of the great strengths of the Western esoteric movement and should be cherished and encouraged. Not only is that diversity a source of strength, it's also one of the hallmarks of a vital, vibrant, and viable spiritual movement. I'm not suggesting that having our own traditions is a bad thing. On the contrary, our own practices and traditions are valid in their own right, but they also benefit from exposure to others. We can learn so much from one another, not in a thieving, appropriative way, but through respectful sharing and mutual benefit.

Negotiating that respectful sharing is one of the challenges of diversity, and part of that respect is acknowledging our differences and not merely tolerating them but cherishing and celebrating them. One tendency we have when encountering people who aren't like us is succumbing to what I call the universalist fallacy: glossing over the very real differences and believing that other folks are really just like us, underneath all the external trappings. The heart of this fallacy is a dismissal of the importance of the culture and traditions which make up those external trappings or, worse, in the conviction that those cultures and traditions are intrinsically lesser than our own. In believing this, we set ourselves up to be badly shaken when the true depth of our differences is revealed, usually through misunderstanding and often accompanied by offending or harming the very people with whom we want to find common ground. An example of this tendency is the assumption that queer relationships are fundamentally like straight relationships and reify all the normative institutions and tropes of straight relationships, a way of thinking that leads to awkward questions about which partner is the husband, when the couple are planning to get married/adopt kids/have a mortgage, and so on. We can see another example in the practice of equating all cultural indicia from across the globe in one-for-one organizational systems, like the tables of correspondence of gods and spirits much beloved by some magical and devotional practitioners that impose synthetic relationships on beings who have only the most superficial level of similarity.

Another tendency goes the opposite direction and focuses on the differences between ourselves and others to an extent that overlooks the common humanity we share; given enough time, it becomes a kind of fetishization of otherness. The targets of this fetishization are regarded not as people with interior lives and agency of their own but as objects from which the observer can extract something of value: entertainment, validation, sexual or spiritual gratification, and so on. For queer folks, this tendency manifests as anything from straight culture's obsession with *RuPaul's Drag Race* and *Queer Eye* to, more disturbingly, the phenomenon of chasers who exclusively seek out trans people as objectified sexual partners. Within esoteric spiritual communities, this tendency often looks like white American Pagans commodifying and gentrifying the practices of indigenous spiritual traditions while failing to engage with the cultures from which those traditions arise in any meaningful way.

To frame this metaphorically, imagine walking into someone else's home uninvited in the middle of a family dinner. Now, imagine helping yourself to one of the place settings: not merely sitting down and digging into the meal, but literally grabbing a plate and loading it up with food, then pocketing some silverware as you head for the door. Perhaps you invite them over to your house for dinner some other time as you leave, provided they're willing to sing for their supper. After all, if your food is just as good as theirs—and it is, of course—they have no reason to complain. All meals matter, right?

These tendencies are rooted in the same fundamental fallacy: seeing other people and their cultures as not merely different, but intrinsically less than ourselves and our own culture: less valid, less wholesome, less sovereign and autonomous, less worthy of preservation and respect. The trick in avoiding either of these tendencies is to remember and constantly remind ourselves that our culture is just one of many, and other cultures have just as much right to space and agency as ours. If we can embrace that principle, we can learn to cherish those differences, and they can bring us to a deeper understanding, not only of the people around us, but of ourselves and our own culture.

Inclusivity

To the diversity that acknowledges we're all different, inclusivity responds that we all belong, that we exist in community *with* our differences, not despite them. Being inclusive means acknowledging and making space in our communities for diversity of belief and praxis, age and experience, race and ethnicity, gender and sexuality, and so on. Communities come into being around their own interests, aims, and standards of membership, but inclusivity doesn't demand that we abandon our standards and just let everybody in. It requires being honest about what our standards are and working to ensure those standards are based in the actual, essential identity of the community, rather than on assumptions made about people who aren't like us.

The work of making our communities inclusive might sound like lowering the bar to some ears … and that's precisely what it is, if we're talking about bars to entry based on arbitrary, unreasonable, or untruthful standards. That work lives in the spaces between community, diversity, and inclusivity, which can hold a lot of tension and nuance. Exploring that nuance and tension can be difficult, but it's absolutely essential work which ultimately strengthens our communities, making them more truly reflective of their own identities. To that end, we should consider the challenges of inclusivity and the paradox of tolerance.

In chapter 7, I wrote about taking a sabbatical from both my personal practice and the Pagan, polytheist, and magical practitioner communities as a whole, largely because of the p-word community's dysfunctional relationship with power and consent. In tandem with that criticism was an underlying issue it took a while longer to unpack, a loose thread in the discourse around what it meant to be a community I couldn't locate but nagged at me until I found it and started tugging on it. Once I did, the whole notion of "the Pagan Community" unraveled in my hands.

One of the foundational elements of the Pagan Community myth as I learned it in the mid-'80s was the community's idea of itself as welcoming, accepting, and inclusive. Whatever your quirks, idiosyncrasies, or outright strange behaviors were, the myth ran that you could find a home for them within Paganism. After all, this was a community formed by iconoclasts: hippies, beatniks, visionaries, mystics, dreamers, and other folks marching to their own drummers, following their own flavors of bliss. For someone raised in a repressive culture with no room for non-normative expressions of spirituality, philosophy, sexuality, or gender—say, most of the United States at the end of the twentieth century—encountering this kind of radical inclusivity was an incredibly liberating experience. As a Pagan, I was told, you could believe whatever you believed, and no one would tell you that you were bad, sinful, or wrong for doing so. It was ... well, magical.

Unfortunately, that kind of radical inclusivity also makes it really difficult to develop or enforce shared social norms, standards of behavior, or healthy boundaries.

We often hear the maxim that Paganism and polytheism don't have popes, by which we mean centralized spiritual authorities. (Discordians are exempt from this, of course.) Our traditions tend on average toward non-hierarchical structures in which everyone is considered equal, or toward hierarchies that plateau instead of peaking, where adherents who've reached a certain level of attainment are considered equals, none with any authority over the others. This allows for a great deal of freedom; in practice, it also means that no one has the authority to tell other folks they're doing it wrong. In fact, the entire idea of doing it wrong falls apart, because there's no standard of right and wrong to use for comparison. Each decides for themselves, and none for any other.

That arrangement is basically fine when we're talking about matters of individual practice or belief, but it can go downhill in a hurry in a community setting. The larger interlocking esoteric communities have grappled with the inherent contradictions and problems of building unity around both inclusivity and individualism since there's been such a thing as larger public communities of esoteric practitioners. After all, a community is a group of people united by sharing something in common—an interest, a history, an identity—and it's difficult to share everyone doing their own thing as a common unifying principle, much less to hold that principle while insisting that everyone has to abide by the same set of rules and communal ethics. In short order, we find ourselves faced with a would-be community which not only doesn't share our values, but which holds values we find antithetical to our own.

Fortunately, this problem has a solution: looking to our praxis to derive an ethical basis for shared standards of behavior. As one example, we can look to the work being done in Heathen and Norse polytheist communities, which have grappled with both the background-radiation racism of American culture and the overt, codified racism of white supremacist groups. Such hate-based groups rarely confine their bigotry to racism, of course, but also fold sexism, homophobia, and transphobia into their soufflé of terribleness. The number of polytheist groups and movements such as Heathens United Against Racism who have explicitly denounced and aligned themselves against such ideologies is heartening, but what's especially worth noting is that these groups and movements have grounded their opposition in the texts and traditions they share in common, rather than relying on the presumption of a shared universal ethic. They've had to establish a commonality of belief and identity in order to develop the necessary ethical basis for opposing and excluding hateful ideologies and groups, and part of their understanding of that belief and identity is its exclusion of racism, sexism, homophobia, and transphobia from their standards of acceptable behavior. In short, they are saying, "This is who we are, and this is what we believe. If you would stand with us, we welcome you, but these are the ethical boundaries of our identity. If our opposition to hatred drives you away, so be it."

They are, in other words, being a community, and doing the work of community.

One could reasonably argue that this establishment of shared identity is an act of exclusion—it is. However, it's as radically different from the exclusion practiced by white supremacists as a fruit bat is from a baseball bat. The relevant philosophical principle at work here is what Karl Popper calls the paradox of tolerance:

> *Unlimited tolerance must lead to the disappearance of tolerance. If we extend unlimited tolerance even to those who are intolerant, if we are not prepared to defend a tolerant society against the onslaught of the intolerant, then the tolerant will be destroyed, and tolerance with them.*[95]

Popper's stance wasn't that intolerant philosophies should always be suppressed but that they should be kept in check, through the use of force if necessary, because any failure to do so would inevitably lead to the intolerant enacting violence against

---

95. Karl Popper, *The Open Society and Its Enemies, Volume I: The Spell of Plato* (London: Routledge & Kegan Paul, 1945), 265.

the larger society. He concludes, "We should therefore claim, in the name of tolerance, the right not to tolerate the intolerant."[96]

The ideology of white supremacists is rooted in intolerance as they're literally a hate group: the basis of their identity is hatred of people based on some intrinsic quality—ethnicity, skin color, gender, sexual orientation, and so on. The Heathens and Norse polytheists who exclude them are not rejecting an intrinsic quality but the hatred and intolerance those people have adopted as a weapon against the Other. This intolerance of intolerance is rooted not in hatred and bigotry but in love, the antithesis of those qualities.

The rest of the Pagan, polytheist, and magical communities could learn a great deal from these groups, both about opposing hateful ideologies in their midst and about what it means to be a community. At some point, every community must make a choice about who they are, individually and collectively. They must choose what they stand for, and who they stand with. This doesn't have to mean eroding or erasing differences of praxis and belief for the sake of inclusivity, nor does it have to mean disrespecting those differences to bolster their own identities. It does, however, mean being clear-eyed about what ideologies and behaviors they're willing to tolerate in the name of being accepting, welcoming, and inclusive.

Taken in tandem, the principles of diversity and inclusivity push us to ask ourselves who our communities are truly meant to serve, and what their essential identities are. In his 1971 book *A Theory of Justice,* the American philosopher John Rawls posited a useful tool for exploring those questions: the thought-experiment of the Original Position.[97] Consider the following scenario: you've

---

96. Popper, *Open Society*, 265.

97. John Rawls, *A Theory of Justice* (Cambridge, MA: Belknap Press, 1971), 17.

just been appointed supreme legislator of your society. Starting tomorrow, society will be reordered to your wishes, and all laws, ethical standards, and cultural norms will be whatever you dictate. There's a catch, though: you won't know what position you'll hold in this new society. You'll make your decisions about the shape of this new society from behind what Rawls calls "the veil of ignorance" which prevents you from knowing your own skin color, your economic status, your level of physical or mental ability, your sexual orientation or tastes, even your gender, until the big reveal tomorrow.

Will you construct a society where some groups of people are privileged over others, banking on the possibility that you'll get lucky ... and risking the possibility of ending up at the bottom of the social hierarchy? Or will you try to make society as level as possible, out of enlightened self-interest? Of course, it's pretty obvious that the second answer, the equitable society, is the best and wisest choice. So why don't we make it?

The following exercise takes some cues from Rawls's notion of the original position to examine the choices we make about inclusion in our own communities.

− EXERCISE −
Seeing Ourselves from the Outside

For this exercise, you'll need your journal, a writing implement, and about ten minutes of undisturbed time.

Open your journal to the description you wrote of your ideal community and read over it again. However, don't just reread what you wrote; read it as though you were engaging with the community you just described, but as someone completely different from yourself. If you're white, imagine being a person of color. If you're male, imagine being female or nonbinary. If you're cisgender, imagine being transgender. If you're straight, imagine being queer. If you're able-bodied, imagine being a disabled person: someone who's blind, or deaf, or mobility-impaired. If you're neurotypical, imagine being neurodivergent. How do you imagine your relationship with that community would change if you yourself were different? Would you feel equally at home in that community, or would you feel alienated, excluded, unwelcome? Would you want to spend time with that community, or would you want to seek community elsewhere?

Now, write down both your responses to those questions and your emotional reactions to them, and to the image of your ideal community as viewed from the perspective of someone else. I know those reactions and responses might be intense, even uncomfortable, but I encourage you to be honest with yourself as you write, because they're the entire point of this exercise. Your responses, your reactions, and your image of an ideal community are neither bad nor good; they're just information intended to help you make choices. Knowing what you value, how you feel about it, and how that may be perceived by others is useful information to have, especially when looking at the broader context of community.

This exercise isn't intended to shame people or communities for not being more inclusive or diverse. Rather, it's intended to show where we may have biases and to reiterate the necessity for honesty and transparency about who and what our communities are. The reality is that even the most inclusive communities still make a distinction between us and not-us, and not every community can or will want to accommodate every individual need. For instance, if a group spends a lot of time camping in the wild for devotional rituals, many of their communal spiritual activities won't be accessible to people with mobility issues, or those who rely on technological medical interventions that can't be backpacked into the wilderness, or even those who simply can't afford camping equipment and time off from work. This group could work to adapt and modify their practices to include those with particular needs, or they could reply, with sensitivity and respect, that they've chosen not to change their practices to meet those needs. Neither answer is intrinsically right or wrong, but the way the group responds to the question holds an insight into who they are as a community, and what their values are.

Leadership

Leadership is another of those words for which we all have our own internal definitions, and around which many of us have substantial emotional baggage. I'm certainly no exception. If the concept of community makes me anxious, leadership makes me almost frantic. I detest being ordered around, I'm reactively resistant to being told what to do … and I'm horrified at the thought of others looking to me to tell them what to do. That said, I'm going to enthusiastically endorse the concept of leadership, and I'm going to encourage you to do so, too. This stance may sound contrary or even paradoxical to everything I just said, but hear me out: that endorsement rides on the definition of leadership I use that I am also going to encourage you to use.

If you've followed me this far, you've noted that I've defined community as "all of us," diversity as "we're all different," and inclusivity as "we all belong." To round out these four principles, I'll offer my suggestion that leadership should be defined as "we all serve." Leadership exists only in the context *of* a community and in service *to* that community. In practice, leadership doesn't look like telling people what to do, but providing them with guidance, as a guide leads hikers on a path. Leadership can look like teaching classes in magic, holding a position in your local community organization, or being the high priest/ess/x in group devotional rituals, but it also looks like teaching people how to cook, organizing a fund-raiser for your local community organization, or walking people through setting up and tearing down ritual spaces. Leaders aren't an elite class of omniscient superhuman savants, but members of a community who share their knowledge and skills to empower those around them, or even better, to give those around them the tools and access they need to empower themselves.

This approach to leadership can be a challenging mental and emotional shift for those of us raised in a culture which equates leadership with domination, command, and control. If we expect leaders to tell us what to do, we may find it unnerving to have leaders who instead tell us *how* to do something, leaving the *what* up to us. Similarly, if we expect our leaders have all the answers, we might be stymied by leaders who freely admit the limits of their expertise and experience. In contrast to the sort of top-down leadership prevalent in so much of our culture, this model of leading from within is actually much better suited to modern esoteric communities where the autonomy and sovereignty of the individual are considered sacred. Seeing leaders as guides within the community, rather than dictators ruling over it, also makes life easier on those who find themselves in leadership positions. The mantle of leadership carries with it responsibility for and accountability to the community one leads, a mantle that can become a crushing burden when leaders are seen as more than human. Many of the best leaders I've known were happy to work in service to their community and even happier to set aside that mantle and just be ordinary folks again.

At the same time, people do sometimes actively aspire to leadership. Some try to bring about what they see as positive changes in their communities, and others crave power and position to compensate for gaps in their personal lives. It's even possible to start by taking on leadership with the best of intentions, then find oneself increasingly drawn to the power and positionality for their own sake, or to enforce a particular vision of community … for its own good, regardless of how the community itself may feel about the matter. This insidious self-deception is one of the traps of leadership, but it's possible to dodge or backtrack out of that trap and regain our focus. To do so, I'm going to enlist the aid of my very favorite twelfth-century Grail knight from Wales.

In Chrétien de Troyes's Arthurian romance *Perceval, le Conte du Graal*, the young and naïve Perceval sets out from his native Wales and becomes a Knight of the Round Table. On a trip home to visit his mother, he stays and dines in the castle of the wounded Fisher King, where each course of the meal is preceded by a bizarre procession with a bleeding lance and the Holy Grail of Arthurian legend. Perceval remains silent through all of this instead of asking about this curious procession and awakes the following morning alone. Later, he is chastised for not asking the Fisher King about the Grail and the lance, the questions that would have healed the king and the land itself: "What do these things mean? And whom do they serve?"[98]

These are the questions we should all be asking ourselves and each other. Let's avoid the well-intentioned mistake of Perceval, who walked among wonders but failed to ask what and why they were for fear of seeming rude. Instead, let us practice discernment around what we do as individuals and as leaders in a group, a tradition, a community. Rather than accepting things as they are merely

---

98. Chrétien de Troyes, "The Story of the Grail (Perceval)," in *Arthurian Romances*, trans. William W. Kibler (New York: Penguin Books, 1991), 381.

because they've always been that way or we don't want to rock the boat, let's ask *why* they are as they are, and who benefits by them being as they are. Rather than saying or doing whatever comes into our heads in the moment, let's ask ourselves why we want to say it and what we hope to accomplish by doing so.

In short, let us ask ourselves what these things mean, who they serve, and to what end.

We don't always consciously know the underlying motives for our desires and actions, though, so saying "let's practice discernment" is useless without defining what that practice actually looks like. The following exercise is offered as a tool for working through our own thoughts and beliefs to unearth those answers.

— EXERCISE —
Answering the Grail Question

For this exercise, you'll need your journal, a writing implement, and about ten minutes of undisturbed time.

Consider something you want to do within your community. Maybe you're considering becoming a teacher and taking on students or initiating someone into your tradition or order. Perhaps you're considering starting a new group, coven, tradition, or order. You might be thinking of writing a book or a blog, or starting a podcast. Maybe you're considering offering a class and debating whether or not to charge money. Whatever it is you're considering doing, fix that intention in your mind, then turn to a new page of your journal and write it down in as direct and concise a manner as you can: "I want to _____," or something similar.

Once you've done that, on the line below your intention, write, "To what end?" Then ask yourself, "*Why* do I want to do this thing? What does it mean to do this? Whom does it serve? To what end am I doing this?" Take a few minutes to seriously consider those questions. Follow your train of thought wherever it leads, but remember to bring it back around to the core question, "To what end?" Once you feel you have a solid answer, write it in your journal next to the question, again in a direct and concise manner.

Don't just stop with the first answer, though. Read over your response, recognizing that each answer holds another question nested within itself, then write below it, "To what end?" Repeat the process of consideration, following the rabbits of your thoughts down whatever holes they go, but always coming back to the question. Write that answer down, then start the whole process over again.

As an example, let's say you want to teach. To what end? To pass knowledge on to the next generation. To what end? So that the knowledge, skills, and lore you received from your teachers will be carried on. To what end? So that your tradition won't die out. To what end? To preserve a particular means of connecting with the gods, with nature, and with one another. To what end? And so on. Repeat this cycle of questioning, considering, and responding. Think of the question as a knife peeling away the layers of each answer, cutting away justifications and assumptions to reveal the next question and, ultimately, the truth that lies at the heart of your original intention.

Before long, you may find yourself questioning every belief and article of faith you hold around this issue, and every action you want to take … and that's a good thing. Faith can be a fine thing, but if we are honest in our practice of experiential spirituality, we have to be willing to examine that faith. We have to ask ourselves what we truly believe, and what that belief is for. Similarly, as leaders, we must ask ourselves why we want to do the things we do, and who those actions serve. Once you've delved deeply enough, you may find that what you actually believe is at odds with what you think you believe, and that what you want is at cross purposes with what you believe you want.

Being Careful with Knives

In spite of its helpfulness as a personal exercise, I advise against trying to use the Grail Question exercise on other people's actions or practices. Like arguing with a sock puppet, it might be kind of entertaining if you like that sort of thing, but ultimately it won't be very interesting or useful. Posing the question to those people themselves, and actually getting their answers, is more likely to get interesting and useful results, but that approach has a couple of inherent difficulties. The first is that sometimes people aren't ready to face their core motivations, and if you force them to confront the reality that they're doing something they know in their heart of hearts to be a bad idea, they're liable to become cross with you. Remember the adage about catching more flies with honey than with vinegar, and act accordingly.

The second difficulty is that some people already know their core motivations and are comfortable with them even if you aren't. Such folk simply cannot be reached this way because they occupy a cognitive reality that isn't tangent to yours. For instance, someone who sees magic as a resource to be exploited and monetized is operating from a worldview fundamentally different from that of someone who sees it as part of a quasi-secret tradition of familial kinship and lore or as a set of tools for the spiritual liberation of all humanity. These positions are intrinsically at odds with each other and won't be resolved neatly just because you ask some pointed questions.

Putting Myself Under the Knife

Some of you reading this may be asking, "That's all well and good, Misha, but what about your motives and your discernment? To what end did you write this book?"

That's a fair question. Here's my answer: I wrote this book to engage with the ways in which gender and sexuality intersect with magical and devotional practice.

To what end? To put both my academic training in gender and sexuality and my experience as a magical practitioner and devotional polytheist to use in analyzing what we do as devotees and practitioners of esoteric spiritual paths.

To what end? To examine how those of us in the Pagan, polytheist, and occult communities engage—or don't engage—with our own gendered, sexual lives, and with those around us.

To what end? To make our communities kinder, more inclusive, more accepting places for those of us under the LGBTQIA+ umbrella, and to make it clear to folks under the LGBTQIA+ umbrella that our p-word communities have space for them.

To what end? So that all of us—straight, queer, cis, trans, and otherwise—can find a way to live our authentic lives, as the truest expression of our gendered, sexual, spiritual selves.

To what end? So that I may have done not merely my will but the will of the gods to whom I'm devoted, and to have done needful work worth doing…which, in the end, is as much as any of us can hope to do.

Chapter 11
AN ENDING AND A BEGINNING: WHAT LIES BEYOND THE CIRCLE

WELL, DEAR READER, here we are. We've reclaimed our own bodies, walked through the labyrinth of gender, warmed ourselves around the bonfire of sexuality, engaged in magical rituals to shift our shapes and consciousness, and gazed upon the faces of the Queer Divine. While our time together in these pages is almost at an end, the work we've done together is far from over. In fact, it's never over. This is the work of a lifetime because this is the work of ourselves: of accepting and embracing the joyous burden of our own gendered and sexual sovereignty.

When I first sat down to write this book, my intention was to share some of what I've learned both in my magical and devotional praxis and in my academic work as a scholar in the fields of gender and sexuality studies. My goal in this has been to give you some things of value and utility to apply in the context of your everyday work as a magical practitioner, a spirit-worker, a devotee, and simply as a human being. If you've learned anything at all while working through this book—about yourself, about magic, about spirituality and sexuality and gender, about the ways all of these things come together—then I'll consider my work successful.

So where do we go from here?

As I write this at the beginning of 2019, the Western esoteric movement is experiencing something of a renaissance of queer spirituality, a flowering of queer magic and queer devotional practice. New traditions and streams of practice specifically devoted to queer and trans spirituality are rising, while older forms of practice are opening their arms to embrace queer and trans seekers. In many ways, this is the best time to be a queer practitioner of esoteric spirituality in recorded history.

At the same time, things aren't always easy. As with any change, there's also been pushback against these developments and progress in both mainstream society and, I'm sad to say, the communities which make up the modern Pagan, polytheist, and magical communities. Our communities include hardline traditionalists who view any change in the direction of inclusion as an unacceptable innovation and incursion into their spaces, and exclusionary essentialists whose belief systems preclude any openness of thought or tolerance of diversity. We have sexists, racists, homophobes, transphobes, and other people whose fear and hatred have soured them, like milk left too long on the counter. We have sexual predators who mask their nature with appeals to tradition, to sex-positivity, to whatever else they feel will give them sufficient cover. All of these behaviors are especially pernicious in our communities because they're based in fears which can be magnified by magical and devotional praxis, and because our own theologies and cosmologies can perpetuate outdated paradigms that are toxic when not adapted for modern understandings.

There's still hope, and more than that is what I think of as the momentum of our cultural position. As I said at the very beginning of the book, magic is queer. Magicians, witches, devotees, and practitioners of all the myriad forms of esoteric have excluded themselves from the charmed circle of mainstream religion and spirituality, merely by practicing our own rites and worshiping our own gods in the context of a modern culture which would just as soon believe us crazy, dangerous, or nonexistent. In that, we are surely as queer as *RuPaul's Drag Race*, *Orange Is the New Black*, or *The L Word* ... if not more so. After all, we're queering spirituality simply by being who and what we are without any mainstream media push to normalize our identities and behaviors.

Now that we're almost at the end of the book here, I'm going to confess something to you: I sat down to write this book with an agenda. The Western esoteric movement—Paganism, polytheism, magic, the whole thing—is a big tent with a big table, and we have room at that table for people of every sexual orientation and gender identity, especially if we can all agree to share the table. My agenda has been twofold: to let queer and trans people know that they're welcome and wanted at the table, and to get straight and cis people to scoot over on the bench and make some room.

A core part of this agenda was to inform and educate, to be sure, and to help readers—queer, straight, trans, cis, everybody—find ways to make their devotional and magical praxis resonate with their own lived experiences of sexuality and gender. However, the ideas in this book aren't merely intended to make individual lives easier. On the contrary, I fervently hope these ideas can be adapted and built upon by people in community with one another—queer and straight, trans and cis and nonbinary—to make our communities of practice stronger, more inclusive, more accepting. As prone as some sectors of our communities and traditions can be to conservatism and retrogression, I genuinely believe that we're better served as a spiritual movement and social demographic by making diversity and inclusivity a core part of our values. Doing that work doesn't have to mean a loss or relaxing of standards, though it might well mean taking a close look at what those standards are and discerning whether they might serve some agenda we haven't fully examined. Neither does the work of inclusion and diversity directly result in a loss of identity. It might mean that our identities change and grow over time, but that's a prerequisite of being alive.

Applying the Lessons, Doing the Work

The answer to the earlier question of where we go from here is to do the work that lies before us. The ideas and practices discussed in this book are intended to be starting points, rather than destinations. Where you take them from here, and what you use these tools to build, is entirely up to you.

I do have a couple of suggestions, of course.

Diagnostics, Correctives, and the Annoying Necessity of Daily Practice

I would love to tell you that the work in this book is the sort that can be done once and never again, but I'd be lying. Sadly, for most of us, the work of possessing our own bodies and lived experiences is the kind of work we're going to have to do again and again, throughout our lives, in a variety of contexts. As much as it galls the part of me that would rather sleep in every morning, Robert

Anton Wilson's dictum of *do it every day* remains annoyingly, aggravatingly true.[99]

As such, none of the exercises in this book are intended to be one-and-done, single-use tools. Some of them can be repeated every so often as a diagnostic to help you work out where things may be going off course, and as a way to recalibrate yourself, spiritually and emotionally. The Mirror of Reclaiming exercise can be especially useful as a way of maintaining your sense of sovereignty over your own body in a world which really, truly wants you to believe that your fundamental nature is a piece of property, an asset, a human resource. Others can be adapted for use as part of a daily practice, formally or informally. The Orange exercise, for instance, is particularly well-suited for use as a daily reminder to inhabit your body mindfully and with intention, especially if you adapt it for other circumstances. If you can eat an orange mindfully, you can bring that same mindfulness to drinking a cup of coffee, listening to a piece of music, enjoying the sight and scent of flowers, or any other sensory experience.

Group Work

While the practices in this book have been presented as solo exercises, most of them can be adapted and modified for use with one or more partners. Of course, these exercises do touch on sensitive, even intimate parts of the practitioners' selves, so any group workings would require that the groups are made up of trusting and trustworthy people. The phrase "perfect love and perfect trust" is used in some Wiccan circles to refer to the kind of relationship a coven member should ideally have with the coven. While that's a

---

99. From his introduction to Christopher S. Hyatt, PhD, *Undoing Yourself with Energized Meditation and Other Devices* (Tempe, AZ: New Falcon, 2010), ix.

lovely ideal, perfection might be a bit much to expect. Let's start with reasonable first and see how it goes.

What does reasonable mean in practice, though? To start, it means that everyone has freely given their informed consent: they're all aware of and in agreement with the group's aims, and they're on board with the kinds of practices the group will be using to accomplish those goals, enthusiastically and without coercion. It means the group has discussed what their values are, what the expectations of the group members are, and what the boundaries for acceptable behavior are. It means that when disagreements arise within the group, everyone shares an understanding of how those disagreements will be addressed. All the stuff we discussed about consent comes into play here in spades. Groups intending to do this kind of work don't have the luxury of wallpapering over questions of consent and agency or hand-waving the possibility of abuse or predation.

All of that sounds like a lot of work because it is. Group work can be incredibly effective and rewarding, but it can also be complicated, taxing, and difficult to manage. I've heard it said that the average lifespan of a magical working group is less than two years, and I'm honestly surprised it's that long. Without a strong force to bind a group together—a vision, a mission, a charismatic leader—many people find that it's simply easier to work by themselves, or they prefer congregating in social settings to working together. Unfortunately, many of those binding forces lend themselves all too easily to abuse.

When working groups do click, however, they can be ... well, magical.

The creation, care, and feeding of a magical working group is well out of scope for this book. If you're interested in the subject, though, I recommend two books as useful resources: Judy

Harrow's *Wicca Covens* (Citadel, 2000) and Amber K's *Coven Craft: Witchcraft for Three or More* (Llewellyn, 2002). Don't let the titles and covers fool you! While their magical focus is on Wiccan practice, that's largely irrelevant. They're excellent manuals for putting together a working group of any sort, including advice on managing disputes, handling group dynamics, and knowing how to cope with issues that may come up—including knowing when an issue is above your pay grade.

— EXERCISE —
Looking Back, Looking Forward

For this final exercise, you'll need your journal, a writing implement, and about half an hour of uninterrupted time.

Open to a blank page and free-write for a few minutes on your current sense of embodiment, your engagement with gender and sexuality, and the ways in which those all inform your magical and devotional praxis. Try not to write about the past or how things have changed, but instead to focus on the present and how things *are*.

Once you've reached a stopping place, set the pen down and flip back to the beginning of your journal. Starting with the very first free-write you did during the introduction (page 27), read over the writing you've done throughout this book. Take an account of yourself and notice how you've changed as a result of the work you've done through the previous chapters.

Now, take a few more minutes to free-write about your intellectual and emotional responses to those changes, and about what the process of moving through this work has been like.

One Final Word Before We Go

An epigram variously attributed to Leonardo da Vinci or the French writer Paul Valéry suggests that no creative work is ever truly completed, merely abandoned by the creator. However spurious the attribution or cynical the interpretation, I'm afraid it's all too true in this case. I've only lightly brushed my fingers across the surface of the subjects addressed in this book: the reclaiming of the body, the liberation of gender, the sacralization of sexuality, and the embracing of their rightful places within our magical and devotional work. I could write another hundred pages on each of these issues and still not say everything that needs to be said, nor even everything I have to say.

As mentioned at the beginning of this chapter, what we've been discussing and doing in this book is the work of a lifetime or several lifetimes. Indeed, one can see it as a core component of what the alchemists and magicians of days past have called the Great Work: the healing and reintegration of the self seen both as the refinement of the individual and as an intrinsic part of the healing of the world. No book could hope to capture everything there is to know, much less do, in service to that lofty goal ... and that's exactly as it should be. At most, *Outside the Charmed Circle* serves as only a stepping stone: it is a map, a set of tools, and a few suggestions for places to visit or avoid along the way. My fondest wish is that this book might play a role, however small, in bringing us all to a world where books like this are no longer needed, where none of us are dissociated from our bodies, our selves, and our power.

To that end, I hope this book is a benediction on your path, wherever that path may lead you.

Until next time, dear ones, be blessed.

Appendix A

RECOMMENDED READING AND LISTENING

IF YOU'VE COME THIS far and are wondering what your next steps might be, the following list of books and websites can give you some suggestions for further investigation. This list is hardly comprehensive, and resources change over time. As we learn more, our understandings of ourselves and the world around us evolve. The commonly held orthodoxies of today become the discredited mistakes of tomorrow, and online resources spring up, flourish, decay, and disappear faster than they can be tracked. Consider this list a starting point, a set of beginnings. Where you go from here is limited only by your imagination, your will, your desire, and your access to libraries and the magic of the internet.

The star symbol (★) indicates a book I consider essential in its category, and an excellent starting place for its category.

Gender, Sexuality, and Queerness

★ Meg-John Barker and Julia Scheele,
Queer: A Graphic History, Icon Books, 2016

This is, hands down, the single best introduction to queer theory I've found. It offers a whirlwind overview of the history, psychology, politics, philosophy, and critical theory of queerness grounded in solid academic research and history, presented in an endearing, engaging, non-threatening graphic novel format.

Judith Butler, *Gender Trouble*, Routledge, 2006

This book was my introduction to Butler's work… and initially, I hated it. The writing style was annoyingly opaque, and she never seemed to get to the damned point. Once I broke through the haze of her academic English, though, I found her arguments profoundly convincing, even life-changing. If I could, I would make the first chapter of this book required reading for everyone interested in sex, gender, or society.

bell hooks, *Feminism Is for Everybody: Passionate Politics*,
South End Press, 2000

Written primarily as a brief introduction to feminist thought for men and others new to the idea of feminism as "a movement to end sexism, sexist exploitation, and oppression," this slim volume manages nonetheless to cover an awful lot of ground. From philosophy to reproductive rights, from class struggles to children's books, from hegemonic beauty standards to racial equality, hooks outlines a "radical visionary feminism" that is both intersectional and effective and seeks to create a just, equitable, and courageous world for all people of every gender.

Audre Lorde, "Age, Race, Class, and Sex: Women Redefining Difference," in *Sister Outsider,* Crossing Press, 1984

This essay, written by a self-described "forty-nine-year-old Black lesbian feminist socialist mother of two, including one boy, and a member of an interracial couple," directly engages with the binary confines of hegemonic standards of contemporary culture—what Lorde calls "the mythical norm"—and sets them on fire. In ten brief-but-rich pages, she calls out the interlocked nature of racism, sexism, classicism, ageism, and heterocentrism and underscores the need for an intersectional approach to revolutionary change, which she suggests is necessary for liberation both in the world and ourselves. While the essay is focused largely on the struggles faced by Black lesbians in both white feminist and Black communities, the points she raises are well worth considering for any reader.

Gayle Rubin, "Thinking Sex: Notes for a Radical Theory of the Politics of Sexuality," in *Deviations: A Gayle Rubin Reader,* Duke University Press, 2011

In many ways, "Thinking Sex" was the inspiration for everything in this book, from its analytic approach to the title itself, drawn from Rubin's charmed circle model of hegemonic sexuality and gender. This essay is worth the price of admission all on its own, but the rest of this collection offers a wealth of revolutionary thinking about sexuality, gender, politics, anthropology, and feminism, and is equally worth your attention.

Magic, Witchcraft, and Sorcery
Janet and Stewart Farrar, *A Witches' Bible*,
Phoenix Publishing, 1996

The publication of this book—a compilation of the Farrars' two previous books, *Eight Sabbats for Witches* and *The Witches' Way*—was one of the final steps in Wicca's journey from being a sexy mystery cult to being an alternative religious tradition with a sexy mystery cult hiding somewhere inside it. Accusations of oathbreaking notwithstanding, anyone interested in getting a sense of what traditional Wicca looks like from the inside could do far worse than this meaty tome, which displays a surprising open-mindedness toward queerness for its day while refusing to shy away from discussing the sexual or gendered aspects of Wicca.

Doreen Valiente, *Witchcraft for Tomorrow*, Robert Hale, 1993
Of all the books penned by the woman rightly referred to as the godmother of modern witchcraft, this might be the most personal and idiosyncratic. It's essentially a book of Valiente's ruminations on the history, personalities, and practice of magic and witchcraft, concluding with a grimoire of her own creation, offered as a set of introductory rites and practices for new witches. While I might quibble with some of her historical data and conclusions, this book is a delightful contribution to the body of modern witch lore, and a marvelous place for someone interested in actually practicing witchcraft to learn what Grandmother Doreen thought and taught.

Laura Tempest Zakroff, *Weave the Liminal*, Llewellyn, 2019
This book is, hands down, one of the best modern introductory texts on witchcraft out there and an excellent place to start developing your own practice, though I suspect even staunch tradi-

tionalists and ceremonialists will find much of value here. Rather than advancing any particular established tradition of witchcraft or encouraging a do-what-you-like eclecticism, Tempest puts forward the radical notion of a curated path, encouraging both experimentation and rigor in a manner that will appeal to anyone with a touch of the Magpie approach to their makeup (as described on page 213).

Sex Magic

Frater U∴D∴, *Sex Magic*, Llewellyn, 2018

An updated version of his classic *Secrets of the German Sex Magicians*, this book provides an overview of sexual magic and mysticism rooted in a syncretic, post-Golden Dawn approach which draws on—or appropriates from—a variety of traditions, Western and Eastern. Queer and trans readers will have to do a fair bit of unpacking to get at the good stuff here, and some may find the level of cultural universalism (if not appropriation) off-putting, though Frater U∴D∴ does at least acknowledge the traditions from which he's adopting his terms and techniques. If you're interested in a modern take on ritual sex magic, *Sex Magic* is a decent place to start.

★ Brandy Williams, *Ecstatic Ritual: Practical Sex Magic*, Megalithica Books, 2008

Williams draws on her background as a ceremonial magician and a priestess in both Wiccan and Thelemic contexts to inform her straightforward, approachable, and blessedly inclusive approach to sex magic. Anyone looking to explore an embodied, gender-inclusive, sex-positive practice of magic and devotion would do well to read this book and her other works, *The Woman Magician* and the Williams-edited anthology *Women's Voices in Magic*.

Intersections with the P-Word Community

Yvonne Aburrow, *All Acts of Love and Pleasure: Inclusive Wicca*, Avalonia, 2014

This book kicked over some apple carts when it was first released, and little wonder. Writing as a Gardnerian Wiccan priestess, Aburrow explores the boundaries of sexuality and gender in an initiatory Wiccan context and offers suggestions on ways to adapt traditional practices to make them inclusive of anyone—queer or straight, trans or cis—drawn to the Craft of the Wicca.

Lee Harrington and Tai Fenix Kulystin (editors), *Queer Magic: Power Beyond Boundaries*, Mystic Productions Press, 2018

This anthology showcases a host of queer and trans authors writing about magic, spirituality, sexuality, and gender from a variety of perspectives. For queer and trans readers, this book is a work of revelation and validation, while for readers who aren't queer or trans, it can be profoundly educational, even transformative.

Christine Hoff Kraemer, *Eros and Touch from a Pagan Perspective: Divided for Love's Sake*, Routledge, 2013

Writing from a perspective informed both by her academic background as a theologian and by her experience as a Pagan and a body worker, Kraemer draws on queer theory, philosophy, and Paganisms ancient and modern to outline an erotic theology of the body for modern esoteric spiritual practitioners. Don't be put off by the volume's slim stature or its explicitly academic approach to the subject: this thoughtful and immensely readable text laid the groundwork for a substantial portion of the work in this book, and is key reading for anyone interested in the topics discussed here.

★ Christine Hoff Kraemer and Yvonne Aburrow (editors),
Pagan Consent Culture, Asphodel Press, 2016

This collection of essays, interviews, and resources for discussing and actualizing cultural changes based in consent should be required reading for anyone whose spirituality falls within the range of Pagan, polytheist, and magical practice. It's exactly the kind of serious book that people in these communities claim to want, and it's exactly the kind of book on ethics, consent, sexuality, and philosophy that these communities need. People from other communities, spiritual or secular, will also find a great deal of value in these pages.

Tomas Prower, *Queer Magic*, Llewellyn, 2018

Prower's book is a whirlwind survey of queer and trans spirituality throughout history and around the world. He introduces English-speaking readers to global traditions of LGBT+ magic from a variety of traditional cultures and communities and offers myths, rituals, and lessons to be learned from each culture in a deeply sensitive, sympathetic, and respectful way.

Hugh B. Urban, *Magia Sexualis: Sex, Magic, and Liberation in Modern Western Esotericism*, University of California Press, 2006

Behold, that rarest of birds: an actual academic text about sex magic, written by an academic who engages with the Western esoteric tradition on its own terms. Urban's history of sex, magic, and sex magic covers all the usual suspects (Paschal Beverly Randolph, Aleister Crowley, Gerald Gardner, and so on), but his work engages the subject with far more serious attention than most of us are used to encountering from the mainstream world.

Katie West and Jasmine Elliott (editors),
Becoming Dangerous, Weiser, 2018

This anthology of "witchy femmes, queer conjurers, and magical rebels" isn't a book on how to become a witch. Rather, it's a book about what it means to *be* a witch, written by women and femmes for whom witchcraft is as much a part of their identity as their skin, their sexuality, and their gender. It's an intensely, often uncomfortably personal work, and readers who identify as straight, cisgender, and/or white may find a lot of it challenging. The witchcraft of *Becoming Dangerous* is an unapologetically queer femme magic which exhorts us to live in the real world of the present, to embrace our own true natures and step into our own power: to become dangerous.

Podcasts

3 Pagans and a Cat, 3pagansandacat.com

Car, Gwyn, and Ode, the titular family of Pagans who create this podcast, bring disparate backgrounds and perspectives together discuss a variety of issues relevant to Pagans and polytheists in a warm, lively, and insightful way. Of particular interest for our purposes, they offer some in-depth, nuanced discussion and analysis of issues of gender and sexuality in relation to Pagan and polytheist praxis and current events.

Circle of Salt, circleofsaltpodcast.tumblr.com

Rune and Felix dish out all the salt you could possibly need or want in their podcast, which is equal parts serious occult conversation, incisive social commentary, and a bottomless well of snark. The targets of their cleansing, banishing sprays of salt have included gender, sexuality, heteronormativity, and poorly handled inclusivity in Pagan and magical communities.

Passion and Soul, passionandsoul.com

In this long-running podcast, sexuality educator and author Lee Harrington connects with sex magicians, erotic priestesses, BDSM practitioners, and other pioneers of spirituality and sexuality. Discussions range in topic from sacred sex and grappling with issues of faith to personal reflections on gender and practical suggestions for newbies to the world of kink. The material in this podcast touches on some sensitive subjects, and it's emphatically not safe for work (or young-person ears), but it's a worthy listen which offers some intimate and profound insights for folks willing to go deeper.

Appendix B
QUEER MAGICAL GROUPS AND EVENTS

THE FOLLOWING IS A short list of magical and devotional organizations specifically oriented to the spiritual needs of queer Pagans, polytheists, and magical practitioners. Please note that a mention in this list doesn't indicate affiliation with, membership in, or adherence to the beliefs of any of the organizations listed here. Similarly, a group's absence from this list isn't an indictment or a judgment.

Between the Worlds: Billing itself as "a spiritual gathering for men who love men," the Between the Worlds Gathering is a multi-day festival in southeastern Ohio open to queer men, cis and trans, from any spiritual tradition that could conceivably be called Pagan, polytheist, nature-oriented, or esoteric. The focus of the gathering is to bring queer men together in sacred spaces which are specifically attuned to their spiritual needs as queer men. For more information, visit their website at www.betweentheworlds.org.

Fellowship of the Phoenix: A nationally recognized religious and magical organization that "seek[s] to encourage and reclaim Queer power, healing, and spirit for the individual and the community at large," the Fellowship of the Phoenix identifies itself as "a Queer neopagan tradition and non-profit organization serving the unique needs of our LGBTQ community." As of 2019, they have temples located in Chicago and Seattle. For more information, visit their website at fellowshipofthephoenix.org.

Minoan Brotherhood and Minoan Sisterhood: The Minoan Brotherhood was founded by Eddie Buczynski in 1975 as an initiatory tradition of witchcraft focusing on the spiritual needs of men who love men, drawing on both classical Greek mythology and Gardnerian Wicca. In 1976, Lady Rhea and Lady Miw-Sekhmet founded a related order called the Minoan Sisterhood, based on Buczynski's work, for women who love women. A third order, the Cult of Rhea, constitutes "a meeting ground between the two traditions." The Minoans have groves located across the United States, and in France, Germany, Ireland, and Italy. For more information, visit their website at minoan-brotherhood .org, or join the Minoan Seekers email list at groups.yahoo.com / group / Minoan Seekers.

Naós Antínoou: A Temple of Antinous: Naós Antínoou is a queer, syncretic, reconstructionist polytheist community centered on honoring Antinous, the deified lover of the Roman emperor

Hadrian (see page 132) and other queer divinities from Graeco-Roman-Egyptian and other pantheons. In addition to their devotional and mystical praxis focused on Antinous, the group offers public ritual presentations at Pagan and polytheist conferences to honor queer ancestors and create new and vital myths which engage with the gods and the land. They are explicitly queer and inclusive, open to people of all genders and sexualities. While they are primarily located in the Pacific Northwest, they have members in various locations, and work to promote social and spiritual justice both in their local communities and elsewhere. For more information, visit their website at naosantinoou.org.

Open Source Alexandrian Tradition: Originally founded in 2009, the Open Source Alexandrian tradition has grown into a tradition of syncretic, radically inclusive progressive spirituality based in Alexandrian Wicca and rooted in the principle that magical polarity is unrelated to gender. Their practice is welcoming of people of all genders, sexual orientations, ethnic backgrounds, and any other differences. For more information, visit their website at st4r.org.

Radical Faeries: Founded in 1979 in resistance to the assimilationist trend within mainstream gay culture of the seventies, the Radical Faeries are a countercultural queer spiritual movement rooted in feminism and eco-spirituality. The movement is predominantly comprised of gay men, but there are Radical Faeries of all genders, orientations, and identities. For more information, visit the Radical Faerie resource site at radfae.org, and check out *RFD Magazine* at www.rfdmag.org.

BIBLIOGRAPHY

Aburrow, Yvonne. *All Acts of Love and Pleasure: Inclusive Wicca*. London: Avalonia, 2014.

Alföldi, Andrew. "Diana Nemorensis." *American Journal of Archaeology* 64, no. 2, 1960.

Amber K. *Coven Craft: Witchcraft for Three or More*. Woodbury, MN: Llewellyn, 2002.

Anderson, Cora. *Fifty Years in the Feri Tradition*. Portland, OR: Acorn Guild Press, 2005.

Anderson, Victor. *Lilith's Garden*. Portland, OR: Acorn Guild Press, 2001.

Apollodorus. *The Library*. Translated by Sir James George Frazer. Cambridge, MA: Harvard University Press, 1921. http://data

.perseus.org/texts/urn:cts:greekLit:tlg0548.tlg001.perseus
-eng1:Library.

Aristotle. *Politics: A Treatise on Government*. Translated by William
Ellis. New York: E. P. Dutton &. Co., 1912. http://www
.gutenberg.org/ebooks/6762.

Ball, Siobhan. "Artemis Is the Queer Girl Goddess BFF of Your
Dreams." *Autostraddle*, May 2, 2017. http://www.autostraddle
.com/artemis-is-the-queer-girl-goddess-bff-you-always-dreamt
-of-377958/.

Barker, Meg-John, and Julia Scheele. *Queer: A Graphic History*.
London: Icon Books, 2016.

Beauvoir, Simone de. *The Second Sex*. New York: Vintage Books, 1989.

Betz, Hans Dieter (ed.). *The Greek Magical Papyri in Translation,
Including the Demotic Spells, Volume 1*. Chicago: University of
Chicago Press, 1986.

Blain, Jenny. *Nine Worlds of Seid-Magic: Ecstasy and Neo-shamanism
in North European Paganism*. London: Routledge, 2002.

Butler, Judith. *Gender Trouble: Feminism and the Subversion of
Identity*. New York: Routledge, 2006.

Chaucer, Geoffrey. *The Complete Works of Geoffrey Chaucer*. Edited
by Walter W. Skeat. Oxford: Clarendon Press, 1900. http://
www.gutenberg.org/ebooks/22120.

Chesterton, G. K. *The Thing*. London: Sheed & Ward, 1929.

Chick, Jack. *Dark Dungeons*. Ontario, CA: Chick Publications, 1984.

Clifton, Chas S. "The Significance of Aradia." In *Aradia, or the
Gospel of the Witches: A New Translation*, edited by Mario
Pazzaglini. Blaine, WA: Phoenix Publishing, 1998.

Congregation for the Doctrine of the Faith. *Persona Humana: Declaration on Certain Questions Concerning Sexual Ethics.* http://www.vatican.va/roman_curia/congregations/cfaith/documents/rc_con_cfaith_doc_19751229_persona-humana_en.html.

Crenshaw, Kimberlé Williams. "Demarginalizing the Intersection of Race and Sex: A Black Feminist Critique of Antidiscrimination Doctrine, Feminist Theory and Antiracist Politics." *University of Chicago Legal Forum,* vol. 1989, issue 1. Chicago: University of Chicago Law School, 1989, 139–168.

Crowley, Aleister. *Magick in Theory and Practice.* New York: Dover, 1976.

———. *The Vision and the Voice.* Newburyport, MA: Weiser, 1999.

Crowther, Patricia. *Witch Blood: The Diary of a Witch High Priestess.* New York: House of Collectibles, 1974.

Davies, Owen. *Magic: A Very Short Introduction.* Oxford: Oxford University Press, 2012.

de Troyes, Chrétien. "The Story of the Grail." In *Arthurian Romances.* Translated by William W. Kibler. New York: Penguin Books, 1991.

Dover, Kenneth. *Greek Homosexuality.* Cambridge, MA: Harvard University Press, 1978: 1989.

Edda Sæmundar Hinns Fróða: The Edda of Sæmund the Learned, Part I. Translated by Benjamin Thorpe. London: Trübner & Co., 1866.

The Elder or Poetic Edda, Part I—The Mythological Poems. Edited and translated by Oliver Bray. London: Viking Club, 1908.

Evans, Arthur. *The God of Ecstasy: Sex-Roles and the Madness of Dionysos*. New York: St. Martin's Press, 1988.

Farrar, Janet, and Stewart Farrar. *The Witches' Way*. In *A Witches' Bible*. Blaine, WA: Phoenix Publishing, 1996.

Feynman, Richard. *Classic Feynman: All the Adventures of a Curious Character*. New York: W. W. Norton & Company, 2006.

Fortune, Dion. *The Goat-Foot God*. Wellingborough, Northamptonshire, UK: Aquarian Press, 1989.

Frater U∴D∴.*Sex Magic*. Woodbury, MN: Llewellyn, 2018.

Gary, Gemma.*The Devil's Dozen: Thirteen Craft Rites of the Old One*. London: Troy Books, 2015.

Goldhill, Simon. *A Very Queer Family Indeed: Sex, Religion, and the Bensons in Victorian Britain*. Chicago: University of Chicago Press, 2017.

Grimorium Verum. Edited and translated by Joseph Peterson. Self-published, CreateSpace, 2007.

Grosz, Elizabeth. *Space, Time, and Perversion: Essays on the Politics of Bodies*. New York: Routledge, 1995.

Hammond, Dorothy. "Magic: A Problem in Semantics." *American Anthropologist* 72, no. 6, 1970.

Harrington, Lee, and Tai Fenix Kulystin, editors. *Queer Magic: Power Beyond Boundaries*. Anchorage, AK: Mystic Productions Press, 2018.

Harrow, Judy. *Wicca Covens: How to Start and Organize Your Own*. New York: Citadel, 2000.

Heselton, Philip. *Wiccan Roots: Gerald Gardner and the Modern Witchcraft Revival*. Somerset, WI: Capall Bann, 2000.

hooks, bell. *Feminism Is for Everybody: Passionate Politics*. Boston: South End Press, 2000.

Horace. *The Odes of Horace*. Translated by David Ferry. New York: Farrar, Strauss and Giroux, 2015.

Hutton, Ronald.*The Pagan Religions of the Ancient British Isles*. Oxford: Blackwell, 1991.

———. *The Triumph of the Moon*. Oxford, UK: Oxford University Press, 2000.

Hyatt, Christopher S. *Undoing Yourself with Energized Meditation and Other Devices*. Tempe, AZ: The Original Falcon Press, 2017.

Jong, Erica. *Witches*. New York: Harry Abrams, 1981.

Kamen, Henry. *The Spanish Inquisition: A Historical Revision*. London and New Haven: Yale University Press, 1997.

Keeling, Kara. "Queer OS." In *Cinema Journal*, vol. 53, no. 2, 2014: 153.

Kraemer, Christine Hoff. *Eros and Touch from a Pagan Perspective: Divided for Love's Sake*. London: Routledge, 2013.

Kraemer, Christine Hoff, and Yvonne Aburrow (editors). *Pagan Consent Culture*. Hubbardston, MA: Asphodel Press, 2016.

Leavitt, David. *The Man Who Knew Too Much: Alan Turing and the Invention of the Computer*. New York: W. W. Norton, 2006.

Lee, Stan. *Amazing Fantasy #15*. New York: Marvel Comics, 1962.

Leland, Charles Godfrey. *Aradia, or the Gospel of the Witches*. London: David Nutt, 1899.

Lorde, Audre. "Age, Race, Class, and Sex: Women Redefining Difference." In *Sister Outsider*. Freedom, CA: The Crossing Press, 1984.

Luria, Rabbi Yitzchak. *Sha'ar ha Gilgulim (Gate of Reincarnations)*. Translated by Yitzchok bar Chaim. www.chabad.org /kabbalah/article_cdo/aid/378771/jewish/Gate-of -Reincarnations.htm.

Mackinnon, Sean P., Christian H. Jordan, and Anne E. Wilson. "Birds of a Feather Sit Together: Physical Similarity Predicts Seating Choice." In *Personality and Social Psychology Bulletin*, vol. 37, issue 7, 2011: 879–892.

Macrobius Ambrosius Theodosius. *Saturnalia, Books 3–5*. Translated by Robert A. Kaster. Cambridge, MA: Harvard University Press, 2011.

Magliocco, Sabina. "Who Was Aradia? The History and Development of a Legend." In *The Pomegranate: The Journal of Pagan Studies* 18, February 2002.

Malinowski, Bronislaw. *Magic, Science, and Religion*. Glencoe, IL: The Free Press, 1948.

Marathakis, Ioannis, translator and editor. *The Magical Treatise of Solomon or Hygromanteia*. Singapore: Golden Hoard Press, 2011.

Martin, Judith, Nicholas Martin, and Jacobina Martin. "Miss Manners: A simple 'you' avoids any gender confusion." *The Washington Post*, September 27, 2015.

Mathiesen, Robert "Charles G. Leland and the Witches of Italy: The Origin of Aradia." In *Aradia, or the Gospel of the Witches: A New Translation*, edited by Mario Pazzaglini. Blaine, WA: Phoenix Publishing, 1998.

Muñoz, José Esteban. *Cruising Utopia: The Then and There of Queer Futurity*. New York: New York University Press, 2009.

Nhất Hạnh, Thich. "The Moment is Perfect." *Lion's Roar*, May 1, 2008. http://www.lionsroar.com/the-moment-is-perfect/.

Nussbaum, Martha. *The Fragility of Goodness*. Cambridge, UK: Cambridge University Press, 1996.

———. "Platonic Love and Colorado Law: The Relevance of Ancient Greek Norms to Modern Sexual Controversies." In *Virginia Law Review* 80, no. 7, 1994: 1546.

Osborne, Robin. *Greek History*. London: Routledge, 2004.

Ovid. *Metamorphoses*. Translated by Henry T. Riley. London: George Bell & Sons, 1893. http://www.gutenberg.org/ebooks/26073.

Pindar. *The Odes*. Translated by C. M. Bowra. New York: Penguin, 1969.

Plato. *Laws*. Translated by Benjamin Jowett. Oxford: Clarendon Press, 1892. http://www.gutenberg.org/ebooks/1750.

———. *Republic*. Translated by Benjamin Jowett. London: Oxford University Press, 1888. http://www.gutenberg.org/ebooks/55201.

———. *Timaeus*. Translated by Benjamin Jowett. Oxford, UK: Clarendon Press, 1892. http://www.gutenberg.org/ebooks/1572.

Plaut, S. Michael. "Boundary Issues in Teacher-Student Relationships." In *Journal of Sex and Marital Therapy* 19, 1993, 210–219.

Popper, Karl. *The Open Society and Its Enemies, Volume I: The Spell of Plato*. London: Routledge & Kegan Paul, 1945.

Prower, Tomas. *Queer Magic*. Woodbury, MN: Llewellyn, 2018.

Radin, Dean. *Real Magic: Ancient Wisdom, Modern Science, and a Guide to the Secret Power of the Universe*. New York: Harmony, 2018.

Rawls, John. *A Theory of Justice*. Cambridge, MA: Belknap, 1971.

Robbins, Tom. *Skinny Legs and All*. New York: Bantam, 1990.

Rubin, Gayle. "Thinking Sex: Notes for a Radical Theory of the Politics of Sexuality." In *Deviations: A Gayle Rubin Reader*. Durham, NC: Duke University Press, 2011.

Soledad, Cholla. "Speak of the Devil: Witch Eye Talks with Victor Anderson." *Witch Eye* 3, August 2000.

Starhawk. *Truth or Dare: Encounters with Power, Authority, and Mystery*. San Francisco: HarperSanFrancisco, 1988.

Stephenson, Neal. *Snow Crash*. New York: Bantam, 1992.

Straczynski, J. Michael. "And the Rock Cried Out, No Hiding Place." *Babylon 5*, original airdate October 14, 1996.

Sturluson, Snorri. *The Prose Edda*. Translated by Arthur Gilchrist Brodeur. New York: The American-Scandinavian Foundation, 1916.

Sullivan, Louis. "The Tall Office Building Artistically Considered." *Lippincott's Magazine*, March 23, 1896: 403–409.

Three Initiates. *The Kybalion: Hermetic Philosophy*. Chicago: Yogi Publication Society, 1908.

Tomlinson, Matt, and Ty P. Kāwika Tengan, editors. *New Mana: Transformations of a Classic Concept in Pacific Languages and Cultures*. Canberra: ANU Press, 2016.

United Nations Office of the High Commissioner for Human Rights. *Free & Equal Fact Sheet: Intersex.* www.ohchr.org/Documents/Issues/Discrimination/LGBT/FactSheets/UNFE_FactSheet_Intersex_EN.pdf.

Urban, Hugh B. *Magia Sexualis: Sex, Magic, and Liberation in Modern Western Esotericism.* Oakland, CA: University of California Press, 2006.

Valiente, Doreen. "The Charge of the Goddess." http://www.doreenvaliente.org/Doreen-Valiente-Doreen_Valiente_Poetry-11.php.

———. *Witchcraft for Tomorrow.* London: Robert Hale, 1993.

Wachowski, Lana, and Lilly Wachowski. *The Matrix.* Burbank, CA: Warner Bros. Pictures, 1999.

Walker, Valerie. "Feri FAQs, v. 8.3, 11/10." Last modified November 2010. http://www.wiggage.com/witch/feriFAQ.8.html.

West, Katie, and Jasmine Elliott, editors. *Becoming Dangerous: Witchy Femmes, Queer Conjurers, and Magical Rebels.* Newburyport, MA: Weiser, 2018.

Wilde, Oscar. *Charmides and Other Poems.* London: Methuen & Co., 1913. http://www.gutenberg.org/ebooks/1031.

Williams, Brandy. *Ecstatic Ritual: Practical Sex Magic.* Stafford, UK: Megalithica Books, 2008.

Zakroff, Laura Tempest. *Weave the Liminal: Living Modern Traditional Witchcraft.* Woodbury, MN: Llewellyn, 2019.

———. "What's In A Pword?" *A Modern Traditional Witch*, April 5, 2017. http://www.patheos.com/blogs/tempest/2017/04/whats-in-a-pword.html.

To Write to the Author

If you wish to contact the author or would like more information about this book, please write to the author in care of Llewellyn Worldwide Ltd. and we will forward your request. Both the author and the publisher appreciate hearing from you and learning of your enjoyment of this book and how it has helped you. Llewellyn Worldwide Ltd. cannot guarantee that every letter written to the author can be answered, but all will be forwarded. Please write to:

Misha Magdalene
℅ Llewellyn Worldwide
2143 Wooddale Drive
Woodbury, MN 55125-2989

Please enclose a self-addressed stamped envelope for reply,
or $1.00 to cover costs. If outside the U.S.A., enclose
an international postal reply coupon.

Many of Llewellyn's authors have websites with additional information and resources. For more information, please visit our website at http://www.llewellyn.com.